LIVINGSTONE'S LAKE

Livingstone's Lake

THE DRAMA OF NYASA
AFRICA'S INLAND SEA

Oliver Ransford

Thomas Y. Crowell Company
New York · Established 1834

TO MY FAMILY

First published in the United States of America in 1967

Printed in the United States of America

L.C. Card 67-12052

1   2   3   4   5   6   7   8   9   10

CONTENTS

v

CONTENTS

PART FIVE KWACHA

MAPS AND DIAGRAMS

ILLUSTRATIONS

ILLUSTRATIONS

ACKNOWLEDGEMENTS

In writing this book I have been well aware of the debt I owe to my predecessors who have studied the history of Lake Nyasa. To mention them all would be impossible, but some of their names are recorded under *bibliography*. My grateful thanks for help and permission to use photographs and quote from documents in their care, are due to Mr. T. W. Baxter, Mr. Young and other members of the staff of the National Archives of Southern Rhodesia, as well as to Mr. Gervase Clay, who when Director of the Rhodes-Livingstone Museum (and my sternest critic) suggested many valuable emendations. I would also like to acknowledge the unfailing kindness and help I have received from Mr. Roger Summers, the Curator of the National Museum, Bulawayo, Mr. Graham Guy of the Victoria Museum, Salisbury, Mr. C. K. Cooke of the Historical Monuments Commission, Rhodesia, from Mr. Johnson and his colleagues at the National Free Library, Bulawayo, and from Mr. Stacey and staff of the Bulawayo Public Library. I owe much also to the guidance of my always helpful neighbour Mr. Peter Gibbs, and to the thought-provoking encouragement of the late Dr. George Jamieson. A particularly heavy debt is owed to those who have wrestled with my handwriting, notably to Mrs. H. B. Dugmore, Miss Dorothy Spencer, and my daughter Carol. I wish to make grateful acknowledgement to Mr. John R. Murray for his help especially with things which by right were my own responsibility. Above all I must express gratitude to my wife for her constructive criticism and constant scrutiny of this work, as well as for her patient endurance during the last two years of many moments of unintentional neglect.

I have tried in this book to use the most generally accepted spelling of African names, but have sometimes been influenced by aesthetic motives. Thus I have preferred 'Angoni' to the more accurate 'Wangoni', and 'Yao' to the clumsy 'Wa-Yao', but for the sake of assonance have paradoxically used 'Wankonde' correctly. The name of the Lake (which is the real hero of this book) was spelled 'Nyassa' until Sir Harry Johnston persuaded the Foreign Office to omit the second 's'. Unfortunately the change encouraged a tendency to pronounce the word with three syllables, the first of which was stressed to rhyme with 'fly'. The proper pronunciation is the near bi-syllabic 'Neeya-sa'. The difficulty has now, however, been resolved: officially it is known as Lake Maravi.

I have already suggested that if there is a hero in this book, it is the Lake. If it contains a moral, the only moral to be gleaned from it is that the European still has his part to play in the orderly development of Central Africa.

INTRODUCTION

Few important geographical features in the world can have been
'discovered' so many times as Lake Nyasa. Dr. Livingstone was
the first man to furnish an accurate account of this inland sea,
but long before his time many other pioneers had stumbled upon
it. Bronze-skinned pygmies were the first men to find the lake.
They were followed, centuries later, by black men from the Congo
rain forests, and by Arabs from the red sands of Oman. Almost
certainly the first European eyes to see Nyasa were those of a
Portuguese trader in 1616, but his countrymen failed to exploit his
discovery. Thereafter a long silence settled over the lake; it
lost its flavour of authenticity, and joined the company of other
myths and travellers' tales, like Atlantis, Lyonnesse, and the
kingdom of Prester John. Then, just over a hundred years ago,
Livingstone revealed it again to Europe, and his genius made it
something almost personal to himself, while the lake in return
has illuminated his own character for us. Today his spirit more
than any other man's broods across its waters.

My own 'discovery' of Lake Nyasa was made just before the
outbreak of Hitler's war. Fellow passengers on the boat gave me
tit-bits of information about it during my first voyage to Africa,
and before I even saw Nyasa I knew its area was about that of
Wales, while its length and width in miles were roughly equal to
the number of days and weeks in a year. But no one had prepared
me for its beauty. My first posting as a Government Medical
Officer happened to deposit me in the Angoni Highlands at
Dedza. Only a few miles away a lip of the great African Rift
escarpment dropped sheer down to where the fabulous waters of
Nyasa glistened in the sunshine 3,000 feet below, and every
evening I would go there to stare in bemused wonder at this
Pilgrim's vision.

And my work took me often to the lake. In those days there
were no motor roads descending the escarpment: we scrambled
to the lake shore down a steep zig-zag footpath. And at the
bottom we entered into a new world. For this was the Africa of

I

Burton and Stanley; here we walked through the dried-up jungle of Tarzan and Allan Quartermain—and found a curious satisfaction in having reached it on nothing more sophisticated than a pair of feet.

The vigorous air of the highlands which had smarted in our nostrils, was replaced on the lake shore by a hot humidity that in summer was almost solid enough to push away with the hand. In place of the rare shrunken trees of the open plateau, we walked beneath enormous baobabs and tufted palms, and strange sausage trees drooping under the weight of their surrealistic fruit. And the narrow plain literally teemed with people. It was like an ant-heap that has been disturbed. Naked children, all pot-belly and navel, scampered off in every direction at our approach; big-bosomed women, sweating in crowded maize gardens, put down their hoes to stare at us as we went by; and round every corner of the erratic native paths of tropical Africa, we came upon another group of huts where men lay stretched out asleep or gossiped lazily in the shade.

It was a starkly primitive, jaded, tawny-coloured land, and it had a smell that was all its own. For the whole lake shore was drenched with the heavy linden-sweetness of flowering trees compounded with the fusty antique odours of bats, wood smoke and wet earth; and it pulsated to a rhythm that was unlike anything I had known before. The throbbing sounds of countless human voices rose and fell in time to the everlasting beat of native drums and the thud of pestles pounding maize in wooden mortars, while to them was added the incessant contrapuntal hum of amatory cicadas.

The lake itself was never out of sight for very long. With its spume-splashed rocks and golden beaches washed by gentle sleepy waves it seemed more sea than lake. Instinctively one sniffed the air to catch the pungent smell of salty seaweed, or listened for the cry of seagulls; and their very absence seemed to stress the unusual temper of this lake. For Nyasa is a singularly alien and exotic thing; there is an elemental and undisciplined quality about it that makes it stand outside the range of ordinary experience. We came to think of it as a sleeping giant, liable at any moment to rage with aboriginal fury. Hot springs boiled up along its shores, and hissed like angry reptiles as they poured into its cooling waters; a thrusting landscape of eocene catastrophe trembled through the heat haze from its opposite shore, reminding us of the red-hot world that had fashioned the rift; the ungovernable storms of Genesis would sweep suddenly from a clear sky across its waters, and when the clouds descended a battalion of dervish-dancing water spouts leapt 500 feet up into the air to meet them, as though the very water was trying to escape from some demon hidden in the lake. There is no tide to mix and intermingle the waters of Nyasa, but something similar although stranger—a *seiche*—continually set the lighter oxygenated surface water skidding to and fro across the useless, stagnant layer below, as though the lake was being rocked like a gargantuan bath tub. No life that we know could possibly exist in this deeper water which stretches down nearly half a mile to the lake's bed, yet such is the impression of enigmatic mystery emanating from Nyasa that, after listening to the natives' stories of the monsters seen emerging from it, we found ourselves wondering uneasily what abysmal fauna did in fact live there.

One never seemed to come to the end of the eccentricities of Lake Nyasa. Clouds of midges in their marriage flight blew continuously across the water looking exactly like smoke from a hull-down steamer yet packed together so tightly that they have been known to suffocate a man. Then we were always intrigued by the fickle way the lake's level fluctuated periodically through twenty feet or more and changed the shape of Nyasa from year to year. Many theories were advanced to explain this mysterious variation; people talked glibly about the influence of sunspots, of geological shifts in the Great Rift and even of subterranean tunnels connecting the lake with fountains in (of all places) the Seychelles. Only quite recently has it been realised that Nyasa is nothing more than a dammed-up river whose narrow overflow into the Shiré blocks up periodically with sudd (which a larger hippopotamus population previously scoured free) until the weight of water piling up after a few years bursts through the barrier, and roars away towards the Zambesi.

This capricious fiddling with her appearance is not the only womanly trait the lake exhibits; she possesses an unexpected quality of shyness too. For Nyasa refuses to disclose her full beauty to new acquaintances: it grows instead with intimacy, like the music of a Beethoven string quartet—and then suddenly becomes so precious as to make it difficult to conceive how life befor: its revelation could have been supported. For Nyasa seems anxious to impress the stranger with her sulks and improprieties at first; only later are her separate beauties revealed and even then, like a born coquette, she grants different favours to different men: to some she gives tranquillity, for when the mood is on her, this lake can sleep the deepest sleep of any lake I know; to the vigorous and venturesome she is an exacting mistress who tests their skill in sport; and to artists Nyasa is a never-ending source of inspiration.

It was for her colour that I first came to love the lake. There may be scenes more beautiful in the world than these imprisoned waters, but after driving each evening for weeks on end to watch the sun go down behind her battlemented western escarpment, for me Nyasa became unbelievably lovely and a dazzling reward for all the hot discomforts of the day. She seemed then to be a lake no longer but an enchanted mirror tilted to reflect the languid artistry of a painted sky. Catching at its bright colours, Nyasa held and even enhanced them in the immense silence of her waters. She would glow deep crimson under the setting sun and then almost reluctantly change into cyclamen and silken purple as she waited for the evening breeze to caress her magic texture and set lines of amber ripples swimming slowly towards the farther shore. This was the signal for all the colours on the water to fade like courtiers from an audience chamber, until at last only an imperial presence of molten gold remained.

With regret I would raise my eyes from the water's glory to the distant mountains—and find there a loveliness scarcely less compelling. For these mountains of Nyasa are not the weary drooping things of Europe that have become tired by people staring at them—they are sheer, precise and virile. They shine with unusual iridescence, yet with the same soft insistence on change of colour as the water at their feet. But theirs are pastel shades; on one size pale lavender melts imperceptibly into pearly-grey and on the other into a luminous madonna blue.

4

Yet as we came to know it better and the lake revolved into the damnable heat of an African summer, both my wife and I began to realise that the oppressive air was drawing an unsuspected quality of menace from our beautiful Nyasa. One morning, as we stood beside it, we saw the lake turn blank under a leaden sky, like a mirror left with nothing but the past to reflect. The trans-lacustrine mountains blurred into formless phantoms, while dimly through the haze we could see the trees beside the water go quivering into the stepless dance they would continue until the green light of the setting sun immobilised them for the night as phosphorescent spectres. We saw too that a great lethargy had settled over Nyasa. The majestic fish eagles perched motionless in their trees, all thought of flight forgotten in the breathless heat, and even the flies moved slowly.

It was as though a mask had been pulled away from the lake that morning and suddenly we saw her as an ugly woman scarred from all the cruelties of the past and grimacing with satisfaction at her curious ability not only to captivate men but to set them quarrelling together. Later we came to know that sinister power all too well; we watched it make ordinary people touchy and unreasonable, so that an innocent remark grew into a slight and then into an insult; and we understood why intolerance and brutality had always found fertile soil beside her shores on which to spawn and flourish.

Only a little later as we sat staring rather gloomily at our lake from the steps of a rural dispensary at Chipoka, the village headman came up, pointed to where the sandy beach ended in a tangled swamp-land, and warned us this was haunted by the aboriginal pygmies of Nyasa. They had been annihilated there, he went on, centuries ago by his own ancestors, black men from the north. He spoke of that old massacre as though it had taken place only the week before, and so vividly that for a moment we believed we could hear the triumphant shouts of the victors and the faint whimpers of a defeated people hanging in the air, and even caught the sickly-sweet smell of putrescence. I think it was at that moment that we determined to learn the full story of this lake and to raise the ghosts of the men who long before had turned a scenic paradise into an earthly hell.

Our researches were interrupted by the war and several years went by before we saw the lake again. But we came back to it at Kota Kota, its largest town and the one most evocative of the past. Officially it was ruled by a District Commissioner and a half-caste Arab named Jumbe, descendant of Livingstone's old friend. But the real rulers of Kota Kota were the blood flukes that gave its inhabitants the disease we call bilharzia. These microscopical worms, like all parasites, are very logical organisms. Their own survival depends on keeping their human hosts alive and yet they contrive to reduce them to such depths of apathy as to be physically incapable of throwing off their parasitic yoke. We were horrified to find that the natives of Kota Kota were weighed down by an incredible load of parasites. It was symptomatic of one's emotions at this time that I was looking for some worth-while cause to redeem the wasted years of war. And the pestilential lake shore at Kota Kota confronted me with a task that precisely matched my mood. I still remember the enormous enthusiasm with which I flung myself upon the problem of eradicating bilharzia from the area. It was clearly necessary to find a substance which would interrupt the parasite's life-cycle and yet be harmless to man and cheap to produce. The bilharzia developmental cycle happens to be most vulnerable at that stage when its embryos briefly use freshwater snails as intermediate hosts; if snails are eliminated from an area, so is bilharzia, and my search narrowed down to the discovery of a naturally occurring snail poison. In the freely growing shrub *Tephrosia vogelii* I found what I was looking for. Twenty-four hours after infested pools had been sprinkled with its powdered leaves, their entire snail population were floating on the water—dead. Yet after drinking copious draughts of an infusion of the leaves I was confident about it being innocuous to man. An enthusiastic report informed Medical Headquarters of my experiments and went on to outline a scheme for local bilharzia control, until such time as the Sanitary Engineers could effect permanent eradication. A curt letter in reply posted me to the Shiré Highlands. It was clear that the Hon., the Director of Medical Services, knew how to handle presumptuous young officers who in the army had forgotten Colonial Service manners and protocol.

6

It was a bad set-back. Soon afterwards I resigned my appointment and thought we would never see the lake again. But in 1963 my wife and I returned to Nyasaland on holiday. It seemed impossible that so much could have altered in the few years we had been away. Only the lake remained the same.

For us, its old aficionados, a long voyage round Nyasa had a nostalgic flavour. The remembering lake showed us all her moods again, and, for our last evening put on her brightest clothes. We saw every colour of the spectrum burning in her waters, and others we did not even know existed. At last they began to fade, but more gently, it seemed, than usual, until we were left watching the familiar golden haze rising like incense from the water. Suddenly it was night. A layer of moon-silver spread over the distant mountains of Mozambique and the sky trembled with the myriad stars of Africa. The placid water reflected each shining point of light and as we turned to go below, it seemed that we were moving through a watery universe, divorced from time and space. It was a sublime farewell.

This is an account of some of the encounters and incidents that have taken place beside this lake of stars. Its history has always been associated with that of the Shiré Highlands in the south, through which its only river outlet finds its way into the Zambesi. Its story has been fashioned by the quirks of countless human personalities and by the accidents of geography. The inspiration of an Arab mystic, the unnavigability of the cataracts at Kebrabasa, the stoical courage of a Scottish trader, the infected bite of a single mosquito, the outcrops of gold in Monomatapa's Empire, the suspicions of an invigilator in a dingy mission examination hall—all these and many other caprices of life have played their part in creating the modern Malawi State of today.

In the following pages I have tried to describe the sombre night which encompassed the lake until the arrival of Dr. Livingstone. Our knowledge of this dark era is owed more to legend than to written history; in consequence this period (although long in time) has been considered in a disproportionately short space, and it necessarily lacks the human interest of the contemporary accounts which bring the later historical period of

7

Nyasa to life. The Zambesi Expedition seems to me to have been of such importance to the lake that I have allotted an appropriate number of pages to its story. But the brightness of Dr. Livingstone's vision, after waxing into high noon, gradually faded into a pale afterglow of European imperialism. Now the lake has revolved farther through space into that modern era of African nationalism which they call *Kwacha* or sunrise. Whether it will represent a new night over Nyasa or another dawn still remains uncertain. But if we know what has gone before, we can perhaps more easily predict and understand that future.

Part One

NIGHT OVER NYASA

THE AKAFULA

No one who travels up the lonely road from Zomba into the
Angoni Highlands of Nyasaland ever forgets his first Cortés
vision of the lake. Coming to an open ridge fully 5,000 feet
above sea-level he catches sight of an inland sea stretching into
the distance below him like a fairy mirage. It is very still and
very lonely up there in the mountain air, and there is a strange
theatricality about the scene. It seems impossible for so much blue
water to have strayed so far into this arid continent; it seems
miraculous that the colour and softness of the Mediterranean
have found their way into the very heart of Africa. David
Livingstone when he came upon this lake in 1859 was inclined to
match its iridescent charm with an equally magic name, and he
called it first the 'lake of stars' (although after a subsequent
unpleasant experience upon its waters he suggested that the
'lake of storms' might be more appropriate), but in the end he was
content to retain its African name—Nyasa—which simply means
'broad waters'. Previously its existence had been regarded as
little more than a traveller's tale, although the cartographers
nevertheless all dutifully marked it on their maps, and labelled it
with names like Zaflan, Zambre, Hemozura, Maravi, Nyanja
Grande, Sumba and Uniamesi. Beside it they scattered drawings
of playful salamanders and griffins, and for good measure added
tiny wrinkled mountains that looked like lines of well-drilled
mole hills.

Seen (as first it should be seen) from the mountain road, the
sparkling waters of Nyasa have about them such a quality of
freshness and pristine youth that it is difficult to believe they were
born more than a hundred million years ago. Yet it was during
the jurassic age of reptilian imperialism that some cosmic con-
vulsion left a depression standing on the high tableland of ancient
Africa, which the generous rains of succeeding pluvial periods
turned first into a swamp and then into a circular sheet of water.
From it a stream found a gap through its confining wall of solid

rock and escaped southwards to the sea. That small outlet ensured that the surface waters of Nyasa, unlike those of its brackish sister lakes in Central Africa, would always be sweet and clean.

Once it had been created, the infant Lake Nyasa began to grow like a living thing. For as the great southern land-mass of Gondwanaland sank beneath the sea, it split off Madagascar from the mother continent and then cracked open increasing stretches of the Great African Rift Valley. Into this brutal rent in the earth's surface the lake's escaping waters thundered in a succession of climacteric floods. Five hundred thousand years ago the lake attained nearly its present maturity, and then, like a replete dowager, Nyasa remained content to sit watching the neander-thal world go by. It saw the first hominids come to hunt along its shores, barking and gabbling to themselves, and then watched the stone age men who followed them, fashioning their crude tools from the pebbles and flakes of quartz that lay scattered on the beach. It had no knowledge of the great tides of civilisation sweeping round the Mediterranean at that time, but one day it stirred with interest at the sight of sapient little red men wander-ing about the lake shore. They spoke to each other not in grunts but with formed words. They even had a name for themselves—Akafula—which meant 'diggers from the soil'; with their arrival the human history of the lake had begun.

The appearance of the lake shore has altered less than most of the world's landscapes during the last two thousand years. We see it today almost as the Akafula saw it. Admittedly in their time the yellow jungle scrub of deciduous trees reached right down to the water's edge and no untidy fringe of maize gardens bordered the water, while the wispy waterfalls of Ruarwe and the Livingstone mountains were then majestic cascades. But its general outline had been fixed; the grim Tarpeian rock which men later were to call 'the ender of law suits' already brooded above the water, and the natural sphinx standing beyond the storm-wracked harbour of Liuli already stood there to remind the Akafula of their forebears' stories about the land of Egypt where they had danced to amuse the Pharaoh himself.

But in their time prodigious numbers of wild animals (whose scanty remnants have now withdrawn to forest sanctuaries) shared the lake shore with the Akafula and remained there long enough to delight Dr. Livingstone a hundred years ago. Enormous herds of buffalo grazed the coarse grass of antediluvian beaches in pygmy times, and countless elephants roamed over the wooded ridges of Usisya. The crocodiles we see today basking in the sun on sandbanks beside the lake were far more numerous too when the Akafula lived there, and they perhaps can claim to be the lake's oldest inhabitants, for they knew Nyasa when it was a mere bog perched high up on a dome of veld above Florence Bay. The hippopotami the Akafula hunted still render their lunatic concerts beside the lake each evening, although the numbers in their falstaffian choirs are now also sadly reduced. The same fish the Akafula caught two thousand years ago were those which fed the multitude about the same time beside the sister lake of Galilee at the northern end of the Great Rift, and they still abound in Nyasa to intrigue our modern palates.

If the game was more abundant in Akafula times, the bird life we see now is as prolific and colourful as anything they knew, for the air of the lake shore today is like an enormous aviary. Everywhere the scene is brilliant with shining green cormorants diving into the water for their meals, and families of crested cranes with golden halos on their heads stand majestic amongst the apple-green papyrus. All day long beside Nyasa one can watch the fastidious lily-trotters stalking on enormous feet from one piece of floating vegetation to another, past the stately figures of the white and purple Ibis, whom the ancient masters of the Akafula once held sacred in lower Egypt. And like the pygmies too we watch three mortal days of avian terror each year when migrating swallows settle down briefly beside the lake before flying into the blue transparent south.

But we possess a more precise living link with the Akafula than any of the descendants of animals they watched and hunted. For if the pygmies could come back to the lake today, they would recognise baobabs they once knew, and perhaps marked with their iron knives, standing still in their old places, already considerable trees in their time, yet only now approaching full maturity.

The Akafula were a race of dwarfs who vanished from the lake four hundred years ago. They have all the melancholy fascination of an extinct people, and yet they seem nostalgically familiar to us, for they surely are the charming little people who live in our folk-lore and nursery tales, as gnomes and brownies and pixies. And beside the lake they enjoy a vicarious and almost tangible immortality; one feels they are never very far away. Often, when the sun goes down behind the western rift, an after-image of a little man standing upright in a canoe forms in the golden haze above the lake's molten waters, seemingly only a little less substantial than the lavender mountains on the opposite shore that have been suspended above the water by some singular mirage effect. And sometimes when the *mwera* wind comes screaming up the lake, and pitch-black clouds sail like galleons before it, one can hear the wailing of lost aboriginal voices as they keen together over their fate. The fragile ghosts of the pygmies seem to cluster particularly round the tufted islands which stand like drill-sergeants before the line of Nyasa's western shores, perhaps because they there established the closest intimacy with the lake. But, although the Akafula are nearer to us in certitude and time than the 'little people' of English folk-lore, unfortunately they are scarcely less mysterious, and we would dearly wish to know more about their story.

Some facts, however, we can extract from the fabric of fable that has been woven round the Akafula. They were the hybrid product of a short-lived truce between the first weak parties of black men emerging from the equatorial forests, and communities of migrating Bushmen recently dispossessed of their ancestral homelands in North Africa and Spain. Although the Bantu were later to hunt the Bushmen down like vermin, the two races lived amicably together in the fertile country south of Lake Victoria Nyanza for some centuries during the third millennium before Christ and there they produced a race of little half-breed men—the Akafula.

From their Bushmen ancestors the Akafula inherited telescopic vision, a fleetness of foot that could outstrip many buck, and the genes that caused their mysterious dwarfing. From the Bantu they acquired resilience, initiative and skill in iron working. But the tranquil period of racial co-existence ended when fresh hordes of Blackmen advanced into Akafula territory and set them drifting off after their Bushmen forebears across the Tanganyikan plateau, searching, like them, for a more secure place to live. One must try to imagine the leader of these pygmy people coming wearily to the northern escarpment above Nyasa and turning with a sudden shout to tell his people he has seen their promised land. No one can be certain of the date or even of its century when this the first of the many 'discoveries' of the lake was made, but it must have been some time between one thousand and five hundred years before Christ. From then until the sixteenth century A.D., the Akafula were the rulers of the lake. Indeed, the last of these little people died out in Nyasaland only one hundred and fifty years ago, and as recently as 1870 Akafula families were still being hunted down in Northern Rhodesia.

These aborigines of the lake were very small, and they were very sensitive about their size. The Bantu knew them as the Batwa, but nicknamed them the *Amwandionera kuti* which means 'where did you see me?', for that invariably was the first question they put to any stranger. If they were given the prescribed assurance 'I saw you from a long way off' the pygmies would dance round shouting 'I am a big man after all', but any other answer was taken as a mortal insult to be revenged with a poisoned arrow. These pygmies had not inherited the dirty yellow skin of the Bushmen—theirs was reddish-brown which, after being polished with ochre, shone like burnished copper. But their heads were grotesquely large in proportion to their bodies, they wore long beards, their faces were flat and their noses broad, and there was an almost oriental slant to their eyes. They had long arms, but their legs were short like achondroplastic dwarfs. Nevertheless, in youth the Akafula seem to have been attractive in appearance, and we know they were very vain, always preening themselves and drumming on their chests with tiny fists. One surviving account has even eulogised 'their beautiful and clever eyes . . . and their delicate rosy lips', but everyone agreed that in old age, when the skin hung about their bodies in wrinkled parchment-coloured folds, the Akafula were incredibly ugly.

During their long trek southwards the pygmies led precarious nomadic lives, but beside the lake they slipped easily into the rhythm of its seasons. They prospered and increased. Little settlements of burnt clay huts sprang up, whose fragmentary remains called 'Akafula bricks' can still be picked up along the lake shore. They owned no stock and they had no need to cultivate the ground, for the hills above the lake were dark with game, and the Akafula were splendid hunters. Almost every morning the little men would slip off separately into the forests carrying minuscule bows and a quiver full of arrows dipped in the secret poisons they carried about their necks in calabashes; but sometimes they would make up parties to climb the bleak heights of the Nyika and gouge out its iron-ore from pits which are still to be seen today. Women and children were the food-gatherers of the Akafula community. They spent their days in robbing bird nests and bee hives, in picking wild fruit from the natural orchard of the forest, or in delving for edible roots and shrubs with their digging sticks and primitive iron hoes. And the pygmies became great fishermen. There had been a day when one of them hollowed out a tree trunk and launched it on the lake. After that innovation they harvested its waters with such success that above all else, the remembering eye of native tradition sets the Akafula standing upright in their tiny canoes, paddling across the lake and trailing crude fishing nets behind them.

In their Lilliputian land of Cockaigne there was plenty of opportunity for the Akafula to indulge their addiction for song and dance, and in them there still gleamed a remnant of the superb artistic talent of their Bushman ancestors. They have left many of their paintings behind for us to see on the grey and yellow walls of caves and rock shelters above the lake—not the burning friezes of the Bushmen but schematic patterns of grid-irons, herring-bones, circles, stars, and chevrons which held esoteric meanings for the initiated, and bear witness to their discovery of a way to express themselves in a form of writing, an achievement that was never attained by their Bantu conquerors.

Looking back over their two-thousand-year occupation of Nyasa we can see that the Akafula established a far more cordial intimacy with the lake than any of their successors. But this pygmy golden age was too good to last. Danger threatened first from Europe. For a moment of time during the second century A.D. it seemed the Akafula and their lake were to be committed to the modern world when a venturesome Greek trader from the coast penetrated to the inland seas of Africa. His reports were incorporated by the great Alexandrian cartographer, Ptolemy, in the famous *Geography* he published about A.D. 150. Unbelievably the discoveries of Diogenes were never followed up, but during the next fifteen centuries mediaeval cartographers were content to accept Ptolemy's authority without question or verification and the two oval lakes he had drawn were slavishly copied on to their maps, although increasing errors crept in just as a whispered message becomes distorted while being repeated down a line. Ignorance of the interior was partly concealed by filling it with empires and mythical animals, with long-tailed cannibals and (by a lucky guess) prancing dwarfs. Yet the elliptical twin lakes continued to appear unfailingly, until, in the eighteenth century, reports of Portuguese explorers seeped back to Europe, and the familiar dyak-crees shape of Nyasa appeared for the first time on Europe's maps. By then the Akafula round the lake had long since been exterminated.

For renewed danger had appeared with the arrival of the Bantu in the fourteenth century and a Makaranga host swept down the tsetse-free western watershed of the lake on the way to establish the fabled empire of Monomatapa on the Rhodesian plateau. The Makaranga were tall, well-built people who carried heavy flat-bladed spears and had a taste for human flesh. Long after their passing they were still remembered with horror in the hills above Nyasa. These 'barbarians [the Portuguese pioneers of Central Africa learned two hundred years later] ate everything; human beings, oxen, buffaloes, wild beasts, snakes and dogs; they left nothing behind them but heaps of bones. In the desert they devoured one another'. One clan of these invaders, the Wakatanga, attracted by the fine grazing on the plateau above the lake, settled there and proceeded to raid their pygmy neighbours living below the escarpment. They despised the Akafula for their size, hated them for their retaliatory thieving habits, and feared them for the way they slashed their enemies' legs in battle seemingly more concerned with bringing them to their own size than with killing them. But no people fight more fiercely to defend their homeland than nomads who have found a place to settle down, and during the next two centuries the Akafula more than held their own against the Wakatanga.

But about A.D. 1500 as the Bantu tide began to run more strongly, fresh hordes of black men came swarming over the northern plateau and coveted the fair land beside the lake. These newcomers were later to call themselves the Amaravi. For a time they rested and gathered strength near Choma Hill which rises from the lake shore above the pleasant fishing village of Usisya; then from this base they commenced a war of annihilation against the pygmies. Perhaps because they were facing such impossible odds, our sympathies in the ancient struggle are entirely with the Akafula. There was no question now of their drifting off again before the Bantu threat, looking for new land to colonise. The lake was theirs and they intended to defend it to the end. But slowly they were hunted down its western shore, fighting a succession of fierce rear-guard battles, which even today are all remembered in native folk-lore, and their sites marked by tradition, like battle honours named by famous regiments on their flags. The Akafula made their last stand in the swamps near the present-day railway terminus of Chipoka, and there they died royally, neither asking nor giving quarter. Although some remnants may have escaped from the shambles across the Luangwa and Zambesi and a few slave wives were spared to mingle their blood with the victorious black men, after that lakeside Cannae the Akafula disappear from history. But their affectation, their gay defiance and brilliant hunting skill still live on in a thousand legends. Even today Africans will tell you they have heard the drums of Domasi being beaten by the Akafula to lure men to their deaths, while the supernatural heirs of the pygmies, the Tokolosh, with their hairy tails and penises so long they are carried slung over their shoulders, are still the dreaded (and amorous) 'familiars' of the women of all trans-Zambesian Africa.

In place of the Akafula clay shelters, the large thatched huts of the Bantu now went up beside the lake and far down the banks of the Shiré River. And the forebears of the present inhabitants of Malawi entered into their heritage.

LAKE MARAVI

By far the most important event ever to have occurred in sub-Saharan Africa was the sudden eruption of the Negroes from the high savannah lying between the Sahara and the Cameroon rain forests. What precise sun-burst of energy set that black flood in motion some two thousand years ago is uncertain, but we know of three contemporary circumstances which were at least contributary causes. One was the encroachment of the desert on to the Negroes' homelands, another the introduction into West Africa of food-plants from Asia, and the third was the discovery by the Negroes of the use of iron. The advancing Sahara concentrated the black men within the forests;* their iron implements enabled them to conquer it; and more nourishing harvests recruited their health. Inevitably a population explosion followed, and it shattered the fevered sleep of tropical Africa. Suddenly it became alive with marching men as successive waves of Negroes swirled through West Africa seeking *lebensraum* while others broke off into the Congo basin to make another nucleus of population from which they later fanned out towards the great lakes in the centre of the continent and the upper reaches of the Nile. There they clashed disastrously with Pharaoh's soldiers, and then, as though directed by some benighted compass needle, they wheeled southwards down the high continental watershed. Here they encountered other wandering people—Bushmen from North Africa and lean brown Hamites from the east. With them the Negroes mingled their genes and produced the hybrid race we know today as the Bantu. This progeny differed in appearance from the Negroes of the west according to the amount of hamitic blood they inherited. They were united only by a common basic language and even this became modified into over two hundred vernaculars, each of them so complex that they always tended to hamper thought and its expression.

* Not only did the Sahara dry up; it also separated the Negroes from outside influences.

There was nothing planned or organised about the Bantu advance through Central and Southern Africa. It was as aimless as a summer cloud, and as unpredictable as a chance wind; yet it was as irresistible as the tide. It resulted in the Bantu colonisation of nearly all Africa south of the 'bulge', an area almost twice the size of the U.S.A., and far more wild and inhospitable. What is most remarkable about this immense conquest is that it was uncalculated and haphazard. There was no wild genius like a Genghis Khan to drive the black men down through Africa; they were not inspired by a fanatical compulsion to spread a new religious faith; they were not even obeying a vandal lust for pillage, for they moved into a stone age wilderness, poorer even than their own dark homeland. They were certainly not pioneers; rather they were refugees escaping from kinsmen made even more desperate than they by ravening land-hunger. And so their migration had more the character of a flight than of an advance and the empty horizons of the south represented not a prize but safety. As the pressure behind them mounted during the early Christian era, the first tentative march of the Bantu gathered momentum, and a whirling tangle of competing tribes went stampeding down the sub-continent, fanning out sometimes to avoid a defiant Bushmen outpost, pausing often to maul each other on the threshold of particularly favoured country, even doubling back on their tracks after encountering an unexpected hazard, yet always pressed on again by the turmoil thrashing at their heels. With them these migrants carried the political organisation of the negroes and many of them had inherited an obsession about cattle ownership from the Hamites. By the fifth century A.D. they had bitten their way right across Africa to the Indian Ocean. By the tenth century their spearheads were across the Zambesi and still pressing forward into the green-gold bush.

About this time a dilatory tribe, the Amaravi, uprooted itself from the Luba country of the Congo basin and joined the black migration. According to their own tradition these tribesmen originated from a place called Kapirimtiya, where God had stamped human and animal footprints into a slab of bare rock. Their wanderings (which may first have taken them to the

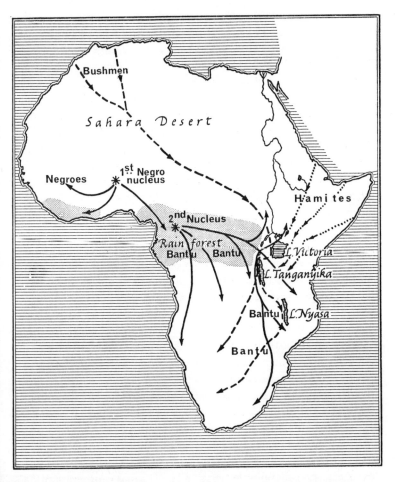

The postulated routes of Bantu, Hamite and Bushmen migrations

Zambesi) ended when they came to the delectable country beside a great lake, which, because of its infestation with tsetse fly, had been neglected by their cattle-owning predecessors. After driving off the Akafula living there, most of the Luba people settled on the lake shore, but some pressed on into the highlands bordering the lake's river outlet, which they called the Cherim or Shiré. The time of occupation must have been prior to 1546 since a Portuguese map of that date shows 'Lake Maravi' on it. But although scattered, these clans, nevertheless remained associated in a federation, and owed loyalty to a single paramount chief. The easy communication provided by the lake and river was an important factor in maintaining their cohesion and it gave them a strength and resilience unusual in sixteenth-century Africa.

The Paramount set up his royal kraal near the southern extremity of the lake and his subjects began to call their country 'Maravi' or 'Malawi' meaning 'flame'. The name was probably derived from the red light thrown over the water by the rising or setting sun, although it is possible that it referred to the glow made in the night sky by the many forges they built, for these people were industrious iron workers. Their country retained that name for more than three centuries, only to lose it during the chaotic nineteenth-century wars, but three hills—Malawi, Malawe and Malabvi—and a Portuguese province in Mozambique continued to enshrine it. Now with independence it has been restored—as Malawi—to the land of the lake.

The Amaravi were typical Bantu—belligerent, strong, energetic and fecund. Like all members of their race they differed in several conspicuous external ways from the other dominant sub-species of mankind, and they had also inherited other less obvious though specialised traits which were almost as important in contributing to their survival as their dark skins. Thus the Bantu have a special blood group pattern of their own, and a unique endocrine balance; a high proportion of their babies are born with a blue spot at the base of the spine which is a rare phenomenon in Europeans; when these infants grow older their bony parts fuse at ages differing from caucasoid and mongoloid children; colour blindness is far less common among the Bantu than in white men, and myopia is extremely rare; the electrical waves emanating from their brains have been shown to exhibit a characteristic racial pattern, while contemporary work has suggested that their brain structure is less complex than that of other races. But these are differences appreciated only by the scientist. To the layman it is their surface features—the colour and texture of the hair and skin, the prognathism and thick everted lips which particularly distinguish the Bantu and their negro ancestors as a separate people. The subject has thorns, and it must be pointed out at once that there is no evidence that the mental capacity of this stock is in any way inferior to that of other races; yet when (in relation to the story of Lake Nyasa) it is recalled that the skin and hair are derived in the human being from the same embryological tissue layer as the brain, it is hardly surprising to find that the colour and texture of Amaravi thought differed in many ways from those of contemporary Europeans and Asiatics. It meant too that the Amaravi were bound to react to circumstances in their own particular way just as it means today, in a wider context, that when African politicians boast of the singular 'African personality', they are speaking of something which is indeed unique.

Both anatomically and physiologically the Amaravi were well adapted to their new environment on Lake Nyasa. After all, similar conditions in the Congo had already sorted out the mutations which could affect their future—encouraging those that were beneficial and eliminating the harmful ones. The racial traits they had acquired accidentally and then preserved by natural selection possessed the same survival value on the lake shore as in the rain forest. The dark skin, the high ratio of surface area to body volume and the crowded sweat glands all contributed to efficient heat regulation and made it possible for the Amaravi to endure physical labour in the heat of a Nyasa summer. Their flaring nostrils were far better adapted to its humid climate than the aquiline noses of a northern race, while the sickle-shaped malformation of their red blood cells (which had been inherited from the negroes) made the Amaravi almost immune to malignant malaria. Only one vulnerable chink weakened their biological armour—the Amaravi possessed no 'built-in' protection against the blood-fluke bilharzia. And in the end these microscopical worms very nearly destroyed them.

But that parasitic Austerlitz lay in the distant future when the Amaravi first settled down beside the lake. Indeed at the time it seemed they were favoured above all others of the Bantu world. They had no concern with the universal African problem of water shortage; the usual dangerous dependence of their race on a vegetable diet was easily avoided by reaping the rich protein harvest of the lake; Maravi's boundaries were defended by barriers of pestilential bush and, provided they could harness the waters of their lake, abundant crops could be harvested for very little labour. Indeed, the Amaravi prospered for many years. Essentially they were cultivators of the soil. The appearance of the Pleiades in the early evening sky was a signal to plant out the millet that provided their staple food. They became skilled iron workers; clay furnaces went up everywhere round the lake and were tended by expert smiths whose craft was handed down from father to son. The pottery produced by the lake women attained a symmetry and utility unusual in a people who had no knowledge of the potter's wheel. Basket-ware of such fine quality was made that it could be used for water storage. Dug-out canoes, perfectly adapted to the dangerous waters of the lake, were hollowed out from msasa trees by men so skilled in 'lakemanship' that one wonders what they might have accomplished had there been an ocean for them to master instead of a land-locked lake.

Maravi was a man's world. Women, as always before the invention of the plough, were the drudges of society, and they were mercilessly exploited. Indeed the possession of a wife was the equivalent of a life pension for her husband and if he were lucky he might acquire several more in this polygamous society, while to pursue an absurd analogy further, it could be truthfully maintained that the pension died with its recipient, for widows were often buried alive with their dead husbands. Thomas Jefferson once wrote of negroes 'that their love is ardent but kindles the senses only', and certainly the women of Maravi found little spiritual or emotional experience in marriage, for it was based quite frankly on motives of economy and succession. They toiled from dawn to dusk in lakeside gardens, and returned to their villages in the evening, bearing on their backs a heavy bundle of firewood and the latest straddling infant. Inside a smoky hut the women then prepared the evening meal, serving up a tasteless pile of porridge, the size of a child's sand-castle, to their menfolk; only much later were they graciously permitted to finish off their leavings. But their duties were by no means finished. For Maravi men did not know the meaning of sexual abstinence; self-denial (if even thought of) was regarded as absurd for they were the honoured protectors of society and the providers of luxuries —which plainly entitled them to life-long incontinence and philandering. Admittedly their moral code spared them the repressions, prudery and hypocrisy of European communities, but it also denied these people the expansion of the human spirit that is consequent on the sublimation of sex.

The long line of the lake diverted the main routes of African travel from Maravi and wrapped it in unusual seclusion to work out its own destiny. This isolation was not altogether a dis-advantage. By the standards and values of the age, Maravi's was a perfectly valid society which might have easily developed into a highly organised Bantu state like those flourishing round Lake Victoria. Indeed for a time it seemed it would. The information we have of the early Amaravi may be scanty but it is always tinged with respect. We find a Portuguese missionary of Sena in 1586 writing with considerable deference about his powerful neighbours to the north. In 1616 a Portuguese trader passes through their country, entertained as he goes by a succession of chiefs. Soon afterwards a Maravi army 20,000 strong takes the field and subdues the enormous tract of country between the Luangwa and Zambesi rivers. In 1624 the Jesuit priest Luis Mariano speaks of the flourishing trade carried on between the Portuguese of Tete and the people of the lake; forty years later Godinho calls their capital a 'Zimbaue' which at least suggests the existence of a well-organised tribal organisation, while in 1667 we find Father Manual Barreto reporting: 'the Maravis are very warlike and are feared among all the kaffirs . . .' and he goes on to say they are 'governed by its Emperor, named Caronga', whose emblem of power was a stool.

Then quite suddenly a dull silence settles over the country of the lake which is broken only by an occasional whisper from it of strife and cruelty. For towards the end of the seventeenth century the Amaravi were overwhelmed by bilharzia, and their pragmatic culture, which had previously protected them as a people, made it quite impossible for them to find a way of delivering themselves from their parasitic bondage.

In the end their very stability had brought ruin to the Amaravi. The combination of a permanently settled unhygienic society and the close proximity of stagnant water provided ideal conditions for the propagation and increase of the bilharzial fluke as well as other parasites like hookworm. The lake people in consequence were bled to incredible depths of anaemia and inertia.

Bilharzia (or schistosomiasis) is a very ancient disease; it has been demonstrated in Egyptian mummies, and doubtless was carried into Central Africa by immigrant Hamites. The patient's symptoms are caused by the invasion of his blood stream by tiny trematode worms and more particularly by the passage of their microscopical eggs through the walls of the affected person's bladder and intestinal tract, or by their deposition in organs like the liver, brain and lungs which are inflamed, corroded and ultimately destroyed. Sufferers from bilharzia bleed continuously from the bladder or intestine until after many years of apathetic misery they succumb to anaemia and intercurrent diseases or to the destruction of vital organs.

The flat worm which causes the disease is barely visible to the naked eye. Male and female forms live together for thirty years or more within their host's veins, in an almost permanent state of copulation; a single female can produce anything up to 30,000 eggs a day. According to the species of the fluke, these eggs are designed to be excreted either in the human host's urine or faeces, and they can only survive if they happen to be voided into fresh water. There they hatch out into minuscule free-swimming embryos which seek out and enter the bodies of water snails which, like parasitic 'hitch-hikers', they use as intermediate hosts, multiplying in them prodigiously to produce swarms of wiggly-tailed larvae. These when liberated into water, in their turn possess the power of penetrating human skin, and once inside their victim's body they mature in their blood-stream into adult worms, and the whole complicated life cycle begins again. Paradoxically it is when the bilharzia developmental cycle goes astray that the parasite causes the most disastrous effects in men. For a proportion of the eggs liberated in the blood by the adult trematodes fail to find their way to the bladder or intestine and finish up instead in dead-end organs like the liver which, if the infestation is heavy enough, are eventually destroyed. The chances of this occurring bear a direct relation to the number of adult parasites harboured by each human host; in other words, bilharzia differs from most diseases in being a quantitative rather than a qualitative disorder.

The lake shore of Nyasa provides ideal conditions for the bilharzia life cycle. Summer rains bring streams tumbling down the escarpment to meander slowly through the flat plain as they approach the lake. In the dry weather as the flow decreases, the streams silt up, and a series of shallow pools are left along their course, which the inhabitants, in preference to the crocodile-infested lake, use as watering points, bathing places, refuse receptacles and, unfortunately, latrines.

For human beings have a curious predilection to perform their excretory processes beside or into water, possibly because the surrounding vegetation affords them privacy. Bilharzia utilises this unhappy tendency. The fresh-water snails which form its intermediate hosts are true mess mates of man and only thrive in foul water. This they found in the heavily-populated lake shore of Maravi three centuries ago, and once the fluke had established itself on this important bridgehead in Central Africa, further conquests followed. Today bilharzia is taking over from malaria as the major scourge of the tropics. Over 150 million persons in the world are now infected, and the number is rapidly increasing. But probably no people were so grievously affected as the Amaravi. For they were re-infected daily as they paddled in infected pools or drew water from them; then by using them as privies they kept the parasitic cycle turning incessantly. Inevitably the people of the lake became riddled with trematode eggs. A brisk haemorrhage from the bladder was regarded as a normal sign of puberty; bellies enlarged to accommodate the swollen and damaged livers. The previous energy of the Amaravi was replaced by apathy as they became weighed down by their terrible load of parasites, and the power of the tribe withered like a blighted tree.

Worse: a vicious circle set in. Less food was grown by the tired people so that malnutrition, evidenced chiefly by the appearance of enormous festering leg ulcers was added to their troubles. And as the Amaravi rotted with disease their way of life which so far had preserved them in a hostile world failed them in the emergency. For their own Bantu culture by now had bred out from them any chance of producing a delivering genius who might find a means to rescue them from their predicament.

A people's behaviour and destiny are shaped by their community culture as well as by racial inheritance and environment. And Bantu culture is a monolithic, stultifying thing, a candle-snuffer of the human intellect. Above all else it taught the Amaravi to discountenance any form of change; their only ambition was to lead the same lives their ancestors had led—for these ancestors were the gods who filled their pantheons.

The design of the Amaravi social system was to integrate the individual not into himself but into a society that felt undivided from the past even by time. In Maravi the dead were just as valid as the living—and sometimes much more powerful. Rather in the way our own attitudes have been standardised today by mass media of information like the press and radio, the cinema and television, so Bantu culture tends to cut down all original thought as soon as it is formulated, like grass being mowed and rolled into a flat lawn; admittedly no weeds can flourish there—but nor can flowers. Every deviation from the norm (except unnatural ferocity towards the helpless) was suspect in Maravi. Twins were often destroyed at birth and the eruption of teeth in an unusual order might lead to infanticide. Any man with talent, ambition, or originality was either killed or driven away from the tribe, and his redeeming genes which might have emancipated a whole nation were lost from the common pool. Even a man with a large head (and presumably a larger-than-average brain) had a poor expectation of life, for it was the custom on the accession of a new chief to provide him with suitable receptacles in which to keep his lucky charms—and capacious craniums were particularly favoured for the purpose. And so, in their determination to

ensure uniformity among themselves, the Amaravi, like other
Bantu people, threw away the divine gift to the human race of a
psyche which is still capable of expanding indefinitely even though
man's bodily shape has already been fixed by evolution. Their
society may have been commendably egalitarian but it was also
the apotheosis of the lowest denominator. The Amaravi became
incapable of producing another St. Augustine, a Caedmon or even
a man whose mind could relate the presence of fresh-water snails
to the disease that was devouring them. And so an extraordinary
people became so ordinary in thought and spirit that they could
visualise no world beyond their own lake shore. They thought of
themselves as the only human beings; and they became so im-
provident that they saw no sense in growing more grain than
provided for their own immediate needs of food and beer.

The most baneful effects of their indigenous culture did not
intrude upon the Bantu individual until the approach of puberty.
Indeed infancy passed in almost ideal psychological surroundings
of marsupial security, strapped and rocked on a mother's back
and, until the age of three, suckled on demand. Perhaps this early
security was and is one of the factors that allows Bantu infants to
pass the accepted milestones of development, like talking and
walking, sooner than European children. At the age of four they
are already useful members of society and able to make a contribution to its economy. Tiny girls can be relied on to look after
the babies of the family, and as soon as boys are able to walk they
become responsible herders of the village goats. But their childish
curiosity, as they grew older in Maravi, was answered only with
magical explanations, and however satisfying these may have been
they did not allow of any speculation. And the laudable politeness
they were taught to exhibit to their elders had the unforeseen
effect of making them inclined to soften disagreeable facts with
untruthfulness. As children they received no hint that their
progress might depend on individual endeavour; instead they
were brought up to believe that the only important things to
learn in life were the intricate patterns of clan relationship and the
performance required of them in elaborate tribal rituals. Privacy,
so conducive to mental expansion, was non-existent; the sole
outlets for their emotions lay in dancing and in a rhythmical form

of music devoid of chords or melody. In any case their intellectual powers could never be properly developed for they knew no method of writing, and the Amaravi grew up in a world of sound rather than in that world of sight which continually inspires detachment, novelty and irrelevance.

And at puberty the Amaravi children become irrevocably engulfed in the mental web of their Bantu milieu. After undergoing bizarre and undeniably exciting ceremonies, they emerged as fully fledged members of the community to stare with their elders in bewilderment at an unfathomable world. The initiation rites of boys began immediately after their first nocturnal seminal emission. They were then secluded in the bush under severe discipline from tribal elders, who instructed them in various skills, venery and folk-lore. At the end of weeks of mind-manipulation and secret ritual (which at one time included eating some part of an enemy who had been killed in battle) the youths returned to their villages to celebrate their manhood. It was the great occasion of their lives; customary rules of behaviour were relaxed and the ceremonies that followed struck foreign observers as intolerably obscene. One of them, the Reverend W. P. Johnson, summed up the missionary attitude by growling, 'the whole thing lends itself to gross immorality'. This perhaps was a little unfair, for the festivities were not very different from those accompanying a Mediterranean carnival, and this was particularly noticeable when the novitiates dressed themselves up in animal skins and masks to be welcomed by the adult men of the tribe into a primitive masonic-type of brotherhood called 'Nyau'.

Girls in conformity with their lower social status underwent less impressive ceremonies. These took place after their first menstruation, by which time most of them had been married for several years, and predictably, the early missionaries found them even more salacious than the boys' initiation. These rites, one of the brethren thundered, are intended 'to inhibit any virtuous feelings in them'; the Reverend Donald Fraser described them more succinctly as 'sin triumphant'; while Henry Rowley, a Magomero pioneer, tantalised the Mission's supporters at home with the information that the girls 'were taken into a hut and what passed there I don't exactly know, and if I did, I don't think

I could describe. It was harm, much harm, I fear.' After their second menstruation the girls went through a course of 'teasing' and were then 'danced' almost naked before the assembled villagers, 'to the glorification' gasps poor Rowley, 'of sensuality'.

The result of all this brain-washing to which the Amaravi were subjected was to make them think alike, behave alike and even look alike. The cult of rigid uniformity set them drifting into something akin to a pre-hypnotic state. Nearly all exigencies and emergencies which could affect their lives had been foreseen, and a pattern of response prescribed for them. But when the unexpected did occur, their reactions inclined to be impulsive, or conditioned by a mass hysteria which was completely deaf to reason.

And because they were unable to rationalise between cause and effect, the Amaravi, like so many western societies before them, became a magic-ridden people. Like prehistoric reptiles attempting to postpone their inevitable extinction by elaborating body armour or elongating their fangs, the Amaravi developed a protective cult of witchcraft to defend themselves from the inexplicable. In their benighted philosophy, misfortune meant that some ancestral spirit had been offended; disaster to a crop came to be regarded as punishment for an offence against taboo, while death invariably was considered the result of necromancy. This faith in witchcraft admittedly provided a substitute for a spiritual belief in God, for, although they vaguely recognised the existence of a Supreme Being, he was so far removed from the world as to be unapproachable and utterly unconcerned with human affairs. And so, lacking a Redeemer, these people filled the darkness instead with evil spirits who were ready at any moment to pounce upon them, and they spent their lives in distracted attempts to appease these fiends of their own creation.

There was no conception of an after-life where earthly virtues would be rewarded and sins punished: in consequence the Amaravi possessed no inner censor of conscience or of fear to mould their actions. And compassion vanished from their souls. Because death was an expression of some demoniac disapproval, even the dying in Maravi could expect no comfort in their last hours; instead they were dragged unceremoniously from their huts and left to expire in the bush lest a greater calamity be visited upon the community.

Yet these people's magical beliefs were not without a certain sophistication. They differentiated, for instance, between sorcerers and wizards. Sorcerers were those members of the community who could cast spells over an enemy by employing 'medicine' or some other well-recognised technique of enchantment, and they were not considered to be particularly malevolent people; after all, they were only using methods that were freely available to everyone and which formed part of the stock-in-trade of the exorcisers of the tribe—the medicine men.

Wizards, on the other hand—and their female counterparts, witches—were considered to be of tremendous danger to the community, and very, very evil. They were people 'possessed' by mysterious innate powers which were constantly working to bring disaster to the tribe. It was believed they could assume forms of animals like hyenas and snakes, and enter huts at night to cast their spells without disturbing the inmates. Some were supposed to be ignorant of their powers and to have obtained them passively, but others were considered to have acquired the art deliberately by performing some weird ritual, like sleeping on their mother's grave. Such monsters were known to be cannibals too, who lusted after human flesh and killed their victims so that they might exhume them later to satisfy their cravings.

Accordingly it seemed logical in Maravi to seek out and destroy these public malefactors as soon as their supernatural powers were recognised—and their children too, in case the black art had been inherited. Thousands of innocent people were poisoned and burnt beside the lake each year. But before any judgement is passed on such fevered beliefs, it must be remembered that only a little earlier nine million wretched men and women in Europe were put to death for practising witchcraft, and that as late as 1705 two witches were executed in Northampton.

Naturally the 'smellers out' of witches—the *Singanga* or tribal medicine men—wielded tremendous influence in the community, and wealth too, for these Bush Torquemadas combined their vocation with herbalism and rain-making. Their procedures of divination were invariably carried out in public, and were considered to be infallible. Usually they took the form of poison ordeals in which the bark of the mwavi tree—*Erythrophlpœum guineënse*—was used. It was cut from the tree on moonlight nights and kept in bags of baboon skin. When required for an ordeal it was pulverised by a special pounder—a *mapondela*—and mixed with the excrement of owls and hyenas. The *Nganga* now took over. He dressed up for the occasion in a mask and a terrifying costume of monkey tails, animal skins and feathers. After mixing the powdered bark with water he executed a convulsive dance, gibbering unearthly incantations, foaming at the mouth and with eyes starting from his head. Around him stood a trembling circle of suspects. Suddenly he would run screaming wildly with outstretched fingers towards some wretch who would be given the mwavi to drink. The victims were chosen with care: they were usually potential trouble-makers, eccentrics, or friendless widows. The poison was invariably accepted eagerly, not only because reluctance would suggest a guilty conscience, but also because the suspects were genuinely anxious to vindicate themselves of the charge of withcraft. Everything depended on the dose of poison administered to them, for a large dose of mwavi was followed by vomiting, which denoted innocence, while a smaller amount was lethal and caused an agonising death that was made more hideous by the insults and blows of the hysterical crowd which pressed round to mock the dying person's convulsions. A dozen might be killed at a single ceremony and their last sight was of a mob of shouting warriors running off to execute their children. Then their bodies, too foul for decent burial, would be mutilated and left for the dogs and jackals to fight over. Sometimes fowls were used as substitutes for the accused—but with no intention of making any concession to humanitarianism; for if they died after taking mwavi, the people they represented were burned to death (and each village in Maravi possessed its burning place) or sold into slavery.

It is difficult for us to comprehend the full horror these poison ordeals hung over the people of Maravi. 'The native life,' Dr. Livingstone once gravely noted 'is one of fear. They are always afraid of something.' As the population dwindled round the lake, loyalties became restricted to family groups, and the earlier cohesion of the tribe blurred and disintegrated into a haze of suspicion and superstition. Only the most sagacious recognised the pernicious influence of the lake. Some time after 1800, one clan drifted off into the hills and ultimately formed the Cewa tribe.* Others like the Achipeta seceded soon afterwards. The remainder sank into increasing helplessness and apathy.

Of course this was exactly the kind of situation that invited aggression. It was like a rich estate whose owner has become too weak to defend it from gangs of thugs, and there were plenty of thugs abroad in Central Africa at the beginning of the nineteenth century. Trouble came simultaneously from Arabs, Portuguese and Angoni. The frail society of Maravi crumpled under their combined onslaught and its last paramount chief is known to have died of starvation. By the eighteen-fifties their nation was nothing more than a rabble of terror-crazed refugees. Even their proud name was lost. Livingstone and his companions knew them as the Manganja—the lake people—and speak of them as a modern traveller might describe the inhabitants of another planet. They were dressed, they tell us, in skins and cloth made from the beaten-out bark of baobab trees. They possessed neither wheel nor plough, nor any better source of light than that provided by burning sticks. No method of writing or enumeration had been evolved. No attempt had been made to irrigate their crops from the immense reservoir of the lake. There were no buildings of stone, no conservation works, and no inscriptions to speak to the Amaravi of their past. Only the arrival of the white men, whom a century later their descendants were to condemn and vilify, saved these people from extinction. Had it been delayed by a few decades the only traces left of the Amaravi for later archaeologists to unearth would have been some scattered teeth, a few iron hoes and the hollowed stone querns they used to grind their corn— nothing more.

The first white explorers on the lake seem to have found the Manganja singularly unattractive. We hear nothing from them of

---

* Bruwer notes in *African Studies* (vol. 9, p. 33) that 'Cewa' can be translated as 'look back'. It may be that this tribe was a separate branch of the Amaravi, who separated much earlier.

the familiar Bantu virtues. Their accounts do not speak of the extraordinary charm of full attention which is one of the attributes of the African, nor of their proverbial hospitality, nor even of their cheerful ability to continue working at dull routine tasks. Even the compassionate Livingstone found little to praise in the Manganja: instead he rails over and over again at their revolting savagery and lack of human feelings. These people, of whom the Portuguese had spoken with such respect two centuries before, were, according to him, cruel, cowardly, dishonest and treacherous, although he was at pains to emphasise that this may have been in part due to the merciless oppression of their conquerors. And the Doctor's companions were even more scathing in their criticism. The virtuous Henry Rowley found himself shuddering at 'the visible presence of evil' when he encountered the Shiré natives. Waller speaks of the Manganja as a 'murderous and bloodthirsty set of rascals', and James Stewart who was later to devote his life to the welfare of the Bantu, displays an odd and contradictory contempt for those he encountered on the Zambesi and Shiré. There were, we learn from him only, 'four things for which they care—dancing, drumming, drabbing and drinking'. He was revolted by the ugliness of 'these dirty degraded people' and some of his descriptions almost scream with a pathological abhorrence. In a flurry of mixed metaphors, Stewart sneers at 'that perpendicular white-turnip-looking brow, pig-chap-looking cheeks and expressionless face'. A woman he meets is pronounced 'ugly beyond expression', and he goes on to tell us 'they are all that, fat, fat, fat, square-shouldered and ox-looking, and when clad in that abominable stuff of bark, are frightful sights for civilised eyes'. Then, rather in the manner of a Shakespearian character, he ends his account with an expostulatory, 'God's image!'.

His feelings on the matter are understandable, for the women of Maravi at the time went to extreme lengths to disfigure themselves, perhaps to appear less attractive to the slavers. They filed their teeth to resemble those of crocodiles, shaved their scalps, covered their bodies with foul-smelling grease and hideous cicatricial tattoo patterns, and threaded discs the size of napkin rings and made of wood, quartz and ivory, through holes in their upper lips which in consequence stuck out 'like pigs' in a perpetual grin. No wonder Rowley gasped that their 'feminine ugliness' was 'almost overpowering'.

It is only fair to say that had the missionaries reached the lake a few years earlier they would have been far less critical of its people. For they saw them when they had reached the very nadir of their fortunes. Only twenty years before, three chain reactions set off from the periphery of Africa at different times had converged on Maravi, and reaching it together, had plunged it into a final apocalyptic fugue of savagery and horror.

3

NIGHTMARE

Disaster for the Amaravi stemmed from three widely separated hinges of world history. The first swung a gate open in Arabia a little before it grew light on June 16th, A.D. 622, when two men riding camels and leading a third padded up to a cave on Mount Thor overlooking Mecca. They dismounted silently and entered. An anxious conversation followed with someone hiding inside, and a few moments later all three men emerged, mounted, and turned their camels' heads towards the north. They rode through the rose-grey dawn to Yathrib, which afterwards would always be known simply as Medina—'the city'—for this third man was Mohammed, son of Abdallah. Although at the time a handful of his friends already believed him to be the mouthpiece of God, Mohammed had recently been obliged to fly for his life from Mecca. But that moment in the cave when he decided to seek safety in Medina marked the turning point in his fortunes; it was also one of those watersheds of the past when the tide of human affairs suddenly changed direction and took an unexpected course. Within a few years the fugitive had become not only the temporal head of a reinvigorated Arab state, but was looked up to by his countrymen as the Prophet. And the faith he preached infused such fanatical energy into the Arabs that very soon they effected conquests greater even than Alexander's. It set Islam sweeping like a bush fire through North Africa and the Middle East; soon Spain and Southern France were afire and the flames were licking at the walls of Vienna; presently even distant China could see the glow of the fire the Prophet had kindled colouring the western sky; only in tropical Africa did it burn slowly and not until the nineteenth century begin to torment and consume the Amaravi.

Another Rubicon of history was crossed in very different circumstances some eight hundred years later when Portuguese soldiers stormed Ceuta on August 24th, 1415. Ceuta is a Moroccan town lying opposite Gibraltar, and its capture brought western men into Africa again as conquerors. It also brought immense prestige to one of their commanders—the twenty-one-year-old son of the king of Portugal. We are inclined to think of this man, Henry the Navigator, as the ideal hero-Prince of the Renaissance, but in fact he had much more in common with the mediaeval crusaders. The prodigies of exploration he inspired in his country-men after Ceuta, were prompted far more by a desire to win con-verts for the Roman Church than by a thirst for geographical knowledge or a determination to monopolise the riches of the Indies. Only after his death did the Portuguese become obsessed with the opportunity for pillage their discoveries had revealed, but it dragged them ever farther into the wilds of Africa and within a century of the capture of Ceuta they were tearing at the wealth of Maravi as vultures will tear out the entrails of a corpse.

Four more centuries went by before the third man who would profoundly affect the destiny of the Amaravi came to the crisis of his own career. On a winter night in 1819, Shaka, Chief of the Zulus, sat waiting in the depths of Nkandla Forest for Zwide, his enemy, to make a false move. Suddenly he saw his chance and he went for it hard and fast. Three days later, after a long running fight against the powerful Ndandwe army, Shaka was undisputed ruler of an empire that stretched from the Pongola river to the Tugela, and from the Buffalo to the sea. And beyond its boun-daries the blooded warriors of his tribe fanned a genocidal storm that raged for years through southern Africa and reached right up to the land of the lake.

Nothing in the story of Lake Nyasa is more remarkable than the way the fire lit by Mohammed the Prophet, the wave of pillage set in motion by Henry the Navigator and the tempest brewed by Shaka the Killer, arrived simultaneously on its shores during the nineteenth century. And by an even wilder coincidence, just behind them there followed a fourth man who would calm the distracted waters of Nyasa and bring peace back to them.

❧ ❧

Islam took many centuries to reach the lake. Its main thrust was directed away from tropical Africa, and carried the Moslems

38

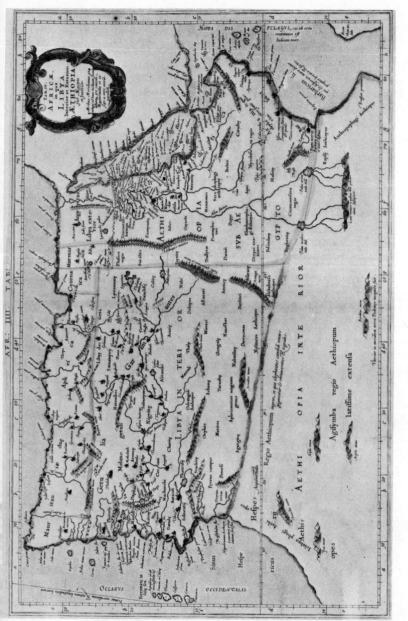

Ptolemy's map, A.D. 150

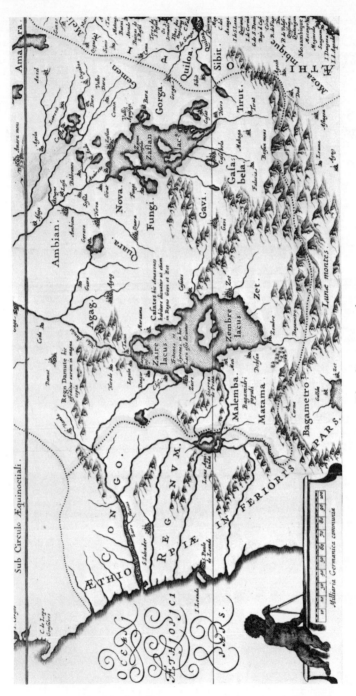

Blaeu's map, c. 1650

to more important conquests in the Middle East and Europe. Although the Arab traders of the Red Sea and Indian Ocean caught a little of the fervour of their kinsmen in the north, they never translated literally the section of the Koran which demands 'when you met those who misbelieve—then strike off their heads until ye have massacred them'. As their exploring dhows crept slowly down the East African coast they were mellowed perhaps by the tropics. By chance they kept pace with the horde of Bantu migrants trekking southwards, and being far more concerned with trade than with conversion, they opened up profitable commercial relations in the eighth century A.D. with these black men and established a succession of trading posts on the coast, of which Kilwa became one of the most important. For a long time the Arabs sailed no farther south than Cape Delgado where their friendly monsoon winds failed them, but a chance gale in 1147 carried one of their boats down to the mouth of the Zambesi. After this happy accident increasing numbers of Moslems ventured up the great river attracted by the wares that natives of the interior brought to them for sale. Even now these Arabs were still unconcerned with conquest or annexation; they were essentially merchants, who bartered their 'trade-wind beads' and Indian textiles for ivory, gold, ambergris and tortoiseshell, which were in such demand in the Mongol Court at Peking that until 1430 regular fleets of Chinese junks sailed each year to the Arab ports of East Africa to fetch them. Only when that distant market collapsed did the Arabs turn seriously to the other valuable commodity they had for sale—slaves—and the darkest chapter in the lake's story began. But before very much of it had been written the Arabs of the Zambesi and Nyasa—whose number has been estimated at 10,000—were temporally evicted by the more powerful Portuguese.

It was only after the Sultan of Muscat had moved his court to Zanzibar in 1840 that Arab influence was again extended to the lake, but now the slave trade they directed grew to the ghastly proportions that so appalled Dr. Livingstone two decades later. This time the Arabs came directly overland from Zanzibar in well organised caravans flying the red flag of the Sultan. Although in Tanganyika they engaged directly in the slave trade, even setting up a number of independent sultanates, those Arabs who turned down into Maravi country preferred to work through Bantu agents.

One tribe, the Yao, turned out to be particularly useful to them in this respect as 'hunting dogs'. They were a warrior people whom an accident of history—the overrunning of their homes beside the Rovuma river by the more numerous Makwa some time in the eighteen-fifties—had made splendidly available to the slavers. For the Yao, drifting southwards in distracted kinship groups, had been taken in as honoured guests by the Amaravi. Their hospitality was poorly repaid; they were succouring a people whom nowadays we would call fifth columnists. As soon as the Yao had regained their breaths they erupted like a succession of time bombs, attacking their hosts and setting themselves up in their places as robber chieftains round the lake's south-eastern shores. These activities happened to coincide with the arrival of Zanzibar Arabs armed with numerous flint-lock guns (which the invention of percussion cap had made redundant in Europe), and the Yao were delighted to discover they could sell their demoralised Amaravi subjects to them as slaves.

A flattering admiration for their new business associates soon drove the Yao to adopt the Arab dress and manners and even their religion. For there was much in Mohammedanism that appealed to them, and, indeed, to all Bantu. It was far more easily comprehensible than the rival (and less compromising) faith of Christianity: it had no racial bias, and could be readily adapted to embrace many of the pagan beliefs that stood at the very root of Bantu thought. Thus Islam maintained the propriety of the chattel-concept of women, it permitted plurality of wives, and was admirably tolerant of divorce. Moreover, conversion required only the repetition of a few readily learnt words, while the prospects of a moslem Paradise, where the faithful were attended by quartettes of luscious virgins, seemed far more attractive than the cloudy Christian Heaven where only damp winged figures awaited them. It is little wonder then that despite the heroic efforts of Christian missionaries, nearly a third of the inhabitants of Africa today have turned to Islam for their faith.

But perhaps more than for these benefits, the Yao of the eigh-

teen-forties were attracted to Islam by the immense prestige conversion gave them, as well as by the guns it immediately placed in
their hands. And encouraged by their profitable association with
the Moslems, they began to raid farther into Maravi to obtain
their human merchandise, carrying with them a musket frontier
and internecine fighting far round the southern lake and into
the Shiré Highlands.*

By the time the white men reached Nyasa, the Yao (whom they
called Ajawa) had set themselves up as a ruling aristocracy in a
dozen little gunpowder principalities at the southern end of the
lake, and there was truth in the Arab proverb 'when you play the
flute at Zanzibar, all Africa as far as the lakes dances'. In each of
their capitals there lodged an Arab or half-caste slaver who was
the chief's admired friend and the organiser of his raids, and now
Arab dhows sailed across Nyasa, where only canoes had gone
before, bringing loads of shackled victims to Yao strongholds
like Makanjira and Mponda. For, only twenty years after their
eviction from the Rovuma, the Mohammedan Yao had become
the grandees of the lake country.

Even today in their long white *khanzus*, and red fezzes or
beautifully embroidered skull caps, the Yao stand out sharply
from the other people of the lake. They have preserved a remarkable air of dignity; their brown Bantu eyes are brightened a little
by the wisdom of the East and there remains a suggestion of
arrogance in their bearing.

In the hey-day of their power they must have appeared still
more striking; all the early missionaries speak of their superior
intelligence and physique. Henry Rowley, comparing them with
the Manganja, writes that a Yao man was 'at once seen to be
physically the superior, his face was broader, his frontal development more masculine, and the organs of causality fuller', and he
seems to have been genuinely relieved to find that the Yao women
were fitted to cope with these supermen, for they, he adds gravely,
'were large of stature, full-fleshed, and sensual-looking to the last
degree'. But, like all the other Europeans, Rowley was appalled
by the Yao's ruthless brutality. Young speaks of a chief he met as

* When it suited them the Yao also traded slaves with the Portuguese from the
Zambesi.

41

'one of the old type Ajawas, haughty and detestable for his cruelty', and not unnaturally the missionaries were always inclined to take the side of the Manganja against them.

One is apt to think of the Europeans and Arabs of Central Africa as being entirely responsible for the enormous crime of its slave trade; nothing of course could be further from the truth and it is salutary to remember that many Bantu tribes shared their guilt, particularly the Yao who carried the fires of Islam to Lake Nyasa and set it burning along its southern and eastern shores.

Although they were separated from each other by eight centuries, the effects of the Portuguese and Arab intrusions into Central Africa bear a curious resemblance to each other. Both added immeasurably to human knowledge of the continent, each degenerated into a squalid man-hunt for slaves, and yet in both their brilliant beginnings the clear notes of crusading trumpets could be heard. For the Portuguese explorers whose caravels first crept down the Atlantic coast of Africa and then broke into the warmer waters of the Indian Ocean, regarded themselves above all else as soldiers of the Cross. The Pope himself had imposed on them the duty of seizing and converting the heathens of Africa, and had even granted plenary indulgence to those who perished on this holy errand. Unhappily their original eagerness to spread the Gospel was very soon replaced by a less becoming interest in the acquisition of ivory, precious metals and slaves.

In their search for these profitable commodities the Portuguese moved rapidly into the history of Lake Nyasa. As early as 1518 the first authentic news to reach the west for thirteen centuries about an inland sea in the centre of the continent was obtained from natives living on the Congo. And when the white men a little later began the exploration of the Zambesi, which seemed to offer them easy access into the interior, they heard a great deal more about it. At this time the Amaravi were driving the pygmies down the lake's shore and had not yet given it their name, so the Portuguese followed the old cartographers by calling it Lake Zaire. Joao de Barros is the first chronicler who gives us any details of its character: its length, he tells us perfectly correctly, is 'a hundred leagues', but he adds excitedly (and less harmoniously with the facts) that it 'sends forth three rivers, viz. the Tucuy, the Zaire and the Zambere, which lower down is called the Cuama'. Of these de Barros identified the Tucuy with the Nile, and so endorsed Ptolemy's original concept of that great river rising from a lake in the far interior. Not unnaturally these early Portuguese on the Zambesi displayed considerable interest in such a geographical phenomenon as the Nile source lying only a few days march away to the north. Visiting Amaravi traders were continually questioned about their lake and between 1565 and 1586 several reasonably factual descriptions of Nyasa were sent back to Lisbon.

Although they had come originally to argue and convert, the Portuguese remained on the Zambesi because they recognised the trading possibilities of the interior. Before long they established profitable relations with the lake people—and inevitably this brought them into conflict with the Arabs already settled in the region. Trouble was sparked off at Sena in 1571, when all the Christians' horses and oxen brought out with great difficulty from Europe died from what we can guess now to have been trypanosomiasis. But the mystified Portuguese suspected the Arabs of poisoning their animals, and when one of their grooms (following the judicious applications of a red-hot iron to his chest) confirmed their suspicions, the Moslem inhabitants of the town were put to death in particularly brutal circumstances except for the single Arab who under torture was persuaded, suddenly, of the advantage of the Christian faith.

But reports of the Manica goldfields soon diverted Portuguese interests from Maravi into the opposite (and apparently more lucrative) direction of Monomatapa. And the more they heard about the fabulous wealth of this Bantu 'Empire' which then extended over most of modern Rhodesia, the more they became convinced that in its eastern Manica Province lay the Ophir of King Solomon. The Portuguese began to see themselves as new Conquistadors whose exploits would soon eclipse those of Pizarro and Cortés. But the dream of this other Eldorado nearly destroyed them for they stormed after it into the unknown bush

43

completely ignorant of its deadly fevers. And when their fumbling attempts to unearth the 'talents of gold' they had read about in their Bibles ended in disaster, they reacted with the blind fury of lunatics, and revenged their sufferings and frustration on the Zambesi natives. Now we read far less in their chronicles about Maravi: their pages are filled instead with a consuming lust for gold, the repeated tricks of fate which denied it to them, and the atrocities they committed in such futile retaliation. One cannot help being repelled by these accounts written by the first generation of white men in Central Africa. The same demented treacheries and reprisals, cruelties and beheadings, floggings and mutilations recur in them over and over again, so that in the end the old dossiers cease to be of interest as historical documents but blur instead into incomprehensible friezes of suffering and bloodshed.

By 1525 several hundred Europeans were prospecting in Monomatapa's country, sometimes working alone, but more usually in small partnerships like the later pioneers of the Klondike and Rand: and of them only a few survived to find their way back to the pestilential settlements of Tete and Sena, there to devise some less lethal way of earning their livelihood. And unable to exploit the country's mineral wealth, the only profitable course open to them was to take over the Arab's trade in its 'black ivory'.

It was the sort of situation that would inexorably lead to the brutalisation of their minds and the sapping of their energies, and it is only fair to recall that the Portuguese made two brave attempts to disentangle themselves from the deadlock by dispatching well-organised expeditions to conquer Monomatapa in 1569 and 1608 and so redeem the failures of the earlier prospectors. There is no doubt that the captains who led these ventures were very brave and very determined men, but their rank and file were recruited from local slavers and the sweepings of Lisbon's prisons, all of them soggy with drink and lusty for women. They marched on foot through the sweltering heat of the Zambesi bush in the heavy armour of the sixteenth century carrying the banners of Christendom before them. Tsetse fly prevented the employment of cavalry with which the contemporary Conquistadors of the New World were winning their campaigns, and the soldiers

44

were no less vulnerable to malaria and dysentery than their predecessors. Accordingly the catastrophes which overwhelmed these expeditions differed from the previous ones only by their larger magnitude. And with their failure, the tide of Portuguese expansion in Central Africa hesitated, receded and then stagnated.

For by now the mother country had become dangerously overextended and no new infusion of blood was available to replace the tremendous toll taken by tropical disease and savage warfare. The Christian outposts in the bush withered like palsied limbs and sometimes died, and all there was to show in Lisbon at the end of a century of effort, were a few ounces of gold dust which had somehow slipped through the embezzling fingers of the king's agents at Mozambique. There is no doubt that a great deal of haphazard exploration was accomplished in Zambesi and Maravi country during the sixteenth and seventeenth centuries, but because it was inspired by avarice rather than by discovery for discovery's sake, the last thing the Portuguese frontiersmen wanted was to reveal its secrets to the outside world.

Yet before the Portuguese settlements in Mozambique sank into complete degeneracy, an event occurred which briefly illuminates the Maravi scene, and nearly altered the whole history of the lake. For in 1616 a white man found his way to Lake Nyasa.

The circumstances that led to his journey require a brief description. During the pandemonium of the Manica gold rush, a hidalgo of the Zambesi, Diogo Simoes Madeira, chanced upon the silver mines of Chikova, and by the judicious use of flattery spiced with an occasional threat, succeeded in persuading the Emperor of Monomatapa to cede them to the King of Portugal. These mines were almost as much a part of the legend of Africa as the gold of Ophir, and the ore extracted from them seemed to confirm their fabled wealth. Madeira's problem was to get his news—and samples—to the royal court at Lisbon. He was on the worst possible terms at the time with the Captain of Mozambique, through whose hands they would normally pass, and he knew that even if the Captain refrained from stealing the silver, he would certainly forward it as coming from himself in order to secure royal favour. Happily Senhor Gaspar Bocarro, a wealthy trader on the Zambesi, suggested a solution to Madeira's predicament by offering to pioneer a route to the sea at Kilwa which would by-pass Mozambique. From Kilwa, Bocarro was confident he could find a boat to take the ore samples to Lisbon by the east coast route.

Madeira was delighted with the idea and Bocarro at once proceeded to prepare for his journey with remarkable speed and efficiency. Bocarro seems refreshingly different from all the other men who opened up the African interior: indeed there is something deeply impressive about the 'savoir faire' and sheer physical toughness which allowed him to march in fifty-three days through 800 miles of unknown, hostile country, with far less fuss and equipment than that of the later Victorian explorers. Fortunately the journal he kept of his travels was preserved, edited and 'set down . . . in case anyone should have occasion to attempt this journey again'.

In it we read that Bocarro first purchased a thousand Katangese copper bangles, as well as other trade goods; then, having engaged a retinue of carriers to carry these passports of African travel, he set off from Tete on March 16th, 1616 with his precious silver samples. He marched downstream for two days before turning northwards from the river to avoid Sena. Next day he slept at Bawe, whose name has been retained in a Mozambique railway siding, and within the week had reached the capital town of Maravi, where we are told, he was lavishly entertained for a fortnight by the reigning chief named Mazura or Hemosura. This town according to Bocarro was one days journey from Lake Malomba, so presumably it was situated in the vicinity of present-day Balaka. With guides lent to him by Mazura, Bocarro, we learn, then 'set out from Mazura and went and slept at Moromba, a town of Mazura, and he gave the Governor thereof, who was called Inhamocumba, cloths and beads worth about two *cruzados*; and the Governor gave Gaspar Bocarro three other Kaffirs to accompany him and be his guides. Near this town of Moromba,' his account continues, 'is the great river Manganja, or a lake which looks like the sea, from which issues the river Nhanha, which flows into the Zambesi below Sena, and there it is called the river Chiry. From Moromba Gaspar Bocarro set out with three additional guides, and travelling along the river Nhanha, he slept along its banks, and the next day crossed to the other side in boats which the native kaffirs have there.'

This is the earliest first-hand description we possess of Lake Nyasa; unfortunately it is sadly lacking in detail and we are not even certain whether Bocarro actually walked down to the shore and stood beside its waters. But as he trudged on over the hills which lie beyond present-day Fort Johnston, he must have seen them glistening below him. Within two months he was at Kilwa only to discover that the Arabs had closed the Red Sea to Portuguese shipping. So Bocarro's silver samples never reached Lisbon and one of the earliest masterpieces of African travel, which has been largely ignored by history, ended on a depressing note of anticlimax.

And no other white man followed him to the lake. For it was in no one's interest to advertise a journey which had been undertaken clandestinely and anyway had failed in its purpose. In any case the Portuguese of the Zambesi were in no mood to become involved in any more exploratory adventures. Not only were they 'played out' but soon after Bocarro's visit, his friend Mazura came raiding into the country lying between their settlements and the lake—and twenty thousand spearmen on the rampage make unattractive travelling companions. Rather nervously the authorities in Mozambique prohibited trading in firearms with *os Maravis* to the north, and tried their best to avoid contact with them. And in truth there was very little incentive for the Zambesi Portuguese to involve themselves in any dangerous activities: fortunes were to be made simply by loafing in their settlements and enormous feudal estates beside the great river, stirring only to bribe some truculent chief to leave them in peace, or to drive a hard bargain with the black slavers who brought them shackled captives for sale.

For the Portuguese preferred to play a passive role in the monstrous traffic of slavery, sending Africans and Mulattoes to do the dirty work of catching men and women. In consequence only those unfortunates who could not escape their agents ever saw their white tormentors. To the majority of the lake people the Portuguese were a shadowy menace living beyond the hills, sinister human spiders who spun webs to trap them. Admittedly these terrifying white people introduced valuable crops to them like maize, cassava, sweet potatoes and rice, and even initiated them into the delights of the guitar, but these enduring benefits scarcely compensated for the massive infection of syphilis which went with them, nor for the indoctrination of the Maravi chiefs in new refinements of cruelty, let alone for the interminable internecine war loosed upon the lake shore to produce the raw material needed to fill the slave pens.

The Portuguese settlements on the Zambesi were ruled by terror; in them the whipping post was by far the most conspicuous object; Tete, Sena and Zumbo were nothing more than funnels through which the bewildered Amaravi were poured on their way to Mozambique and the plantations of Brazil. In them even today one is uneasily conscious of the imprisoned fear and hatred that in the past was fastened upon each street and house, like escutcheons of the Prince of Darkness. There, lulled by the lazy rhythm of their river, the white nabobs of Zambesia slipped into lives of such debauchery that one sometimes wonders whether any other Christian community has plumbed equal depths of degradation. These white men's homes were a strange mixture of palace and pig-sty; their time was divided between attending flamboyant church ceremonies, sleeping with African women, supervising mass floggings of their black serfs, drinking vast quantities of hard liquor and shaking with the rigors of malaria which destroy the mind before the body.

Of course there were exceptions: some of the officers who governed Mozambique were very upright men and one has the greatest admiration for the priests, eager for martyrdom, who disappeared at intervals into the bush with only their Bibles and lofty thoughts for company. The trouble was that no merchants or explorers travelled with them, and since the Portuguese knowledge of Lake Maravi came to depend entirely on hearsay, it tended to diminish. In 1627, only eleven years after Bocarro had walked there in a week, we find a missionary, Luis Mariano, informing his superiors in Rome that 'The Lake of Hemosura is 97 days distant from Tete'. But however inaccurate Mariano's account may have been, it is of interest to us because it is the first to describe the Murchison cataracts on the Shiré: it continues

'From Moravi to the Lake is half a league, as I have been assured by one who had noted every particular. From the lake flows the river Cherim [Shiré], extremely gentle at first, but its bed being afterwards divided by numerous rocks, the stream becomes too furious to be navigated. Moravi lies between the lake and the Zambezi: the town is well peopled, and there are merchants in it with whom we carry on a great trade.' He goes on to give some advice to future travellers (which is still appropriate to the tourists of today): the lake, he says, 'is four or five leagues wide, and in some places the land cannot be seen across it. . . . There is a great abundance of fish in it; the depth is eight or ten fathoms, and the Mozambique winds raise a great sea in it; so that whoever would go there for discovery ought to go in April or May.' The good priest obviously regarded a journey to the lake as a most hazardous undertaking, but he bravely concludes his report with 'Nevertheless, I shall not hesitate to proceed on it, having [and here he means 'if I were given'] the holy commands to do so.'

But if the silence about Nyasa was deepening, in one respect the Portuguese 'image' of the lake grew clearer: its irregular oval shape, hallowed for fifteen hundred years by Ptolemy, is suddenly replaced on their maps by the familiar caterpillar outline. This is first seen on a map printed by de Lisle in 1722. Hassins repeats this shape in 1737, while de la Rochette, who had evidently read Mariano's account, goes a little further by annotating his map of 1782 with the information that the lake people trade with distant Malindi, that its water is 'full of fish' and he even describes the local winds.

It was not until the last decade of the eighteenth century that the Zambesi Portuguese were roused from their long torpor by the news that the British had occupied the Cape. Suddenly they saw that their old conquistadorian dream of a 'viagem a contra-costa' and a trans-continental empire stretching from Mozambique to Angola was threatened by these energetic newcomers to Africa. It became vitally important that they accomplish the 'traversa'—the crossing of the continent—before the British could do so, for only this would give them a valid claim to the tremendous block of territory that today constitutes Rhodesia and Zambia. A promising start was made in 1796 by a half-caste named Pereira, who pioneered a route from Tete to the kraal of Chief Cazembe near Lake Mweru in the centre of the continent. Pereira (who answered more readily to the name of 'Terror') trudged there up the watershed which runs northwards between Lake Nyasa and the Luangwa River. Unfortunately the 'Terror's' sense of direction was decidedly shaky, and when he engagingly announced that he had travelled westwards to Cazembe's, and added that at one point he had been only fifty miles from Lake Maravi, the cartographers obligingly accommodated his information by slanting Nyasa obliquely to the west across their maps, forsaking the correct northerly meridian formulated by de Lisle. It was a mistake that was to plague geographers for the next sixty years.

Two years later a formidable expedition led by the celebrated Francisco Lacerda set off from Tete along the same route intending this time to march to the Atlantic. Lacerda entered present-day Nyasaland a little to the east of the road to Misalo, and crossed the headwaters of the Bua and Rusa Rivers. But like Pereira he never saw the lake nor did he get any farther across the continent, for the familiar tragedies to the expeditions of two centuries before were now dismally repeated. Lacerda himself died of malaria near Cazembe's kraal, and of his followers, only a few half-crazed survivors eventually stumbled back over the nine hundred miles to Tete.

The 'traversa' was, however, successfully accomplished only a little later by two pombeiros or half-caste traders, during the years when Europe was reeling through the tremendous calendar of Napoleonic victories. The pombeiros set off from their master's estate near Loanda in 1802 carrying a letter to the Governor of Sena. Eight years later they turned up in Tete with a story of such incredible hardships that hardly anyone believed it. Nor was the journal they had kept of their journey likely to alter that scepticism for as its editor laments it was 'wholly deficient . . . in the scientific elements of geography'. In any case people of colour were not considered to qualify as explorers in those days, so the communication they opened up between the two Portuguese colonies did nothing to substantiate Lisbon's claim to the country they had traversed. All the pombeiros in fact accomplished was to attract embarrassing attention to Portuguese methods of rule in her African colonies.

For all at once the outside world was anxious for more information about Central Africa, and its interest was catered for by an English naturalist named Thomas Bowdich who, having forsaken the mild pleasures of taxidermy, devoted himself instead to a rewarding exploration of Lisbon's dusty archives. The results were summarised in a book published in 1824, in which he tells us that Maravi 'is a little more than sixty leagues north of Tete. At the short distance of half a league from this town is a lake, which winds in a north north-east direction, being four or five leagues wide, and in some places more; but its length far exceeds the breadth, as it is known to reach Mombaca. . . .' This is the first we hear of Nyasa from an English source, but twenty years later Mr. Desborough Cooley went over the same manuscript material again and published his own version of the mysterious interior, first in the *Journal of the Royal Geographical Society* and subsequently in a book which is both remarkably dreary and wildly conjectural. Cooley wags a reproving finger at the scarcely more speculative accounts of the early Portuguese, whose errors he ascribes to their naïve acceptance of reports from natives whose 'unwritten languages', as he justifiably sighs, 'fluctuate perpetually', and he goes on to complain too of the infuriating way the names of African villages and rivers are liable to change several times in a single generation. But although Cooley provides an admirable summary of the little that was known about Maravi on the eve of the Yao and Angoni incursions and Livingstone's arrival there, his conviction that Nyasa and Tanganyika were a single lake slanted (in conformity with contemporary Portuguese opinion) north westwards across the map, led him to flounder into a mass of other fallacies.

Cooley's book was written during that polemical arm-chair era of African discovery when the explorers give us the impression of being far more concerned with pulling each other's geographical theories to pieces than with adding any contribution to the world's knowledge. Bowdich was severely castigated by Cooley, whose greater scorn however, was reserved for the two foolish

Germans who had recently reported the existence of two snow-crested mountains in the latitude of the equator. Poor Cooley in his turn fell foul of the redoubtable Captain Burton. Yet still these men's intelligent guess-work was slowly pulling aside the veil of ignorance which hid Lake Maravi from the world: and in Central Africa itself increasing numbers of Portuguese were travelling up Pereira's old route into Maravi country, avoiding the more direct river approach because they believed the Shiré to be closed by sudd and hostile natives. One of these travellers, a respected judge of Tete named Senhor Candido de Costa Cardosa, returned home at the end of 1846 from a long journey during which, he told his friends, he had made an exhaustive exploration of the 'Nyanja Grande' or Lake Maravi.

What makes this journey so remarkable for us now is that Dr. Livingstone, after freely publicising its accomplishments, later for reasons that have been glossed over by his biographers, succeeded in persuading the British public that in fact Candido had never been anywhere near the lake.

Candido was one of the gentlemen who welcomed Livingstone on his arrival at Tete in 1856, towards the end of the Doctor's own triumphant 'traversa' of the continent. Livingstone had already been told by an Arab trader about a great lake lying north of the Zambesi, and had been very tempted to visit it. So when he learned that Candido had recently seen the legendary Lake Maravi, Livingstone listened with great eagerness to his account of it and then opened his diary at a blank page and persuaded his new friend to sketch a rough map there to show its approaches; from the handwriting it is clear that the Doctor then annotated it himself. The information obtained from Candido was later recounted in letters to several friends, and repeated at length in the book the Doctor wrote in 1857 about his missionary travels.

Yet although he himself had originally drawn attention to Candido's visit to Lake Nyasa, only two years later Dr. Livingstone went to great pains to deny it had ever taken place. There are some curious aspects about this sudden change of front which have never been satisfactorily explained, and probably Livingstone himself would have found difficulty in accounting for all his conscious and sub-conscious motives for doing so. But perhaps we

Livingstone's annotated copy of Candido's sketch map of the approaches to the Lake

can find a clue to his new attitude by recalling that once, in a ruminative mood, the Doctor confessed, 'some of the brethren do not hesitate to tell the natives that my object is to obtain the applause of men. This bothers me, for sometimes I suspect my own motives.' And in 1859, Livingstone had a very good reason to wish to obtain that 'applause of men'; only a few months earlier his government-sponsored and much-vaunted expedition which had been intended to establish a centre of Christian civilisation in the Batoka Highlands, had foundered on the shiny black rocks of Kebrabasa. Livingstone felt the humiliation of that failure very deeply, less perhaps for personal reasons than for the effect the loss of personal prestige might have on his *idée fixe*—the emancipation of Central Africa. He believed his reputation could only be restored by producing some new trophy of exploration from the apparent failure of the expedition—and what could be more suitable for the purpose than the discovery of one of Ptolemy's great lakes? Admittedly to claim that discovery would make it necessary to discredit all the accounts of the Portuguese pioneers who had visited the lake before him, and in particular, Candido's, whose journey he himself had so foolishly advertised. But at least it was in a good cause, and it was by no means a difficult task: Portuguese inefficiency could be relied on to provide him with all the ammunition he required.

So within a week of visiting Lake Nyasa himself, we find Dr. Livingstone drawing attention to several obvious absurdities in the account his former friend gave him of the lake. For Candido had said his 'canoes were punted' across a 'broad and shallow lake' with 'a strong current', from which 'two rivers issue forth' in whose centre there was a hilly island named Murombola, and which 'lay 45 days to the N.N.W. of Tete'. In every one of these particulars Livingstone was now in a position to assure the public Candido had been entirely wrong, and he proceeded to deal with each of them in turn. For Nyasa, he now revealed, was in fact narrow and far too deep to allow punting, it had no current, was drained by a single river, while the mountain named Morumbala (which presumably Candido had meant) lay not in the lake but two hundred miles away near the confluence of the Shiré with the Zambesi; and finally, instead of being '45 days to the N.N.W.

J. A. Vinter, lith. from a photograph by Monson.   Day & Son. Lith.rs to the Queen.

yours Affectionately
David Livingstone

The Ma-Robert

of 'Tete' the lake was situated to the north-east and a mere one hundred and fifty miles away.

It followed then that if Candido was not a liar, he was a fool who had visited a minor lake and jumped to the conclusion he had found the great Nyasa. Livingstone himself said he inclined to the second more charitable explanation. 'To me it is clear', he mused in a letter written in the September of 1862 to Sir Roderick Murchison, 'that if he is a true man, there is still a lake between Tette (*sic*) and Tanganyika, for Candido invariably points to the N.W. or N.N.W. of Tette.' But his rising indignation with Portuguese counterclaims to priority of discovery can be sensed in the appendix Livingstone wrote two years later in his *Narrative of the Zambesi Expedition*, where he snorts, 'A broad shallow lake, with a strong current, which Senhor Candido declared he had visited N.W. of Tette, is assumed to be the narrow deep Lake Nyasa, without current, and about N.N.E. of the same point.' It was practically the last card the Doctor had to play in the game, he had taken every trick and from then on the discovery of Lake Nyasa was firmly embedded in his legend. In fact, the only remaining point at issue concerned the identity of the lake Candido had so foolishly mistaken for Lake Maravi. That small controversy continues.

Yet still the feeling persists in one's mind that Candido was not the sort of person who would lie deliberately or mislead a friend. The few descriptions we have of him suggest an honourable and reliable man, while Livingstone himself goes out of his way to tell us, admittedly after their first meeting, that he was 'intelligent', 'very kind and obliging' and that 'his statement may be relied on'. So as one casts about for a way of reconciling Candido's account with the truth, several points come to the mind at once: to begin with Livingstone was not fluent in Portuguese and may have misinterpreted some of Candido's remarks; secondly we know that an unusual number of earthquakes were recorded in Nyasa country soon after Candido's journey, and they, together with the cyclical variations in its water level may have greatly changed the lake's appearance—and that of its appendage, Lake Malombe—between 1846 and 1859; finally it must be remembered that Candido, like the Africans today, regarded the 'Nyanja Grande' as a single unit made of Lake Nyasa, Lake Malombe, and the Shiré River, whereas Livingstone and the geographers who followed him saw them as three separate entities.

So now remembering these points we must reconsider Candido's account of his journey. The only part which conforms to the description he gave of his crossing place as being surrounded by 'level plains covered with grass' is that shallow portion we now call Lake Malombe and which he considered to be an integral part of the 'Nyanja Grande': this can easily be punted across, and in it there is an appreciable current. Thus Livingstone's most damaging piece of criticism is disposed of at once. We come now to the damaging suggestion that when Candido declared there was a hilly island in the centre of the lower end of the lake, he had seen (and was speaking of) the mountain Morumbala two hundred miles away and had assumed the elephant marsh at its foot to be Lake Nyasa. But was this suggestion by Candido's detractors justified? It was prompted by the name Murombola (so similar to Morumbala) which Livingstone had written beside the island on Candido's sketch map. But in his account of the meeting, Livingstone notes that the island is also called Murombo, while Kirk wrote of it as Marumbo after questioning Candido on the subject. The likelihood is that Candido was speaking of Malombe, which Bocarro had called Moromba, and we know (on Sir Harry Johnston's authority) that an island once stood in the centre of Lake Malombe exactly where Candido had drawn it. All in all, Candido's statement substantiates rather than discredits his claim.

Much capital was made too of Candido's apparent error in saying that his lake was drained by two rivers. But the context in *Missionary Travels* suggests that this particular piece of information was not recounted as a fact, but based on hearsay evidence. And when this same subject was discussed with Kirk, Candido's description was very differently interpreted: 'No river flows out of it', he said of the lake 'it is merely expanded.' Nothing could have been much closer to the facts. This still leaves Candido's misleading information about the distance and direction of the lake from Tete to be explained. But he never seems to have told Livingstone how he reached Nyasa: certainly he did not go up the 'impassable' Shiré river, and it is most unlikely that he took the direct overland route as Livingstone seems to have concluded, for in 1846 it was being ravaged by Angoni war parties. The strong probability is that Candido followed the familiar Luangwa track to the kraal of Chief Mwase at Kasungu, who is known to have been friendly to the Portuguese at the time; from there a short march down the escarpment would have brought him to the lake shore whence his exploratory travel would have been completed by canoe, safe from the marauding Angoni. This journey of five hundred miles might well have taken '45 days' to accomplish, and it would have started off in a north-westerly direction.

But most important of all for the rehabilitation of Candido's integrity is the fact that on his map he correctly names the Shiré as the outlet of the lake and precisely identified the Cewa ('Shiva') and the Yao as inhabiting its opposite shores. By doing so the 'old Judge' completely demolishes Livingstone's lofty assumption that he visited quite another lake and assumed it to be Nyasa. It follows of course that the Doctor's claim to have discovered Lake Nyasa before the Portuguese is unfounded—although this hardly detracts from his real achivement, which was to bring that lake to life.

๖   ๕

As in the case of the Arabian desert eleven centuries before, so the African wilderness in 1787 brought forth a reforming genius —Shaka Zulu. Shaka was not the prophet of a new faith, rather he was the apostle of a concept of war unknown before in Bantu Africa—total war. To those of us who have lived at the same time as the monsters of the Third Reich, Shaka seems a familiar figure, a half-crazed creature who dreamed wild, impossible dreams of conquest—and then accomplished them. But unlike the Nazi leaders he possessed a high gift for strategy and tactics and these make him stand out like a Colossus in the abject Bantu world of his time. Men living today in southern Africa still shudder when they recall his name, and speak with awe of the devil's wind he blew through the sub-continent—the *mfecane*.

It raged far afield and when it reached Maravi it was still strong enough to choke the life out of its inhabitants.

Shaka was loved by no one and feared by all. He was a ruthless egocentric with a penchant for impaling anyone who annoyed him. When a sharp attack of dysentery abruptly removed his mother from the Zulu scene, this black Oedipus watched unmoved as seven thousand of his courtiers were slaughtered to bear her company to the Zulu heaven; then he turned and ordered her domestic cattle to be killed so that their calves might share with him the sufferings of orphanage. Whole regiments would be commanded to commit mass suicide for some trivial offence, yet somehow Shaka's very cruelty added to his stature—at least in his subject's eyes. Historians estimate that during his lifetime, this single man was responsible for the death of two million of his fellow Africans, as well as for the dispersal and disruption of scores of previously autonomous tribes.

A strange air of unreality surrounds Shaka's memory; where one can comprehend the agony of an African village or even the sufferings of a single tribe the very number of Shaka's victims produces a sense of mental blockage in us, not so much from scepticism as from sheer incomprehension of such senseless inhumanity. But then, of course, it has always been accepted that Shaka was a madman; what made him so dangerous was that his madness never lacked direction. He was very resolute and very enterprising, and remarkably unfettered by convention. More than anything else he wanted to horrify the world he knew, and that obsession turned Shaka into our supreme example of a human catalyst who could change the character of a whole people. For under his influence peaceful pastoral tribes became engrossed with blood; killing for them became a cult and an end in itself; a people for whom inheritance had always been determined by matrilineal succession turned into a patriarchal warrior society. The ancient battle-affiliations of clan were disregarded, and Shaka's levies found themselves enrolled, according to their age, in impis whose names still reverberate like distant drum taps through southern Africa. He replaced his warriors' throwing spears with short stabbing assegais, introduced huge ox-hide shields, trained regiments a thousand strong to manœuvre like a single man, and taught them a technique of close-in fighting, which together with his own revolutionary tactics, made them invincible. Zululand under his rule became a Bantu Sparta whose army has had no equal in the long history of savage warfare.

After the defeat of the Ndandwe army in Nkandla Forest in 1819, one of the Zwide's generals, Zwangendaba, succeeded by hard running in escaping from the rout and into the history of Lake Nyasa. Gathering together the remnants of his small Angoni clan from their huts beside the White Umfolosi River, Zwangendaba fled with them into the country of the Swazis. He commanded only a few hundred defeated warriors, and they were hampered by their women. But they wore the gaudy trappings of Shaka's impis, they carried his new weapons and not unnaturally they were mistaken for and protected by the prestige of the Zulu kinsmen who had defeated them. And they were as dangerous as wounded leopards; the tribesmen through whose savannah land they marched stared at the Angoni like hypnotised rabbits and fled before even being attacked. No spur to courage is so sharp as the sight of flying heels, and the Angoni fought their way through Swaziland and modern Rhodesia with growing confidence, snowballing all the time in numbers, as they incorporated warriors and desirable women into their ranks from the tribes that went down before them. Like the Matabele, who had also abandoned their homelands to escape forcible incorporation into the Zulu empire, the victorious Angoni sped through the yellow sunlight of Africa with predatory joy and in such perfect step that Shaka himself might have been watching them. Head-dresses of raven feathers danced to the rhythm of pounding feet, kilts of monkey tails swayed in time with their furious pace, goatskin fringes bobbed up and down at knees and ankles, shields of black and white oxhide were held before them like the prows of Viking boats, and stabbing assegais were steadied above their shoulders ready to 'drink the blood' of the terrified human creatures who ran before them. All the old vigour of ancient Africa seemed to have been reborn in the Angoni. Leaving a broad tract of scorched earth behind them, they turned aside to fight the Portuguese near the sea at Lourenço Marques, then drove westwards into the Transvaal where they met and were repulsed by Mzilikazi's Matabele. Deflected northwards, they retraced the steps of their migrant ancestors in a sort of Bantu riptide. No wild animals could have behaved more savagely; they killed with terrible ease and were nourished by rapine and slaughter. One rickety kingdom after another collapsed before them; Zimbabwe was pillaged in 1834 and the great Mambo, successor of Monomatapa, was defeated in battle, and skinned alive.

Fifteen years and many killings after the Angoni had fled from their homes in Natal, they stormed up to the Zambesi. Of only one thing were they afraid—water—and so the crossing of the great river was an event of such tremendous significance that their descendants still speak of it with awe. A few clans managed to scramble across at the Kebrabasa rapids which only twenty-three years later were to turn Livingstone's attention to Lake Nyasa, but the large majority, after propping up their courage with a mammoth beer drink, crossed the river near Zumbo. Their safety was assured by Zwangendaba who struck the waters with his spear and parted them. This Mosaic miracle has been precisely fixed for us in time by occurring during a solar eclipse at two in the afternoon of November 19th, 1835, and Angoni tradition goes on to tell us that one of the chief's wives was so overcome by the experience that she was prematurely delivered of a son on the farther river bank. She called him Mombera, and he grew up to be the patron of Dr. Laws who later wrote of him that, 'like Cyrus of old, God seems to have called him and used him for the special purpose of admitting the Gospel to his people, though he knew it not'.

Once across the Zambesi, all central Africa lay helpless in the sunshine before the Angoni. Replete with confidence, they split up into several divisions, the better to exploit their opportunity. The very helplessness of their victims goaded them on. One clan wrote their own amazing odyssey by marching thousands of miles to Lake Victoria Nyanza, but the majority followed Zwangendaba to the southern shores of Lake Tanganyika where he died in 1845, having rivalled his old preceptor Shaka by causing a million deaths. Quarrels over the succession now further divided his people; following different chiefs and after some intricate marching and counter-marching, as well as bloody

fighting among themselves, the Angoni eventually filtered back
into the fertile country on both sides of Lake Nyasa. The lake,
which only a short time before had stirred uneasily to the sound
of Yao slaving trumpets, now turned distractedly to catch the
wilder notes of Angoni war drums beating down its northern
shores.* Enough Maravi victims lived here to satisfy even Angoni

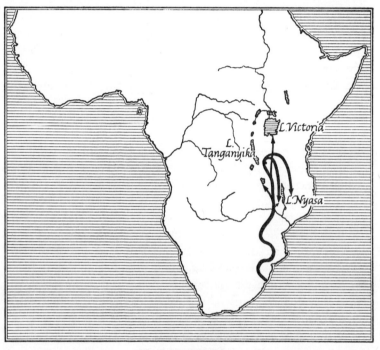

The Angoni Riptide

appetites, and soon the lake was echoing to continuous tocsin
shouts of 'koto, koto'—'danger, danger'—as it earned its name
anew with its water staining red with blood and catching the
reflection of burning villages.

The grotesque terror the Angoni inspired in the Amaravi
reminds one of the hopeless despair which overwhelmed the
romanised Britons during the Norse invasions. But the Angoni

* The Angoni were also known as the Bututa, Landseens, Mafiti, Maviti, Mazitu,
Magwagwara and Zulus.

were more ruthless than any Vikings. The loot they could not carry away they burned. No one survived their raids except youths who could be recruited into their army, and girls of marriageable age. Older men were bludgeoned to death or speared, while the crones and unwanted women were left to die in the bush after their breasts had been lopped off, a process which, according to an appalled English visitor to Angoniland, took 'twenty-four to forty-eight hours'.

The Amaravi fled like flocks of terrified sheep before the impis—often into the arms of the slavers in the south. Presently, bored with slaughter, the Angoni settled down like great birds of prey beside the lake and set up little kingdoms of their own. But they could not rest for long; as one of their own historians has told us 'to the Angoni war was like work and his heart rejoiced to think of it', and every year when the campaigning season came round they went off again on another raid of arson and plunder which set fresh mobs of panic-stricken refugees stampeding down the lake shore. An early missionary, Dr. Elmslie, who lived among the Angoni, tells us in his memoirs, 'I have seen an army, ten thousand strong, issue forth in June and not return till September, laden with spoil in slaves, cattle, and ivory, and nearly every man painted with white clay denoting that he had killed someone. . . . Around Bandawe', he goes on, 'more blood has been shed than can be related.' Other observers write with awe of even larger armies setting off on these 'annual event' campaigns, covering fifty miles without difficulty day after day, and at the end of the 'season' surging back to their chief's kraal yelling praise songs for the warriors who had been the first to hack their way into each separate stockade, and clutching in their hands the weapons and clothes of the men they had killed. Harvest time was dreaded by the Amaravi: 'The Angoni,' a European visitor of 1899 was told, 'used to come when the grass was long, sometimes we were warned by the drums in the next village and then we fled and hid ourselves in caves in the hills. At other times we knew nothing until we saw the heads of their spears in the long grass. They killed all the old people and the children and took our young men and women.'

The Cewa in the hills above the western lake possessed a few firearms and they managed to fight off the Angoni from mud forts they called *machemba*, whose vestiges can still be seen around Kasungu. And the Yao were usually strong enough to protect their slave preserves from the invaders. But the only safety for the Amaravi lay in the waters of their lake. For the Angoni had never overcome their fear of water. A fugitive had only to wade out into the lake up to his knees and he was safe. Many settled like frightened birds on inaccessible rock ledges above the lake, reminding Dr. Elmslie 'of sea-fowls on the cliffs around our coasts'; others lived in huts built above the water on flimsy stilts, or fled to tiny off-shore islands pasturing their cattle on the mainland by day, and swimming back with them each night.

By the middle decade of the nineteenth century the whole Nyasa lake shore had become a pandemonium of violence and fear and anonymous atrocity. Fighting impis and gangs of slavers led by Yao gunmen or Portuguese mulattoes milled about through a famished land engaged on an enormous man hunt, and from the far north the more highly organised Arab slavers of Tanganyika were already probing down towards the lake. This was the lowest ebb of its fortunes. The forces released by an Arab mystic, a Portuguese Prince and a Zulu King had arrived together in Maravi like scavenging guests at a carrion meal. Yet in the perverse way of history, hope was about to be born again, for immediately after administering the poison, Fate prescribed the antidote. The sky was already paling with the dawn of a new era at this moment of the lake's greatest misery as a fourth man came trudging towards it. He carried with him the prestige of a prodigious feat of exploration and he was possessed by a passionate determination to relieve the sufferings of Africa. He stood at last beside the dying lake, picked up a handful of sand from her shores and let it trickle through his fingers, stooped to dip his hands in her water, and vowed to free her from her bondage. It was the morning of September 17th, 1859; the man was David Livingstone. He had led a Christian civilising mission to the great lake, and at last its long dark night was over.

Part Two
DAWN

4

GOD'S HIGHWAY

Dr. Livingstone's place in the story of Lake Nyasa is a very special one. No other man is so identified with it. He was already famous when he first came to the lake because of several splendid achievements of exploration, and his most recent journey had set all his countrymen talking about him. Indeed it is difficult for us now to appreciate the tremendous sensation Livingstone's trans-African journey made on Britain in 1856; and it is almost impossible to realise the incredible heights of prestige to which it raised him. The British people seemed more stirred by his exploit than by anything that had occurred since Elizabethan times, and when the Doctor landed at Southampton that winter, they accorded him the sort of welcome a later generation of Americans was to bestow on Colonel Lindbergh. For Livingstone's journey had taken him to places which to the Victorians seemed as remote as outer space is to us today. Moreover, it had differed from all the other great feats of exploration in being inspired by genuine altruism rather than by self-interest. And so nearly everybody believed that in this missionary-explorer they had found an authentic Christian hero, and the more they stared at his distinctive figure, the more they discerned in it those very characteristics they considered most distinguished in their own race. In particular, they admired the incredible courage that shone through Livingstone's modest demeanour, his wholesome candour and the deep sense of religious dedication which had driven him through the wilds. And when it seemed the Doctor was a devoted family man, the common people from whose ranks he had come, took him to their hearts, and accorded him a unique and permanent place in their affections. What they did not know or even suspect was that Livingstone's character, far from being simple, was most extraordinarily complex; they had not the faintest conception that many of his undoubted virtues were marred by less admirable characteristics. For Livingstone was a strange amalgam of contradictions. Although on matters of principle he was invariably a man of iron, in practical affairs he was often a hopeless prey to vacillation; his modesty sometimes gave way to vanity and brusque assertiveness; candour was occasionally replaced by deliberate misrepresentation, and his legendary composure at times succumbed to such fits of desperate irascibility and callous unconcern for others that it was eventually to estrange him from his family and bring his next venture into Africa to tragedy. Dr. Livingstone in fact remains one of the most ambivalent characters of his age and it is this which makes him perhaps the most interesting of all the great Victorians.

However much they may have misinterpreted Livingstone's personality, the British people were nevertheless perfectly justified in giving him their unstinted admiration for a prodigious feat of exploration and endurance. Armed only with a walking stick, magic lantern, sextant, compass, nautical almanac, tattered Bible and unbounded faith, he had tramped alone right across the breadth of Africa between 1854 and 1856. But this journey was really only the logical sequel to several earlier and less publicised expeditions which during the previous ten years had carried Livingstone northwards from his mission station in Bechuanaland to seek a healthier and more rewarding site for his work (and one where incidentally he could escape from the hostility of the Boers and the bickerings of his colleagues). Beyond the further limits of the Kalahari desert the explorer had stumbled, Columbus-like, upon a new world, had come to a country of lush plains and healthy uplands woven together by a network of navigable streams all leading into a 'glorious river'—the Zambesi—which lay much farther to the west than anyone had previously imagined. By discovering that the deep interior of the continent, instead of being a desert, was a land of exuberant fertility, Livingstone had made the greatest 'breakthrough' in all the history of African exploration. And what perhaps was of even greater significance, he then revealed to a horrified public that a new and peculiarly vicious trade in slaves was being conducted there by both the Portuguese and Arabs in previously uncontaminated country.

It was perfectly in character for Livingstone to be convinced that God had led him purposefully into central Africa as His

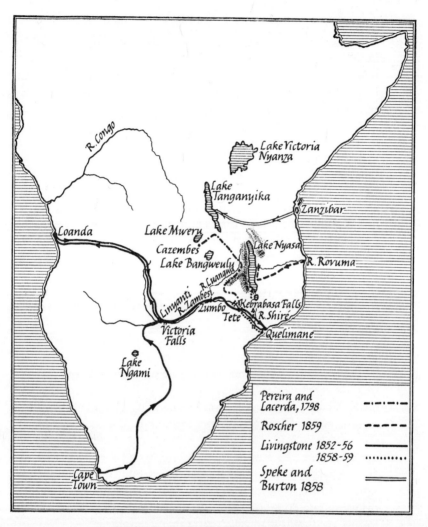

Pereira, Roscher and Livingstone's journeys

instrument to suppress what he later called 'this devilish trade in human flesh'. From the time of this revelation, the Doctor belonged no longer to his missionary society, nor even to his family, but to a wider and more noble purpose. He seems to have realised almost at once that to destroy the slave trade he must somehow make Central Africa accessible to the outside world, and lead civilised commerce as well as evangelism into it. The first and fundamental need, he saw, was to pioneer a practical approach from the sea. 'I shall open a path into the interior,' he informed his brother-in-law about this time, 'or perish'. It was his dominant thought. In 1852, he freed himself for the task by sending his family home to Britain; then he made his way back to the same Makololo tribe which had befriended him when he had come first to the Zambesi. Their capital town of Linyanti happened to be situated almost exactly half-way between the Indian Ocean and the Atlantic. From it Livingstone set out to discover his 'path into the interior', going first westwards through present-day Angola. His equipment for the journey by any standard was pitifully inadequate. He was nearly penniless and practically defenceless, yet he passed in safety through a succession of hostile tribes that had never seen a white man before. He brushed aside the peremptory demands for toll of 'a man, an ox or a tusk'; instead he claimed help from a succession of unwilling chiefs and somehow he obtained it. His way took him through wild unknown country. Often he was half starved and racked with fever. He marched under a scorching sun or in drenching tropical rain. Yet he was able to write down in his journal everything of significance he saw. Nothing escaped his notice; bizarre customs, mysterious diseases, botanical curiosities, strange animals, all were so meticulously recorded that later explorers complained he had left nothing new for them to describe. But what most particularly distinguished this journey was the way the Doctor carefully charted his route and made a series of amazingly accurate astronomical observations to pin-point on his map every village, stream and geographical feature he passed. On this first great journey we see Livingstone at his most impressive. He literally revels in his new untrammelled freedom. Every night he would make his bed up in the open and lie there staring at the stars, and listening to the tuneless songs of his Makololo and their Lozi porters as they crouched round a smouldering fire.* He was unaffected by loneliness or the lack of books. His mind instead was absorbed with his crusade and a host of strange experiences. And he was almost mystically happy, because he knew his pilgrimage was willed by God. Each morning he would rouse his carriers and start off again, usually on foot but mounted sometimes on an ox of vicious manners named 'Sinbad'. The Makololo marched behind him with their loads, vastly intrigued by this white magician whose legs, they said, were wrapped in 'bags', and in doing so gave a new word for trousers to the English language. At last they burst upon the Atlantic near Loanda, and were at once overwhelmed by the hospitality of the Portuguese whom later the explorer was to load with such abuse. One sees now that this was the turning point of David Livingstone's life. Personal safety, common sense, family ties, and the tremendous temptation of a fame he could already claim, all directed him to accept the offer of a passage home made to him by the captain of a British cruiser. But Livingstone would have nothing of it. He was obsessed still with a compulsion to discover a practicable route from the sea to his chosen mission ground, and after the difficulties he had already encountered on the journey to Loanda, he knew it could not lie in the west. Accordingly he must return to Linyanti and seek his 'path into the interior' to the east. In any case he said he was bound by a sense of duty to return his porters safely to their homes. And with a feeling of dull awe at the temper of this man, we see him turn his back on civilisation again and plunge once more into the wilds.

Another arduous march that lasted a whole year brought the explorer back to the country of the Makololo and it was while resting there that he began to interest himself in the chain of great inland lakes which he heard lay to the north. Then, towards the end of 1855, Dr. Livingstone left Linyanti again and set off eastwards down the course of his 'glorious river', the Zambesi, his way made easier now by reports preceding him that he was not only a powerful magician but the Son of God. Very soon he came

* Only the two leaders were true Makololo; the remainder came from tribes that had been conquered by them.

to the most splendid sight in all Africa, the 'smoke that thunders', which later he renamed the Victoria Falls. Beyond it, difficult hilly country temporarily deflected him from the river with disastrous results which were only to become apparent a few years later. At Tete he came again to country known to the geographers, and by now the worst of his journey was over. The river below Tete is navigable and so after learning more about the great lakes in the interior from Senhor Candido and an Arab trader, Livingstone travelled swiftly downstream leaving his 'faithful Makololo' behind to await his return. Almost exactly four years after setting out on his pilgrimage from Cape Town, he reached the Indian Ocean at Quelimane, having accomplished what nearly everyone believed to be the first crossing of the African continent. Fragments of news about his journey had been reaching England for some time, and its latter part had been followed by an attentive public rather in the way that nowadays we read about the fortunes of a test team touring Australia. One of Her Majesty's cruisers had been sent to Quelimane to bring him home, and Livingstone was gratified to discover that almost overnight he had become a celebrity whom all Britain was waiting to honour.

A heavy mood of uncertainty and discontent had settled over England at the time of Livingstone's homecoming. All the old values which for generations had been part of the national life, now were being held up for scrutiny and debate. It seemed wrong there to permit a system to continue any longer which could allow such extremes of wealth and poverty to exist together in one land; nor was it considered right that a small privileged class should continue to rule the country alone, especially after the shocking exhibition it had made of directing the recent war in the Crimea. This new mood of criticism and the resulting demand for reform was by no means confined to Britain; rather it was a symptom of that widespread restlessness which only a few years before had plunged the people of half a dozen European states into rebellion against their autocratic governments. And by now it had spread across the Atlantic. Already John Brown had staged his massacre at Pottawatomie Creek, and in the rising dispute concerning the ethics of American slavery, even the voices preaching tolerance sounded increasingly intolerant. At least the subjects of Queen Victoria could congratulate themselves on reacting to the temper of the time more peacefully with restrained political demonstrations and an unhealthy preoccupation with the merits of rival religious doctrines. But deep down in their hearts one can sense that the British people in 1856 were searching for a worthy cause to champion, and a dedicated man to follow. And on to the stage at this moment stepped Dr. David Livingstone.

With him he carried an entirely new concept of the people of Central Africa, and, what was more, a practical formula for the redemption of their souls and bodies. Take 'Christianity, civilisation and commerce' into the interior of Africa, he cried, with something of the fervour of a modern evangelist, and the slave trade will be destroyed at its source. His mood was so infectious that a wave of public enthusiasm went surging through the country, and when it appeared that Livingstone was anxious to lead the new crusade himself, his progress through the kingdom took on something of the character of a triumph. A gentle rain of civic honours and academic distinctions began to descend on his modest head and although he declared he was horribly embarrassed by all this 'lionising' and by the 'public spouting' for which he was in such demand, it must be admitted that in his heart of hearts he rather relished his new-found fame.

The tremendous vogue for Livingstone persisted even after England had been shattered by news of the Indian Mutiny and the appalling massacres at Cawnpore. If anything the flattery and the favours increased as it became widely believed that at Loanda the Doctor had deliberately placed a duty to his Makololo porters before his own safety and anxiety to rejoin his family. At meetings held up and down the country, stern resolutions calling for the suppression of the slave trade were passed and everywhere breathless chairmen were standing up to call for volunteers for the newly opened mission fields. High society clamoured for the Doctor's notice; even the Duke of Wellington, who was not much given to blandishments, pressed some of his favourite water filters upon the embarrassed explorer, his offer being accompanied by a covering letter from the President of the Royal Geographical Society which gushed, 'believe me, my dear friend, that no transaction in my somewhat long and very active life has so truly rewarded me as my intercourse with you'. A royal summons brought the Doctor to Windsor one day and although Prince Albert was a trifle cool, the Queen proved charming and was moved to helpless laughter on learning that all the African chiefs the explorer had met had been anxious to know how many cows she possessed.

Even staid businessmen caught the fever when they heard about the rich coal deposits in this new country, its unlimited cheap labour and the fertile soil which was waiting, it seemed, only for capital investment to grow enough cotton to make Britain independent of the American cotton fields. Indeed, it became modish that summer in the country's Chambers of Commerce to discuss projects that visualised long lines of paddle steamers toiling up the Zambesi carrying trade goods together with the Gospel into the interior, and returning a little later packed profitably with bales of cotton. Never before had the business world contemplated an opportunity like this to practise an altruism that seemed almost certain to pay a handsome dividend, and its magnates soon were lining up to offer their support to any new venture Dr. Livingstone might have in mind.

And because Livingstone by now had made it quite clear that his recent 'geographical feat' was but the prelude to a more ambitious enterprise, the feeling was growing that this should be sponsored by the Government. Certainly he would not go out again under the auspices of the London Missionary Society, for the only jarring note in all the tempest of applause that had greeted him when he emerged from Africa strangely enough had come from the directors of his own missionary society, who had intimated bleakly and fatuously that in future they were 'restricted in their power of aiding plans connected only remotely with the spread of the Gospel'.

Then in the autumn of 1857 Livingstone's book *Missionary Travels and Researches in South Africa* appeared and the enthusiasm for the explorer rose to an even shriller pitch. For there had never been a book quite like this before and it was an immediate and tremendous success. In this massive volume of 300,000 words Livingstone recounts his adventures in a curiously restrained style which contrives to make each reader feel that he especially has been taken into the author's confidence. The book was written in great haste and is badly constructed, but somehow this gives to it a peculiar flavour of artlessness and candour. Moreover, the author has a rare and natural gift for lucidity, and the reader finds it remarkably easy to visualise his immense fertile plains filled with game and cattle 'as fat as prize beasts', the system of majestic rivers he saw, and the extensive fields of wild cotton growing beside the Zambesi. Sometimes when Livingstone is stirred by the memory of some particularly vivid scene or incident, his prose in *Missionary Travels* takes on an almost lyrical quality, but suddenly he will break off into a taut description of the evils of the slave trade; it seems then that, were he speaking instead of writing, the author's voice would tremble a little, and the reader finds it impossible not to share his superb indignation. When the book is finished and put down, it leaves the impression that south central Africa is a primitive Arcadia, gorgeous in colour, peopled by friendly tribesmen, and endowed with boundless untapped wealth. Of course nothing in 1857 could have been much further from the truth, but the naïveté of Livingstone's style completely hides the fact that he had deliberately embellished the things he deemed creditable to the country, and had ignored those that might be considered detrimental.

What strikes us today as so extraordinary is the way nearly everyone accepted the author's account of the new country without question. Only a very few readers were sceptical. But those few included the formidable Robert Moffat, who once declared his son-in-law's book to be 'a pack of lies'. And, as we shall see, James Stewart, who stands second only to Livingstone in his service to Africa, came to believe that the author of *Missionary Travels* had been guilty of culpable exaggeration, even of 'accursed lies', when he described the Zambesi country in such glowing terms.

The truth of the matter was of course that when he wrote his book Livingstone was so dazzled by his vision of the redemption of the oppressed inhabitants of Africa, that almost instinctively he discounted all the difficulties lying in his path and saw only its ultimate fulfilment. Thus hardly anyone realised at the time that many of the more unpleasant experiences which had attended Livingstone's progress across Africa had been carefully omitted from the account he gave to the public, although each one was carefully recorded in his own diary. Even so one would have expected some of the readers of *Missionary Travels* to have known that its author had not hesitated in the past to gloss over facts damaging to himself, as occurred for instance when he drew a veil over the actions which had provoked the Boers to sack his mission station at Kolobeng in 1852. What perhaps is more surprising is that not even the hard-headed businessmen who read his book, or the politicians at the Foreign Office, bothered to ask why the Portuguese (who after all had been established in Mozambique for three hundred years) had accomplished so little in the exploitation of the country if the Zambesi really was as easily navigable as the Doctor claimed after a single rather casual inspection. And so although at least the cotton steamers of the commercial houses never materialised farther than the drawing-board stage, by the time the truth about the Zambesi became known, several bands of unfortunate missionaries had already set out for the Utopia of Central Africa, to be decimated in due course by malaria and dysentery.

However much one searches about in one's mind to find a human synonym for Livingstone, he remains unique. No other historical figure in the least resembles this man; he is singularly himself, a freakish deviation from the norm. At first sight he was unprepossessing, yet there was something about him which made even perfect strangers turn round to take a second look. Possibly their attention was caught by the determined set of his mouth and grim expression on his face; more probably it was the odd quality that made him seem remote even to those who knew him best, and which set him above the ordinary rules of life. He was a sturdy man of middle height with one arm crippled by a lion and hanging loosely from his frame. His face was tanned and deeply lined as though he had known much suffering. An oversensitive mind was hidden behind a mask of brusqueness. Although he could be very gentle to those he believed might help him to further his fairy dream, most people found him unapproachable to the point of rudeness. Indeed one is sometimes repelled by the unlooked-for streak of inhumanity David Livingstone occasionally exhibited, even to his own family. Of his courage there could be no doubt. Sir John Kirk who accompanied him on some of his most perilous expeditions once wrote that his friend 'did not know what fear was' and in this he was perfectly right. Livingstone's fearlessness was a peculiarly personal thing, bred from a deep conviction that the Lord Himself had ordained him for some special purpose. This concept is revealed in a striking passage in his diary: it tells of Livingstone during his trans-African journey watching a throng of armed natives preparing to oppose his crossing over one of the tributaries of the Zambesi next morning. One must visualise him brooding that evening over the dangers that lay ahead and then in flickering candlelight turning for comfort to his Bible which fell open at St. Matthew's Gospel. 'Felt some turmoil of spirit', he wrote with fervent underlining a little later in his journal, 'in view of having all my efforts for the welfare of this great region and its teeming population knocked on the head by savages tomorrow. But I read that Jesus came and said, "All power is given unto me in Heaven and earth . . . Lo, I am with you always, even unto the end of the world." It is the word of a gentleman of the most sacred and strictest honour, and there's an end on't. I will not cross furtively at night, as I had intended. It would appear as flight, and should such a man as I flee?' Next morning Livingstone continued on his way unafraid and unmolested, his antagonists completely nonplussed by his imperturbability.

The Doctor possessed powers of physical endurance scarcely less remarkable than his fearlessness. But it was not so much his stamina which drove him across the breadth of Africa as the unwavering belief that he had some special place in God's scheme for the continent. The intensity of his feeling about it comes out more in his lectures than in his book or correspondence. He was a nervous speaker, yet his harsh and awkward delivery was accepted as another sign of passionate sincerity. His tour of 'public spouting' up and down the country ended with a famous speech on Central Africa delivered in the Senate House at Cambridge towards the end of the year. No one who was present ever forgot the profound effect it made. At first his words came with more than usual hesitance but as his voice gained gradually in strength and significance, his audience sat spellbound. 'I know that in a few years I shall be cut off in that country which is now open.' He shouted prophetically at its conclusion, 'Do not let it be shut again! I go back to Africa to try to make an open path for commerce and Christianity. Do you carry on the work which I have begun. I leave it with you.'

These impassioned words inspired the formation of the Universities' Mission which was to play such a large part in the story of Lake Nyasa, and they also contributed to the British Government's decision to sponsor Livingstone's next venture into Africa. Before the House of Commons rose that year for its Christmas recess, the Chancellor of the Exchequer stood up to announce a generous financial grant towards a new expedition of exploration and evangelisation to be led by Dr. Livingstone to the Zambesi. The Foreign Office appointed him to the official (although geographically somewhat vague) post of 'H.M. Consul at Qualimane, for the Eastern Coast and the independent districts of the interior',* while across the road the Admiralty became engrossed in plans for the new venture. And so amid high hopes was born the 'Zambesi Expedition' of 1858, which was to end nearly six years later in tragedy and disillusionment and whose only positive achievement was the rediscovery by Europe of Lake Nyasa.

❧ ❧

Whatever schemes the Naval enthusiasts may have been formulating, Livingstone right from the start insisted he preferred the expedition to be planned on a comparatively modest scale, and the Government were quite prepared to fall in with his wishes. 'Just come here and tell me what you want,' Lord Clarendon told him grandly, 'and I will give it to you.' The Doctor replied with a lengthy memorandum.

He proposed, it said, to carry the expedition from England in a steamer of such shallow draught that it would get right up the

* This is the form given in Seaver's authoritative biography of Dr. Livingstone, but the Commission in the Rhodes-Livingstone Museum is slightly differently worded.

Zambesi as far as Tete, and so cut down the time spent in the unhealthy lowlands. At Tete a small wood-burning launch would take over, and provide transport to an upland site near the confluence of the Kafue and Zambesi where headquarters would be installed. The expedition would then devote itself to exploration, evangelisation, instruction of the local natives in agriculture, and the harassment of the inland slave trade.

It all sounded delightfully simple and practical to Lord Clarendon, and after he had given the document his approval with a scrawled 'This seems a very estimable plan', preparations were quickly completed. A steamer named the *Pearl* was chartered at Liverpool and began loading the expedition's surveying instruments, preserved foods, calico bales (which were the cumbrous currency of Central Africa a century ago), and sections of a small launch for use on the upper Zambesi which had been provided by a Scottish philanthropist at cut-price and christened *Ma-Robert*— the name given to Mrs. Livingstone by the Bechuanas after the birth of her eldest son.

Then the Doctor turned with noticeably less enthusiasm to the selection of his assistants. He insisted on limiting their number to six, and he chose them in a remarkably casual and off-hand manner. One suspects that this pose of unconcern was either a gesture to indicate how unimportant he considered them in his scheme, or stemmed from a subconscious lack of confidence in himself as a leader of white men. For, as soon became apparent, Livingstone was pitiably inept at handling subordinate Europeans.* He distrusted them: he viewed their illnesses as malingering, and disagreement as defiance. Their reaction was predictable, and to those of us who have been brought up on the conventional Livingstone legend, it comes as a shock to find that far from moving through the story of the Zambesi expedition graciously, sustained by the admiration and respect of his companions, Livingstone came to be detested to a greater or lesser degree by each of them in turn. Even Kirk, loyalest and most charitable of men reached the conclusion that Livingstone was not only dishonest and a 'hypocrite', but 'out of his mind', 'a most unsafe

* Dr. Livingstone on the other hand had no difficulty in remaining on friendly terms with those he considered his equals or superiors.

79

leader', and 'about as ungrateful and slippery a mortal as I ever came in contact with' who 'would give all for a C.B. or better a K.C.B.'—and this was relatively mild censure compared with the unrestrained criticism of some of the other members of the expedition.

They were an odd sextet, the men whom Livingstone chose to accompany him on his Zambesi venture; their mutual antipathies combined with Livingstone's churlish behaviour to produce the curious atmosphere of brittle asperity which characterised the expedition. It is worth while then to pause for a moment and consider the characters of these six men.

As second-in-command of the expedition Livingstone chose a naval officer, Commander Norman Bedingfeld, whom he had met briefly at Loanda. It is by no means certain that Livingstone by then had heard the rumours that pursued Bedingfeld all his life about his having been court-martialled twice, and even dismissed from his ship on the charge of 'contempt and quarrelsome conduct towards his superior Officer'. But even if they were untrue (and strangely enough Bedingfeld was inclined to boast about them) these canards happened to fit in very well with Bedingfeld's character. He was an odd oafish creature, filled with a great humourless conceit. Having decided he was indispensable to the expedition, he proceeded to antagonise everyone connected with it by an inexcusable exhibition of boorishness. No one really knew what his real motives for joining the venture were; presumably he pictured himself in a dignified naval uniform and pose, standing on the bridge of an exploring steamer as it cruised comfortably up a broad tropical river and carried him to inevitable promotion and distinction. But there was also some weird aspiration wandering through his mind of finding the ten lost tribes ('as if', commented the Doctor drily when he heard of it, 'we had not plenty of Jews already'). Quite early during the voyage from England, Livingstone assures us he had misgivings about his second-in-command. They began, he says, 'when I saw him seasick', and increased after he had made the disconcerting discovery that 'Bedingfeld was an awful bore. . . . His *private* devotions must needs be performed in the most *public* place in the vessel.' For his part the pious Bedingfeld was strongly critical of

Livingstone's lack of Sunday observance and threatened to expose it to the Press. The truth was that the temperaments of the two men made it utterly impossible for them to get along together for any length of time, and even before they had reached the Zambesi, they were quarrelling in public and calling each other liars to their faces. It was all very petty, very undignified and very ridiculous, and the Doctor himself seems to have realised this when he told Bedingfeld they must both stop acting 'like boarding-school girls in a pet'. A little later he came to the quaint conclusion that Bedingfeld's irascibility might not be entirely his own fault but due to a 'peculiar condition of the bowels' brought on by 'the change of climate'. Unfortunately he only made things worse when he followed up this hunch by writing to Bedingfeld: 'I earnestly and most respectfully recommend you try a little aperient medicine' and proferred his second-in-command a box of pills. Bedingfeld, having taken fresh offence instead, replied with indignant letters of resignation. The Doctor stood it as long as he could and then fired off a formal notice of dismissal in return. Bedingfeld's reaction, according to Livingstone, was as unusual as everything else about him for, we are told, he 'commenced dancing and singing as if overjoyed' before being packed off home in disgrace. 'I never before met with such a bare-faced dirty hypocrite', Livingstone summed up the character of his 'naval donkey' after he had gone, adding with that curious habit of alliteration which came to him so easily when thoroughly aroused: he 'was constantly carping, complaining and raising objections,' and if this was not enough, we learn too in one of the most crushing of parthian shots, that Bedingfeld 'suffered from venereal irritable bladder'.

If Bedingfeld lasted the shortest time of all Livingstone's original companions, Dr. Kirk for the next five years wears an air of aggrieved permanence in the expedition, and he became in fact, if not in name, Livingstone's understudy. Kirk was just twenty-six, strong, healthy, and experienced in travel when he was chosen to join the expedition as its doctor and botanist, and he performed his duties very well. If one had to search about for a single word to describe his character, probably 'reliability' would be the most appropriate. One gets the impression in him of a young man of unusual earnestness and maturity, and can glimpse already the great powers which later were to enable Kirk to play an immensely important part in the history of East and Central Africa. Of all the men who worked with Livingstone during the next few years, Kirk alone does not seem a pygmy standing beside a giant, and of them all, he was the only one to leave the expedition with an enhanced reputation.

It is far more difficult to form a clear impression of George Rae, the expedition's engineer. He drifts through the story of the next few years like a faceless wraith, seldom mentioned yet always present, quietly gossiping about his colleagues, complaining about some slight, plugging a leak in the *Ma-Robert*'s hull, or tinkering with her engines. Half-way through the course of the expedition he takes himself off to England, ostensibly to superintend the construction of a new steamer, but glad really to have found an excuse to sever his association from what he realised now to be a doomed enterprise. And then the strange alchemy of Livingstone's vision touches him again and we see the Glasgow engineer almost in a trance coming back to join the Doctor— and he is the only one who stays with him to the end.

Over the figure of the geologist to the expedition, Richard Thornton, there still hangs an aura of avoidable and dismal tragedy. James Stewart, who came to know Thornton well, describes him as being 'young and clever rather than able, opinionative and active, and would work if one but knew how to get the work out of him'. It soon became clear that Dr. Livingstone was the last man to manage that. The instructions he gave to this young man who was scarcely out of his teens, were difficult to follow and sometimes contradictory, so it is no wonder that his 'geologising' turned out to be disappointing. Moreover, Thornton suffered from repeated bouts of malaria on the Zambesi and seems to have been overcome by the inertia and capricious appetite which continued fever so often induces. His geologist, if Livingstone's account is true, 'lay in his tent all day and gorged himself with food', and was 'a disgrace to the expedition and English name'. This is all very well; the trouble was no one ever seems to have enquired why the wretched Thornton behaved in such a way. Instead he was handed a notice of dismissal from the expedition on account of his incurable 'lethargy'. He seems to have accepted his expulsion with remarkably good grace, and once he had only himself to rely on, accomplished several creditable feats of exploration. Then unbelievably he drifts back to the Zambesi again to rejoin Livingstone, as though, like Rae, he could not escape from his spell. Only a little later he is killed by his old enemy malaria at the end of a hazardous and rather gallant journey to bring help to the despairing band of missionaries that had followed Livingstone out to Central Africa. He lies today beneath the large baobab tree on the banks of the Shiré where Livingstone buried him below the lake a hundred years ago, the only one of the six original members to perish during the course of the expedition.

Thomas Baines, the fifth member of the party, was a much older and more experienced man. Already by 1858 he had gained some distinction from his work as an artist during the Kaffir wars and the North Australian Expedition, and when Livingstone engaged him as his painter and storeman, he seemed a most fortunate and suitable choice. Thomas Baines came from Kings Lynn and he possessed many of the traits of the typical East Anglian. He was an unassuming, self-sufficient and thoroughly likeable man. If there was a flaw in his character it was his pliancy; he was far too easy-going. Baines' appearance, judging by photographs, strikes one as being mildly comical; he was slightly built but tried to make up for it by wearing his hair in long Byronic locks and growing a vastly impressive curling beard. His eyes seem a shade too dreamy and mild for the man of action he professed to be; his expression suggests naïve bewilderment and irresolution, so that one knows at once why his acquaintances often referred to him as 'old Baines' and 'poor Thomas Baines'. He seems the sort of man who in a London restaurant would find difficulty in catching the waiter's eye and would be certain to leave with short change. The proper role for him, one feels, would have been that of a happily married proprietor of a village grocer's shop in his native Norfolk. Yet there was a quality in him which drove him all his life away from comfort into the wilds of Africa.

Baines' task of organising and supervising the expedition's

widely scattered stores would have proved difficult even to a skilled accountant and certainly he was quite unfitted to cope with it. Very soon Livingstone was finding fault with his work as a storekeeper and criticising his painting. Even so Baines was as flabbergasted as Thornton had been to receive a notice of dismissal; it accused him of carelessness, theft of government stores, 'painting Portuguese portraits' without permission (Livingstone's indignation shows again in the alliteration) and (unbelievably), of 'skylarking with the Portuguese'. In due course the wretched man was sent off to the Cape, pursued still by the Doctor's emnity and spite. There is something desperately pathetic about the way Baines, for the next seven years, tried to persuade Livingstone to withdraw his accusations, but the Doctor's malevolence continued and as late as 1870 we find him writing to Baines' mother (whom he referred to as 'the old hag') to demand the return of some articles in her son's possession which he claimed were his. And in fact the unfortunate Baines was never completely cleared of the charges until after his death when it became perfectly clear they had been groundless.

Whatever we may feel about its other members, the student of the Zambesi expedition very quickly perceives that the sixth of them—the Rev. Charles Livingstone—was the curse of the whole enterprise. What perhaps one finds even more surprising is the length of time it took for his brother David, the persecutor of Bedingfeld, Thornton and Baines, to reach the same conclusion. As a youth Charles emigrated to America and entered a theological college where, in due course, he became ordained. Seventeen years passed before the pastor of the family came home to see his parents and his visit happened to coincide with his brother's triumphant return from Africa. Charles was promptly enrolled in the Zambesi expedition as 'general assistant' and 'moral agent to lay a Christian foundation for anything that may follow', while Lord Clarendon and his colleagues in the Cabinet were given to understand that this younger Livingstone would prove additionally useful both as a photographer and consultant for the cotton industry that was contemplated for Central Africa. Psychologists, however, will see David Livingstone's decision to take his brother along with him to Africa as a manifestation of a subconscious doubt concerning his own ability to direct and command Europeans. For Charles was to be the trusted staff officer through whom unpopular orders would be transmitted, and a shield against the criticism the older man dreaded. Charles turned out instead to be a scourge for his brother's back. He is the classical 'tell-tale' and very quickly assumed an almost hypnotic dominance over his brother and became the vindictive *eminence grise* of the expedition. Perhaps a clue to Charles' reason for establishing himself as his brother's moral censor rather than as his 'moral agent' comes out in a sentence from one of his letters which reads: 'The Dr. is the last man to see through a spurious article',—for Charles was convinced that most of his fellow officers were what nowadays we would call 'phonies'. He was furious when they failed to treat him with deferential respect, and retaliated by carrying malicious stories of their 'transgressions' to his gullible brother. The dismissals of Thornton and Baines can with certainty be traced to Charles' trouble-making and it was not until long afterwards that Doctor Livingstone himself sadly confessed, 'the one mistake of the expedition has been bringing Charles into it'.

The journals and correspondence of Charles' companions, however, almost from the day they left Liverpool, are soured by outbursts of indignation about the venom of this man they called 'the long one'. Thus we find Kirk, in a letter to a friend, rather melodramatically describing Charles as 'a sneaking mischief-maker, a plotting low scoundrel', while his diary gives us several revealing glimpses of the 'moral agent' as he saunters along the winding native paths of Africa in a clean well-cut suit (for Charles is the dandy of African exploration) and a large felt hat with an umbrella held over his head, occasionally stopping to aim a kick at one of the porters or to hold up the march by insisting on 'a snooze every half-hour or so'.

The most charitable thing that can be said about Charles Livingstone is that during the expedition his mind was unbalanced by a desperate homesickness to which was added a genuine concern about his family's safety in America after the outbreak there of civil war. Repeatedly in his letters he complains that his mail from home has gone astray. He was obsessed with waking visions of his wife and children, would sit for hours over their photographs and then go to bed and dream of them all night long. But however much one may be inclined to sympathise with him this hardly excuses his spite and invective which were responsible for so much of the unhappy atmosphere under which the expedition laboured.

Apart from these, his 'official' companions, David Livingstone decided to take his wife and six-year-old son Oswell along with him on the new venture. He was confident his party would pass quickly through the unhealthy Zambesi country into the Barotse highlands and ran little risk from fever. No doubt too he hoped Mrs. Livingstone would smooth away some of the difficulties he expected to meet in handling his staff. Indeed the story of the Zambesi expedition might well have made much happier reading if Mary Livingstone had been able to spend more time with it. But none of its members were thinking very much about difficulties or social friction when they travelled up to Liverpool that February in 1858 to join the *Pearl*. They were filled instead with excitement and perfect confidence that they would accomplish great feats together. Not one of them had any inkling of the miseries that lay before them; no one dreamt that Livingstone's project would have fared much better had he travelled alone.

Everything was ready by the first of March, and then, even before the expedition had properly got under way things began to go wrong. First of all Dr. Kirk heard his father had suddenly died, and for a moment he hesitated about continuing in the venture. Then a series of vexatious delays held things up for several days and it was not until March 12th that the *Pearl* slipped her moorings and crept down the Mersey in a depressing flurry of sleet and snow. Soon afterwards Mrs. Livingstone fell ill, apparently from a severe attack of seasickness, and several weeks went by before she realised she was pregnant. Even Dr. Livingstone shrank from the thought of confining her in the wilds of the Zambesi and he decided to leave her behind at Cape Town so she could journey up to her parents' home at Kuruman to have her baby. 'This is a great trial to me', her husband noted a shade ungraciously in his

Commander Norman Bedingfeld

Dr. John Kirk

Thomas Baines

Bishop Mackenzie

Thomas Baines' painting of the *Ma-Robert*

diary after hearing the news, 'for . . . she might have proved of essential service to the expedition in cases of sickness or otherwise.' Meanwhile the European members of his staff were becoming increasingly dismayed by their leader's shyness and obvious lack of confidence in them, an impression that was not improved off Madeira when they each (with the exception of the favoured Charles) received three double foolscap pages filled with insultingly elementary instructions. Their morale, however, improved at Cape Town which gave them a tremendous reception, as well as a civic banquet and a contribution of eight hundred guineas for their work. And a month later they came at last to the mouth of the Zambesi and could feel the great adventure had really begun. It was May 14th, 1858. Although they did not know it at the time, a greater blow against slavery than theirs even then was being prepared in the prairie towns of Illinois where the great voice of Abraham Lincoln was turning the American problem from a moral into a political issue.

But before they could get any further there was an unexpected and heartbreaking delay as they searched the pestilential swamps at the river mouth for a practical channel through the Zambesi delta and three dreary weeks went by before they discovered one at Kongone. And when they won through at last to the river proper, Livingstone, who had missed seeing this part of its course during his previous journey, had to admit it was much shallower than he had anticipated. Only too obviously there was no hope of getting an ocean-going ship like the *Pearl* through these shoals, and all the sanguine expectations of steaming comfortably and quickly up to Tete had to be abandoned. It was all very depressing, and the wan little party felt sadly abandoned as they watched the *Pearl* steam away to other duties. Everything now depended on the *Ma-Robert*, and at once it turned out to be hopelessly inefficient, 'only fit', according to Livingstone, 'to grind coffee in a shop window'. Ruefully they nicknamed their launch *The Asthmatic* and bundled their stores on to its decks to carry in relays up the river. It was a wretched time; Baines and the younger Livingstone went down with severe fever, and they were not helped by Dr. Livingstone's well-meant advice that its best remedy was increased physical exertion. Moreover it transpired that the tribes higher up the Zambesi had rebelled against the Portuguese and were likely to become dangerous, while the expedition itself seemed bedevilled by such numerous quarrels that Livingstone noted gloomily in his diary that his officers were all showing a 'disposition to blame each other' for everything that went wrong. Bedingfeld in particular was being most difficult and it was a relief to see him go at last. But it was the Zambesi itself which was the greatest enemy now. Far from being easily navigable, its course everywhere was interrupted by sandbanks and shifting shoals on which the *Ma-Robert* grounded with maddening frequency.

The next few months are a confused story of short river journeys past unhealthy mangrove swamps with ghostly fever trees shimmering in the heat, of everlasting woodcutting for the insatiable bunkers of the *Ma-Robert*, of hauling it endlessly over sandbanks, and of incessant manhandling of stores. Every now and then some members of the party would go back to Kongone to pick up fresh equipment or mail which rarely arrived on schedule and they began to hate the lower river. All of them, to a greater or lesser degree, were becoming worn down by boredom, dissension and unaccustomed hardships. Each in turn was tormented by fever, heatstroke and prickly heat, and it was not until two grim months had gone by before even the advance party got as far as Tete. Another eight weeks of misery and toil saw them a few more miles farther up the river at the Kebrabasa cataracts, and then the most crushing blow of all fell. For here, clearly, the Zambesi was quite impassable to any ship.

This probably was the worst moment of all Livingstone's life. He had staked everything on the Zambesi being 'God's Highway' into the interior, and the check at Kebrabasa meant the destruction not only of his dreams but of a much cherished reputation for infallibility. There was wild talk of blasting a way through the rapids with dynamite and of chartering a more powerful boat from England. He was full of recriminations. Everyone was reproached for the set-back, especially the absent Bedingfeld who had chosen the puny *Ma-Robert* instead of a more suitable ship called the *Bann*. But however much Livingstone fulminated on these matters, it was impossible to exonerate himself from the blame. The truth was, that to avoid the difficult country lying below the Victoria Falls, he had neglected to explore this particular part of the Zambesi during his trans-African journey. What was even more humiliating, because he had made an elementary miscalculation in the river's fall, Livingstone had not even suspected that such formidable cataracts existed here. All the fine talk and glowing assurances about an easy route into the interior had been disproved. The extravagant praise lavished on him now was seen to be undeserved, and Livingstone knew he had been made to look extremely foolish. One can only surmise the intensity of his mental agony as he contemplated the cataracts for he was quite incapable of sharing it with anyone. All he could do was to withdraw further into his shell and make some rather pathetic excuses and explanations in his diary: 'Things look dark for our enterprise', runs one such entry; 'This Kebrabasa is what I never expected. No hint of its nature ever reached my ears'; and again: 'The honours heaped on me were not of my seeking. They came unbidden.' But even as he brooded over the disappointment, Livingstone's perspective broadened. Might it not be possible, he asked himself, that the Lord had intended to lead him up not the Zambesi, but one of its great tributaries instead? His vision might yet come true, might even be more splendid than he had anticipated. Impetuously David Livingstone decided to abandon the upper Zambesi and take his launch up the river Shiré, which long ago he had heard led to a great inland sea called 'Nyasa' or 'Nyinyesi'—the 'lake of stars'. And so, amid the crushing pains of a great man's frustration and despair, the sleeping lake was awakened into its new life.

5

A SPLENDID LAKE

Within a few days of coming to his new resolution, Livingstone set off to explore the Shiré with Kirk, Charles and Rae. They took the *Ma-Robert* out of the Zambesi into the wide mouth of the Shiré on New Year's Day, 1859, and the date seemed a happy omen. For all that had been so mysteriously wrong with the Zambesi was wonderfully absent in this new river. The explorers cruised comfortably upstream, delighted with the river's navigability, entranced by its scenery and fascinated by the masses of wild game wandering about its banks which set Livingstone writing (with characteristic parenthesis) that they had seen 'a prodigious number of elephants . . . five or six herds of them at once. My companions estimated them at 3,000. (I think 800 or less.)' The purpose of this first visit was merely reconnaissance and the establishment of friendly contact with the suspicious natives living in the valley. But the white men were back again a few weeks later, and this time they felt confident enough about their reception to leave the boat and begin the exploration of the superb mountain country to which the river had led them. All who have toiled for months through the humid heat of tropical lowlands will understand how their spirits rose as they watched the blue mountains before them growing closer every day. Difficulties became more easily borne; thus when firewood ran short everyone applauded Livingstone's happy inspiration of feeding the launch's bunkers with the dry elephant bones that lay about. Their renewed sense of purpose is reflected in Livingstone's journal and sometimes in it one even catches an echo of the lyrical prose of his earlier writings: 'When will this fertile valley resound with the church-going bell?' he asks one day, and on another laments the doubts which a little earlier had been allowed to corrode his faith, and cries: 'It is presumptuous not to trust in Him implicitly, and yet this heart is sometimes fearfully guilty of distrust.' In this more buoyant mood Livingstone simply brushes aside the unwelcome discovery that the course of the Shiré is interrupted by a series of rapids scarcely less formidable than those at Kebrabasa. He makes them sound less intimidating by calling them after his friend, Sir Roderick Murchison, so that they have almost a 'home county' ring to their name and reassures the authorities in Whitehall that a short road will easily by-pass them. And as his party climbs up into the cool mountain country beyond, they find another England, only one blessed by a more genial sun. As Livingstone adds to his dispatch, it is clear to him now that the appointed destination of the expedition was not the upper Zambesi after all, but these more promising Shiré highlands. In memorable phrases the Doctor describes the fertile valleys and the lovely tree-crowned hills which indeed have a charm and tranquillity met nowhere else in Africa. Even Charles was enthusiastic: 'I never saw such a fine country', he informs a friend, 'we are all in raptures about it.' But in the midst of all this beauty, Dr. Livingstone finds an unanticipated and hideous horror. Even at the moment of their coming, the highlands are being ravaged for the first time by slaving parties. His hyperbolic pen seems indefatigable now as his friends at home are informed that the Shiré possesses all the advantages so signally lacking in the Zambesi. It is a river, they learn, 'admirably adapted for steam navigation' and it passes through cotton fields, 'four hundred miles in length', but it leads, he says later, into a 'land of darkness and of the shadow of death'.

There is no doubt for him now about where his duty lies. Again and again from the Shiré Highlands, Livingstone writes to explain that the slave trade is an affront to God and its suppression must now take precedence over mere feats of exploration. His letters are intended to inspire his friends, and silence his critics. The same message runs through them all: 'We are in the centre of the slave market and it is against this gigantic evil that my own mission is directed'. And he hints that for this purpose, 'our own honest poor might with advantage be settled here'. And now, with the whole concept of his expedition changed, Livingstone's mind begins to dwell on the futility of continuing to employ a geologist and a painter on the project. As his doubts about their value increase, he can think of little else except the redundancy of

Baines and Thornton, and how much better things would be without them. The idea of their dismissal grows into a petulant resolve and then into an obsession. And so, as he moves in hesitant stages toward the discovery of the great lake, we must picture Livingstone not as the sublime figure of the legend, but as a man a little unbalanced, as a man consumed not so much by a vision as by rankling grievances and unfounded bitterness regarding the two unsuspecting junior officers of his expedition.

Livingstone came upon a lake named Shirwa during this first foray into the Shiré Highlands, and heard it was separated from the greater lake beyond by only a narrow strip of land. On the way back to the boat he seems to have obtained a brief view of this larger lake, for after musing about its name ('We patronise Nyinyesi—the stars—as Nyanja by which they sometimes call it means every large water'), he goes on to say in a letter to his old friend Cotton Oswell: 'well, we went down the Shirwa valley and in crossing over the range which separates it from the Shiré valley we got a glimpse of the end of the lake.' But in fact six more months went by before Livingstone reached his lake of stars. First there were stores to collect at Kongone; then repairs to be effected on the launch. But all the time he was in a fever of impatience, for Livingstone had heard of the discovery by Burton and Speke of the sister lake of Tanganyika and he was afraid they might turn south and anticipate his discovery of Nyasa, which by now he had come to regard as something especially his own. Fortunately for his peace of mind, the Doctor had no suspicion that a much greater threat to the priority of his discovery, at that moment, was being made by an obscure German youth named Albrecht Roscher, who even then was slowly approaching Lake Nyasa from the east.

It is one of the supreme ironies of the story of the lake, that, having lain practically unknown and undisturbed by Europe for centuries, it should have been independently 'discovered' by two men within a few weeks of each other. Although Livingstone got there first by the narrow margin of seventy-two days, one feels that Roscher has never received the credit due to him for an achievement which in its way is just as remarkable. Roscher was only twenty-two when he was commissioned by the exiled king of Bavaria to investigate the rumours about the inland seas in the centre of Africa. When Livingstone was standing appalled below the rapids at Kebrabasa, Roscher was already at Zanzibar organising his own expedition. He was inexperienced and working on a desperately small budget, and he wasted a good deal of time trying to engage porters for the long journey inland. The delay cost him the honour of the lake's discovery. In the end he decided to join an Arab caravan setting out for the interior to hunt slaves. He had a dreadful time; the Arabs robbed and maltreated him and he was continuously ill with fever. Yet Roscher struggled on gamely and at last was rewarded by the sight of the blue waters of Nyasa when he came to the village of Nusewa.* Only several weeks later did he hear about the arrival of a group of white men at the southern extremity of the lake, and realised that after all he had not been the first European to see it. For the next four months Roscher remained by the lake exploring its beautiful eastern shore. Then at last in the March of 1860 he turned back to begin the long march to the coast, leaving behind his heavier loads and personal journals which unfortunately have never been recovered. Only three days later Roscher was murdered for the sake of the few poor possessions he was carrying. His porters escaped and eventually reached Zanzibar. The white man, they said, had been wakened one morning by the sounds of a scrimmage outside his hut. A group of savages were waiting for him at the door and a moment later Roscher was dead with an arrow in his neck and another through his chest. Surprisingly enough, when one considers how lightly the Sultan's yoke lay across the interior of Africa, the murderers were all arrested and brought back to Zanzibar where they were publicly hanged. Albrecht Roscher's bones still lie near the lake at Kisoongoonie. If he was not the lake's discoverer, at least he has the melancholy distinction of being the first of the many white men who spilled their blood there.

Not until the August of 1859 was Livingstone able to steam up the Shiré for the third time. Now they moored the *Ma-Robert* to a tree on Nkanamoyo island at the foot of the cataracts and, in

* The modern Losefa.

93

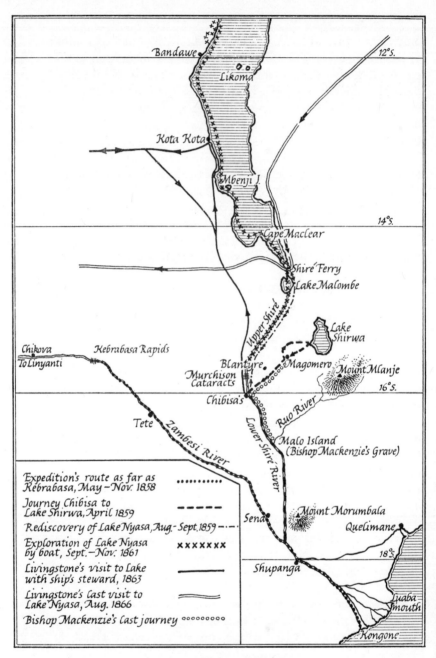

12°S.

Bandawe

Likoma

Kota Kota

Mbenji I.

14°S.

Cape Maclear

Shiré Ferry
Lake Malombe

Upper Shiré

Lake
Shirwa

Chikova
To Linyanti

Kebrabasa Rapids

Blantyre
Magomero
Mount Mlanje

Murchison
Cataracts

16°S.

Chibisa's

Tete

Zambesi River

Ruo River

Lower Shiré River

Malo Island
(Bishop Mackenzie's Grave)

Expedition's route as far as   ••••••••••
Kebrabasa, May – Nov. 1858

Journey Chibisa to   – – – –
Lake Shirwa, April 1859

Rediscovery of Lake Nyasa, Aug.– Sept. 1859 –·–·

Exploration of Lake Nyasa   xxxxxxx
by boat, Sept. – Nov. 1861

Livingstone's visit to Lake   ————
with ship's steward, 1863

Livingstone's last visit to   ════════
Lake Nyasa, Aug. 1866

Bishop Mackenzie's last journey ∘∘∘∘∘∘∘∘∘

Sena

Mount Morumbala

Quelimane

18°S.

Shupanga

Luaba
mouth

Kongone

Livingstone's Zambesi Expedition

Livingstone's words, 'left the ship, on the 28th of August 1859, for the discovery of Lake Nyassa'. It was the summer of Magenta and Solferino and of John Brown's insane conspiracy which led him to Harpers Ferry and immortality. And it was the vital central period of the Zambesi expedition too, and nothing in its story is more remarkable than the extraordinary mental state under which its leader laboured at the time. For that matter, every member of the party was unusually moody and dejected. The 'moral agent' according to Kirk was being 'horribly disagreeable' and they had all been depressed by the drowning of one of the *Ma-Robert*'s native crew in the Shiré a little time before. But it was Livingstone himself who was strained by the greatest emotional tension, and occasionally one wonders whether he was wholly sane at the time of the lake's discovery. Certainly we see him in the worst light of his whole career. Nothing pleases him and no one is spared his criticism—not even brother Charles who had left behind some essential item of photographic equipment so that we have no visual record of the great achievement. Nor are the African crew-men of the *Ma-Robert* exempted from his wrath; one of them after being 'insolent' receives a beating from Livingstone 'with a flat piece of wood'—and then for days afterwards the Doctor's conscience is so troubled by his own degradation that in his journal more space is devoted to the incident than is written about the discovery of the lake. Livingstone raves too about the iniquities of the Portuguese who, he realises now, are conniving at the slave trade, and one can almost sense his feeling of relief when he finds the *mot juste* and describes them as 'an utterly effete, worn-out, used-up syphilitic race'. One day his rancour is turned on Dr. Kirk. It is a remarkably petty incident and would be hardly worth recording were it not for the light it throws on the peevish working of Livingstone's mind at this time. Kirk had been collecting botanical specimens on the river bank and was delayed in coming back to the launch. After waiting for twenty minutes Livingstone, at Charles' instigation, decided to teach him a lesson for 'sporting', and took the boat up-river, leaving the frantic Dr. Kirk to stumble along behind them on the river bank until his punishment was considered adequate. Always at Livingstone's elbow now, one can sense his demented brother

Charles, whispering never-ending calumnies about the misconduct—even the orgies—of their companions. Perhaps because
both of them were outside the range of his spoken anger, Livingstone's most bitter animosity became directed at Thornton and
Baines. Psychiatrists in their jargon have coined the word 'projection' to express the subconscious transference of a man's irritation
from the true culprit on to an innocent scapegoat, and what was
happening now was the projection of all Livingstone's resentment
about his humiliation at Kebrabasa on to the two men waiting for
him at Tete. Livingstone (as Kirk once remarked) was 'a man who
takes small intense hatreds', and now his fury seems nearly to
consume him as his scorching pen dispatches letters dismissing
each of them in turn. Thornton's crime was of being 'inveterately
lazy' and meeting remonstrances with 'sneers at Scotchmen'.
Livingstone goes on to tell a friend that Thornton 'has several
times had hysteria, the fits of laughing & crying, rising in throat
and flatus, resembling exactly that met with in females', and elsewhere he speaks in his queer alliterative way of Thornton's 'complete collapse consequent on change of climate'. Yet it never
occurs to this devout medical man that the kindest course would
have been to invalid his geologist home; instead he is allowed to
drift off by himself to search for an illusory silver mine on the
Zambesi, and ultimately to join a German expedition climbing
Kilimanjaro.

But a more vindictive punishment is reserved for Baines, who
Livingstone asserts has not only been lazy, but dishonest too, and
whose sins therefore must be broadcast to the world. 'Baines
turned out a thief,' he briefly informs his brother-in-law, 'so I
turned him off'; but a massive volume of incoherent evidence
about the painter-cum-store-keeper's crimes is forwarded to
London, while Mr. Oswell is startled to learn from his indignant
friend that 'The only one likely to be cut off is our miserable
artist. I left him at Tette by way of sparing him exposure to
malaria in the lower Shiré and he took to stealing our stores and
drinking and debauchery.'

One would have expected the Doctor's rancour towards Baines
would have been softened by his triumphant discovery of the
lake, but instead he seemed to grow even more vindictive. The

weary Kirk and Rae were dispatched to Tete to arrest the criminal and search his baggage for irrefutable evidence of his misdeeds. Although nothing was found that could be accounted really incriminating, there was no question of giving Baines any respite, for the Reverend Charles had succeeded in extracting some form of confession from the unhappy man, although admittedly at a time when Baines was 'heady' with fever. The 'thief' was brought down to Kongone in disgrace to wait for a boat to take him away. There he was treated like a pariah; 'I do not allow Baines to come to our table', the pious Doctor notes in his diary, 'but send him a good share of all we eat ourselves', and almost apologetically goes on to admit he has allowed him an awning to shield himself from the sun during his solitary meals. There still remained one more dreadful philistinian scene of accusation and disavowal before the wretched thing was over; then Baines was allowed to escape to Cape Town, a sick, discredited and shattered man.

᷒᷒   ᷒᷒

This final purging of unwanted members from the expedition, however, still lay several weeks in the future when Livingstone, 'a little before noon of the 16th September 1859' saw the gleaming waters of Lake Nyasa stretching out like a sea into the far distance.* Popular imagination, always so concerned with shaping itself according to its own sentimental wishes, has created a pleasing scene for this great moment of discovery: it sets the solitary figure of David Livingstone, his mind filled with fine and lofty thoughts, tramping alone up to the crest of a ridge, to stand there in enchanted surprise at the sight of the great lake; far below him a group of faithful Makololo porters are to be seen struggling to keep up with this superman; a Yao tribesman, however, happens to be conveniently at hand and he steps up to tell the explorer the lake is named 'Nyasa'. Curtain. The tableau in its time has been enacted in a hundred different village halls, and is one of the most precious items of the Livingstone myth to have been handed down to us. The true facts about that morning, however, are rather different: Livingstone's thoughts at the time

* They did not actually reach the lake until September 17th.

97

were anything but elevated; he had already seen the lake some months before, and for years had known its name; he came to it not by windswept hills but through the fetid swamps of Lake Malombe; instead of travelling alone he was accompanied by a group of querulous white men; only a few of the 'faithful' porters were true Makololo and far from being paragons they were already learning the lessons which soon were to turn them into the most merciless pillagers in all the new country Livingstone had found.

But the discovery of the lake was a dazzling achievement—of Livingstone's whole career second only in importance to that of the Victoria Falls. 'It is a splendid lake', the enthusiastic Kirk described it at the time, and these five words perfectly express nearly everybody's feelings about Nyasa, for it is always an exquisite pleasure to stand and gaze over its glistening waters which have caught and even improved upon the bright iridescence of the Mediterranean Sea. But Livingstone was curiously unimpressed by the lake. No such quality of poetry creeps into his description of its discovery as occurred when first he saw the Victoria Falls and wrote: 'Scenes so lovely must have been gazed upon by Angels in their flight.' Perhaps he was not quite certain whether his really were the first European eyes to behold the lake, although to the end of his life he would claim the priority of its discovery in the face of substantial evidence to the contrary. His accounts written at this time seem far more concerned with the geological terraces round about it than by the marvel of finding so much water in the centre of the vast aridity of Africa. Moreover, he was worried about the safety of his 'precious punt' which he had left '. . . in a sinking condition', and practically unguarded below the Murchison cataracts, and he informed his companions there was time for them to spend only a single night beside the lake. A little later the four white men spread their blankets out between the pendant branches of an enormous banyan tree that stood close to the site of present-day Fort Johnston. A large slave caravan happened to be encamped nearby, and in the evening 'an awful blackguard looking lot' of Arab slavers came strolling over to talk with the white men; they offered them some malachite for sale as well as three little black girls at a little more than a shilling each. The incident was not without importance; with it came the realisation that Providence had guided Dr. Livingstone to the lake at precisely the most vulnerable point on all the great slave route that led from the headwaters of the Congo to the distant Indian Ocean. It is not difficult for us to imagine Livingstone lying there that night listening to the lapping waves and composing in his mind the dispatch which would ask the British Government to station a gunboat on the lake near the Shiré ferry for the purpose of 'cutting off slaving at its source'.

The long return march to the *Ma-Robert* was made in excessively hot weather and after it even the Doctor confessed to feeling 'useless', and directed a hopeful enquiry to Quelimane about purchasing donkeys there for future overland journeys. Although free from malaria thanks to their quinine pills (which we learn from Livingstone were 'dead shots'), each of the white men went down in turn with dysentery, which Livingstone blamed on the cook being over-liberal with mulligatawny in the soup, while the less credulous Kirk was certain they had all been poisoned by a native chief. Not until October 6th did the ragged little group of men stagger into Chibisa's village with dull eyes, hollowed cheeks and yellow-grey complexions, and set the *Ma-Robert* chugging downstream on yet another of the interminable trips to collect stores. Although by now Livingstone had decided that Nyasa (he invariably spelled it Nyassa) was to be the setting for his endeavours in Africa, almost two whole years went by before he came back to the lake. To us in the twentieth century who have cast off the leisurely use of time our grandfathers knew, Livingstone seems to have allowed an absurdly long interval to elapse before resuming the whole thread of his purpose in the continent. But the Doctor believed his first duty lay in leading his Makololo home from Tete where he had left them three years before. And as if that was not enough, his erring intuition had persuaded him that, besides the Shiré, the Rovuma river (which lay outside the jurisdiction of the Portuguese) also drained Nyasa, and he was determined to explore it. But the delay did not really matter very much. From now on Nyasa would always be thought of in association with David Livingstone—which was wholly fitting, for of all the men who have come to its shores, he is the only one whom posterity would label as truly great.

🌿　🌿

The Makololo play a surprisingly important and, on the whole, an honourable part in the story of Livingstone's travels and the history of the lake. They did not come from a homogeneous and long-established tribe. Rather they were members of a temporary association of several separate tribes that had been welded into an 'empire' by foreign invaders from the south. They lived in terror of the Matabele. During the nineteenth century these Matabele (and their kinsmen the Angoni) were the Huns of Central Africa, and to pursue the analogy further, their blood-thirsty King Mzilikazi was its Attila. Livingstone owed his ascendancy over the Makololo to his having married the daughter of Robert Moffat—for Robert Moffat was about the only man in Africa who could influence and restrain Mzilikazi. In fact the Makololo regarded Livingstone's friendship as a sort of insurance against the emnity of the Matabele. The porters who accompanied him on his trans-African journey had been charged to serve him well, and indeed, on at least one occasion had saved his life. 'They were', he once wrote fondly, 'a jolly rollicking set of fellows with a great deal of the soldier in their character' and Livingstone always regarded them as superior to any other Africans he knew, a feeling incidentally which was shared by very few other white men. Towards the end of his first great journey Livingstone had left ninety of his Makololo porters at Tete when he went on to Quelimane by canoe. There they settled down to await his promised return, slipping happily into the debauched ways of the local natives and their Portuguese masters. Although they gave Livingstone a tremendous welcome when he returned to Tete in 1858, most of them were genuinely dismayed two years later when he announced he felt 'in honour bound' to lead them back to Linyanti. Charles Livingstone and Kirk, who were going too, contemplated the tremendous journey with a concern at least equal to theirs, and were scarcely comforted by the Doctor's calm assurance that their walk would only take six months. As usual when he was travelling on foot, Livingstone's estimate proved astonishingly accurate. He left Tete on May 16th, 1860, with the few Makololo he had persuaded to go home (and even some of these deserted at the first opportunity), and he was back again six months and one week later after a man-killing march which had lowered the morale of the expedition to breaking-point.

For not only did the journey prove unexpectedly arduous, but at Linyanti the white men had been appalled by evidence of a tragedy for which the Doctor could not escape a good deal of responsibility. Only a short time before, two missionary families had trekked from Bechuanaland to the Makololo country. They had been attracted there by Livingstone's appeal for mission workers as well as his report of a friendly people living in a healthy country and the assurance he would meet them on the upper Zambesi to help them establish their own station. But no missionaries were waiting for Livingstone at Linyanti, only some scattered graves, and the news that the few remaining survivors had already lurched off towards Kuruman, having been plundered by the Makololo and obliged to pay toll at every river drift they came to. Livingstone's comment on the tragedy of the two missionary families strikes one as being particularly heartless: 'A precious mull they made of it', he wrote to his brother-in-law. Perhaps better than anything else it illustrates his occasional inclination to lapse into a curious mood of inhumanity.

But what made the march even more distressing were the Livingstone brothers' repeated quarrels. According to Kirk they indulged in 'abusive filthy . . . language' and Charles even assaulted his brother (whom he now called "the cursing Consul of Quelimane"). Of all the incidents Dr. Livingstone describes in his personal journal nothing is more remarkable than the account he gives of his discovery of Charles' real character. As one reads it, one can almost visualise the Doctor's expression of bewilderment and blank dismay after his brother had suddenly released his 'long pent-up ill-feeling' about him. As is so often the case with a quarrel of this kind it began in a particularly inconsequential sort of way with Dr. Livingstone reproving his brother for tearing his pillow. The highly strung Charles promptly exploded into a tirade of hysterical abuse about the Doctor's lack of leadership, of his attempts to bewitch him, and even of making him 'do all the hunting and carry the game too'. The Doctor, with an effort, managed to control himself and so prevented the puerile family row from becoming public property. He had only his diary to confide in, and there in bemused wonder and a little incoherently, he repeats the vituperation Charles has hurled at him: 'Manners of a cotton-spinner, of the Boers; didn't know how to treat men. An old filthy pillow that I got the benefit of it; that I cursed him, that I set the devil into him, &c., and asked if it was not his work to take time for me, and repeated again and again that I had cursed him. What part of Botony is Sunday cursing. Seemed intent on a row. Would be but a short time in the expedition: regretted that he was on this journey. Would rejoice when he could leave it. So far my brother Charles.' Eventually the two brothers managed to patch up some form of reconciliation, and indeed Charles was allowed to co-operate and is treated generously in the account of the expedition Livingstone later gave to the public; but from now on he is rarely mentioned in the Doctor's private journal apart from an occasional dry entry that Charles is in a 'funk' or 'keeping up his sulks'. In Kirk's opinion he was only 'kept on out of charity'.

Yet once his irritation is forgotten, and his senses quietened by the journey, David Livingstone becomes almost his old alert inquisitive self again. Thus with his inimitable irrelevance he tells us in his journal that a hyrax 'tastes somewhat like partridge' and that a female elephant possesses 'punctae of nipple 12 in number'. From an old native chief he learns that 'Nyassa goes by the name of Chibébe too', and then inconsequentially he asks why it is that 'on passing a large tamarind tree people ran to it and made obscene gestures to it' and adds characteristically that the Portuguese do so too. But however ebullient his own spirits, his companions seem to have been almost on the verge of mutiny when they tramped wearily back into the Tete at the end of the journey. Luckily good news was waiting for them there, and their profound gloom changed suddenly to extravagant optimism. An official dispatch announced the Government's intention of replacing the *Ma-Robert* with a larger steamer that already was on

Private

River Shire 20 Oct
1859

My dear friend,

Two pages of a letter from Livingstone, soon after the discovery of the Lake

Two channel rapids above Kebrabasa, 1858, drawing by Thomas Baines

its way out from England. And better still, they learned that on board this ship, the *Pioneer*, was a band of Anglican missionaries headed by a Bishop; they were the first fruits of the famous Cambridge appeal 'to carry on the work which I have begun'. It seemed to Dr. Livingstone, then, that after all the anxieties and frustrations of the past, the fortunes of the expedition were bound to improve. Only much later would he write that this was in fact the high tide of its small success, and afterwards because of the influence of the Portuguese slave traders its prosperity declined.

Livingstone took the wretched *Ma-Robert* down the Zambesi for the last time (and left it sunk in the river on the way) curiously flattered at the prospect of having a Bishop working under his direction, glad that the neglected task of evangelising the Shiré Highlands could now be undertaken, certain that the advent of the missionaries would enhance the prestige of his enterprise. He did not stop to consider that the irruption of a Bishop, three priests, a lay missionary and a couple of artisans into what was already a remarkably inharmonious company, might complicate his task still further.

☙   ❧

Livingstone and the new Bishop met on February 9th, 1861, and they took a liking to each other immediately. Looking back now it is difficult to think of a more suitable man to soothe Livingstone's difficult mood at the time than Bishop Mackenzie. He seemed to have been born with all the gifts—including tact. Mackenzie regards us from one of the portraits taken of him at this time with all the 'gravitas' of a Roman patrician, yet one knows at once that those earnest eyes will kindle easily with a tenderness that is almost feminine. But there was nothing un-manly about Mackenzie—rather he possessed in full measure that unusual quality we speak of as sensibility. His remarkably hand-some appearance makes Mackenzie seem the very epitome of militant Victorian Christianity. If the balding head gives him something of the appearance of a tonsured mediaeval monk, the luxuriant side-burns stretching down from the curling hair on the Bishop's temples could only have been cultivated by a member of the 'cloth' during the calm unhurried days of a century ago.

Even at University, an unusual athletic prowess that was combined with natural integrity and humility had made Mackenzie
stand out from among his contemporaries. Now with increasing
maturity he seemed able to dominate all those with whom he
came in contact—until he met David Livingstone. And now
here he was in Africa, anxious to follow the Doctor's advice in
every particular. No two men could have been more different
than David Livingstone and Charles Frederick Mackenzie, and
yet they possessed certain traits in common: one of them was
courage, and another a sense of dedication, for the new Bishop
was as determined as his mentor to bring the blessings of Christian
civilisation to the people of Central Africa.

But he had to restrain his eagerness for some time. Livingstone,
when he met the Bishop at Kongone, was engrossed with his
theory that the Rovuma would afford an easier approach to
Nyasa than the Zambesi, and the protesting newcomer found
himself hustled off against his will on an unwanted exercise in
African exploration. Only after three exhausting months was he
back again with the missionary party at Kongone, ready to set
out for the Shiré Highlands. Most of their stores, they were
distressed to find, had been destroyed during their absence but
they were comforted by Livingstone's airy assurance that it
would only take them three weeks to reach their goal. As it
turned out the *Pioneer* proved to be hardly better suited to the
Zambesi than the unlamented *Ma-Robert*, and the fledgling
evangelists during the next miserable eight weeks learned what it
felt like to be members of one of Livingstone's expeditions.
Before they reached Chibisa they, like all their predecessors, had
come to detest the endless boredom of the river passage, its
mangrove swamps and shoals, the long rank grass which lined its
banks, the monotonous heat, the mosquitoes, and the inevitable
fever. One particular seven-mile stretch of the river took three
mortal weeks to negotiate—and beyond it they stuck again,
apparently permanently, on another unsuspected sand bank.
Predictably, they all passed through the mood of disillusionment
that attended everyone who followed in the Doctor's tracks, and
little whispers of criticism could be heard in the steamer as the
half-starved clergymen looked for the 'vast' cotton fields that had

been described so often, or discovered that the small amount of cotton they did eventually obtain was purchased by them for rather more than it would fetch in Manchester. Even the expected herds of game were absent, driven away by the drought; and when a solitary eland did happen to stray near the river, one of the priests drily noted that 'a whole army of natives turned out' in gratified surprise to hunt it down. The feeling of animosity in the *Pioneer* was by no means one-sided: Dr. Livingstone disparagingly referred to the new arrivals as 'the Parso tribe', while the other expedition members believed the clergymen were inclined to eat more than their fair share of the rations—and (if we are to take Charles Livingstone's word for it) one of the missionaries was a 'pilfering parson', and 'a sleepy sort of fellow, a great eater & very fond of jam and jelly', whom they caught one night 'licking the jam pots' when he thought the others were asleep.

But Mackenzie was a benign influence. And he and David Livingstone became close friends. To the members of the expedition he was soon 'quite a brick of a Bishop', and 'a trump of a fellow', while for his part Mackenzie confided to the Bishop of Cape Town that he and the Doctor chaffed each other all day long like schoolboys. At length, their relations strained, but still intact, the company reached Chibisa, and when Livingstone announced his intention of accompanying the missionaries into the highlands to find a suitable site for them to settle, they began to think the worst of their difficulties must be over. They set off from the cataracts in the beautiful crisp winter season of Nyasaland, and even after this lapse of time, how easy it is for us to visualise those men again, striding together towards the lovely rounded Shiré hills. In the van goes Livingstone wearing his rough blue serge suit and peaked consular cap with the faded gold lace around its brim, 'tramping along', as Mackenzie himself observed, 'with a steady, heavy tread which kept one in mind that he had walked across Africa'. Beside him marches the Bishop, a pastoral staff held in one hand, his loaded rifle in the other, while behind them trail the missionaries, a little awed by their strange surroundings and uneasy at the prospect of having to spend the night out in the open surrounded by savages and all manner of wild animals. There is a pathetic quality about this first ill-conceived and quixotically gallant missionary advance into the land of the lake, and somehow one knows that right from the start, despite the air of confidence, it carries the seed of solemn and certain tragedy embedded in it. For the venture could scarcely have been made at a more unfavourable moment; the country for which they were bound was already boiling with Yao slaving parties, and demoralised refugees. In the centre of the turmoil the white men came upon a curious square-shaped mountain named Chiradzulu, looking over a fertile plain towards the dominating massifs of Zomba and Mlanje. In its shadow they found a small, easily defensible, tongue of land jutting out into the river beside the village of Magomero. Almost casually it was chosen as the first U.M.C.A. station; some mud huts were hastily set up and then, satisfied he had served the Bishop well, Livingstone went on with his brother Charles, Kirk and a sailor from the *Pioneer* named Neil, to begin the proper exploration of the lake. With them they carried a small sailing boat.

Nearly four months went by before Livingstone and the Bishop met again, and in the interval Mackenzie had made a decision which in the end was to destroy his mission. For the Bishop, during that time, had changed from an ardent pacifist into a thunderbolt of war and had resolved to protect his Manganja neighbours by attacking the Yao slavers. It was by no means a hasty decision; it was reached only after fervent prayer, earnest discussion and anxious contemplation of all the risks involved. Moreover, the missionaries did not regard it as the initiation of a new course of action; rather they thought of themselves as doing no more than following the precedent set by Dr. Livingstone who, only a few weeks before, had liberated two parties of slaves in their presence. The Doctor describes these incidents in one of the more dramatic passages of his *Narrative of the Zambesi Expedition*, as well as in several letters. He tells us that in the Shiré Highlands on his way to Magomero he suddenly encountered a slave caravan being driven along by half a dozen black slavers who were 'shouting and trumpeting as if they had been returning from performing a capital game before Her Majesty at Balmoral'. At the sight of the white men the startled slavers 'darted off like mad', leaving eighty-four of their captives behind, who were promptly freed from their bonds and slave sticks, which were then used symbolically as fuel to cook them a meal. Amid much clapping of hands, and ululating, the liberated slaves attached themselves to the missionary party, and Mackenzie found himself presented with a ready-made congregation which included the famous Chuma who followed Livingstone to the end. A week later there was a second and more serious collision with the slavers. This time the Yao, screaming 'Nkondo, Nkondo, Nkondo'—'war, war, war'—opened fire on the white men. Now it was the turn of Livingstone and his party to be taken by surprise. 'So little did we intend to fight', the Doctor wrote afterwards, 'that I was unarmed and had to borrow a revolver in case it came to close quarters and after a few rounds our ammunition was expended—but they made off. . . .' As affairs of this sort go it was a very small skirmish, but its date, July 22nd, 1861, is an important one in the story of the Land of the Lake because it marks the first armed conflict there between the forces of evil and the unanswerable logic of humanitarianism. At that very moment the few scattered shots of Livingstone's party were being echoed on a vastly greater scale thousands of miles away as a ragged army of Union troops came reeling back into Washington and the exultant Confederates rode their horses after them through the stream at Bull Run. It seemed then that the anti-slavery cause in America was lost. But Livingstone had no difficulty in winning his own small 'battle'. The white men's fire brought down half-a-dozen slavers, and the remainder drew off hurriedly, with shouted threats of reprisal, leaving another trembling group of captives to swell the Bishop's congregation.

Soon after this skirmish, and the 'settling' of the Bishop, Livingstone moved off from Magomero leaving Mackenzie and his clergymen to their own resources.

For a few weeks the missionaries were content to sit quietly at Magomero, examining their consciences, and they made no attempt to check the atrocities of the slavers they could see going on everywhere around them. But in their letters one can detect a rising note of anger and resentment which eventually was bound to break out into action. Ominously we learn they are indulging in shooting practice, and we read one day of the Bishop losing his temper and striking a lazy porter with his crozier and using its crook afterwards to haul him to his feet. Then, after the Bishop had repeatedly 'heard the accounts of barbarities perpetrated', the inevitable occurred: 'Mackenzie's blood', in Kirk's memorable phrase, 'rose and theories vanished'. There was a hurried conference with the local chiefs, and afterwards we find Mackenzie writing almost gaily that he had 'consented at last to head an army' against the slavers. (He did not add that he was seriously considering sending home for military aid to help him in his campaign.) This was a very different thing from Livingstone's acts of self-defence. The missionaries deliberately set themselves up against the slavers as the rulers of the highlands—and now they proceeded to carry the war into enemy territory; they burned Yao settlements and killed those who resisted them, the Bishop himself shooting one recalcitrant chief. There seems something very wrong here, but it is difficult to know what else a man of flesh and blood could have done except defend with arms the Manganja villagers whom the missionaries by now had come to regard as their protégés. And at least for a time the new policy seemed justified, for an uneasy peace descended on the land.

We can see now that a clash between the slavers and the white men was bound to come sooner or later, yet still one feels it unseemly that it was initiated by clergymen. Certainly the High Church sentiment at home, led by Pusey, was overwhelmingly critical of the Bishop's action, holding it to be no part of a missionary's duties to shed blood however great the provocation.* The question of whether the Bishop was justified in using force to oppose the slavers is one of those perennial ones which can be relied upon to divide English opinion more or less equally. Even today the argument is still open. Charles Livingstone, to his credit, was always on Mackenzie's side. After hearing of Pusey's criticism he clarified one aspect of the controversy when, with heavy facetiousness, he pointed out 'all very well Mr. P. but if you were in Africa & saw a host of murderous savages aiming their heavily loaded muskets & poisoned arrows at you, more light might enter your mind . . . and if it didn't, great daylight

* In a speech, Pusey called Mackenzie's conduct 'a frightful thing', explaining that 'the Gospel has always been planted, not by doing, but by suffering'.

would enter your body through arrow & bullet holes'. On the other hand, David Livingstone was disinclined at first to support Mackenzie's militant policy. In a letter to Murchison we find him wondering anxiously, 'What you will say to gentlemen killing those who they are sent out to convert'. But his opinion slowly changed and a year later he is writing cautiously, 'to my mind the case here was one of necessity, of dire necessity, and not one clergyman or layman would engage in it willingly any more than he would choose to perform the office of the common hangman'. But it was only after Mackenzie was dead and Livingstone had meditated beside his grave that he summed up his, and perhaps our own, feelings in the matter better than anyone else could have done: 'At first', Dr. Livingstone wrote, 'I thought him wrong in fighting, but don't think so now. He defended his 140 orphan children when there was no human arm besides to invoke.' It was the kind of epitaph his 'good Bishop' would have appreciated.

Bishop Mackenzie's troubles still lay in the future when Livingstone set off across the Shiré Highlands with a small gig to make a detailed exploration of his lake of stars. He launched her on the Upper Shiré and rowed slowly northward: it was September 2nd, 1861, before his party emerged from the river and became the first white men to sail on the broad waters of Nyasa. One would have expected the next few weeks to have included some of the most splendid experiences of Livingstone's career, and it is vaguely disturbing to find instead that both he and his companions looked back with grim distaste on this first voyage upon the lake. For one thing it was appallingly hot that summer and there was little protection in an open boat from a scorching sun whose ferocity seemed accentuated by reflection from the water. All of them suffered from fever or rheumatism. They were often endangered by the furious and unsuspected tempests that lash the lake, and they were distressed by the sea-sickness its short steep seas induce. Nor were matters improved by a robbery which reduced them to their underclothes and a starvation diet. Then again the natural beauty of the setting was obscured by a shimmering heat haze as well as by the smoke of countless bush fires, so that they hardly even glimpsed the blue mountains on the opposite coast. Moreover, the prospects for European settlement in the malarial country round the lake were a great disappointment to Livingstone. The lake people were mostly surly, even hostile, and on one occasion the explorers had to draw their guns to avert a murderous attack. Elsewhere, however, they found the natives living in such abject misery that the white men's hearts were seared with compassion and anger. For although they found areas round the lake where a teeming population seemed reasonably prosperous, raising crops of rice, sweet potatoes, maize and cotton, the southern shores of the lake had been made into an abomination by the brutality of the slave hunters, whose activity Charles gasped was 'going on just now at a fearful rate'. And in the north, things were even worse; there the startled explorers found the country had been devastated by a worse horror—the ferocious Angoni. Here, as the Doctor grimly notes, the beaches were 'literally strewed with human skeletons and putrid bodies'.

During this first exploration of the lake, Charles, Kirk and Neil travelled in their sailing boat, while the Makololo porters did their best to keep up with them along the winding shore, insisting as they went further northwards that Dr. Livingstone accompany them for protection. And so instead of a quick and easy exploration, the white men considered they were doing very well to cover six or seven miles a day. Nevertheless, a great deal of work was accomplished. The southern shores of Nyasa were accurately charted and whimsically compared to the boot shape of southern Italy. Then, because the eastern side was closed to them by war, they crept slowly up the western coast taking soundings, making astronomical observations, measuring heights and mapping every stream and hill. At dusk they would meet again to make their beds up for the night among the rushes on the beach, so that today nearly every settlement on the south-western lake shore can, with probity, post a notice claiming 'Livingstone slept here'. The insatiable curiosity of the people of the lake was something new to them, and embarrassed, even irritated, the explorers. They were watched with the same childish attention 'as was manifested', wrote Livingstone later, in one of his rare moments of jocularity,

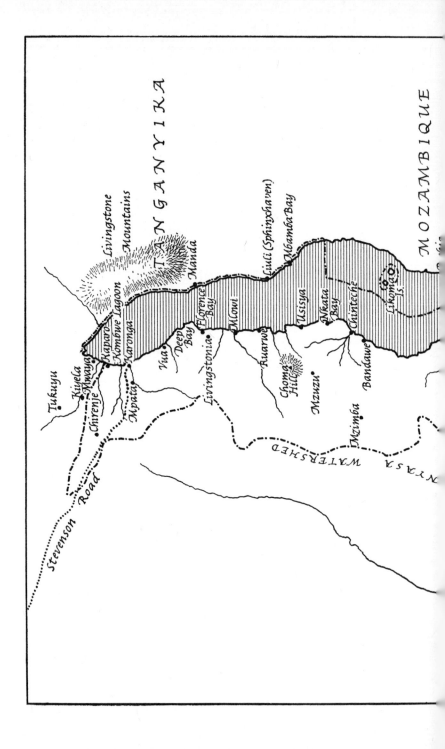

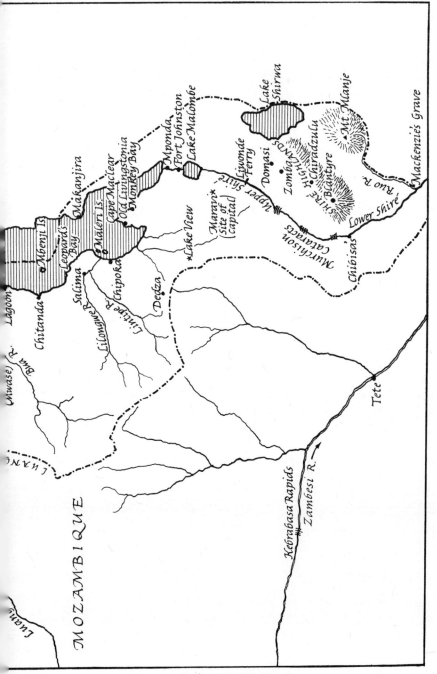

Lake Nyasa and the Shiré Highlands

'when the hippopotamus first appeared at the Zoological'. Their pink skins in particular intrigued the natives who would come crowding round to touch the *chirombos* (wild animals) at every stop, which set Charles complaining: 'black humanity perspiring is not pleasant while one is eating'. The Doctor's daily bathe was certain to attract a large audience and one morning after watching him lathering his head with soap, a small boy came running back, shouting to everyone that this strange magician was taking out his brains.

Livingstone for his part was just as inquisitive as any of the natives. Everywhere he went, he demanded information about the length and shape of the lake. The answers he received were wildly contradictory and confusing. 'How far is it to the end of the lake?' he asked one native chief. 'Who ever heard of such a thing?' came back the scornful reply, 'Why, if one started when a mere boy . . . he would be an old grey-headed man before he got there.' He heard the lake turned round to the west and divided in two, but next day that it ran eastwards to the sea. Another time he was told that it issued from a rocky gorge, and he gave it up after learning from someone else of its 'coming back to the point from which one starts'.

At Chitanda's, not far south of Chia Lagoon, the explorers wakened one morning to find they had been robbed during the night of all their spare clothes as well as most of the calico-currency on which they had to rely for buying food, the only piece remaining being one small bale Dr. Kirk had been using as a pillow. The well-equipped Charles naturally came off the worst of all the travellers; a letter he wrote soon afterwards gives us some idea of what a well-to-do explorer in Victorian days carried with him: 'The people of Nyassa resemble the most highly civilised nations in having expert thieves among them', he informs his confidante, Mrs. Fitch, for from him they had managed to get away with 'the waterproof cloak & leggings, 3 pairs of trousers, 3 pr of the new socks you sent, 1 pr of Hoppies new boots, new undershirt & 3 shirts, a fine leopard skin I had recently bought, some specimens of birds and animal skins, 3 prs of scissors & 2 knives, all my instruments for preparing specimens. . . .' Dr. Livingstone's indignation was expressed more tersely: 'This is the

first time I have been robbed in Africa,' he complained next day
in his diary. Unfortunately it was not the last occasion, for what
little equipment remained to them was stolen a few weeks later
near Kota Kota during their return journey. On this occasion
Charles wakened to see the thief running away, and drew his
revolver; fortunately, perhaps, his gun misfired twice and the
robber got away.

The letters and the journal Livingstone wrote at this time are
disappointingly factual, and rarely kindled by any feeling of
warmth or inspiration, although one entry, in which he associates
fever with the presence of mosquitoes, shows that for a moment
he was within an ace of anticipating the discovery of malaria
transmission by over thirty years. He sadly notes the increasing
extent of the slave trade and that the Arabs had built dhows to
carry their captives across the lake; in a more relaxed moment he
compares the shape of Mbenji Island with that of a thatched house
and then, as he voyages north, his entries nearly come to an end
when his boat barely rides out an exceptionally violent storm
opposite the mouth of the Dwangwa river. He writes afterwards
about the swarms of nkungu flies he sees for the first time, and
records the resemblance of the lake's fish to those in Galilee,
while a letter shows he was the first to recognise that Nyasa was
but one of the great lakes threaded into a gigantic rift valley running down nearly the whole length of Africa.

But as he travels north, the tone of Livingstone's writing
saddens, for as he says himself, the beauty of the scene is hidden
by the misery of the people living in this 'abode of lawlessness
and bloodshed' in which, as Kirk also commented, there had
'been a dreadful slaughter for the shores are covered with skulls'.
'O, when will Christ's holy gospel enter into this dark region!'
the Doctor cries another day, and the poignancy of his despair
seems still as fresh today over the darkening lake as when it was
expressed a hundred years ago.

Livingstone never reached the end of his lake, nor even saw it.
Among the broken hills and ravines that stride upwards from
Nkata Bay, he and his land party became hopelessly lost and for
four days moved in mortal danger. What today is a prosperous
smiling country, in 1861 was an inferno of decaying corpses,

withered crops and smouldering villages. War parties of Angoni roamed everywhere killing, burning and destroying, and several times the lives of Livingstone and his terrified Makololo were threatened by them. At last they made contact with the boat again after passing 'nests of pirates living on bare rocks', but by now Charles and perhaps Kirk too had reached the limit of their nerves and endurance. With a sickening sense of frustration for an unfinished task, the boat was turned about. 'This is the first time I ever returned without accomplishing all I set out to do', David Livingstone informed his friend Murchison with perhaps an understandable refraction of the truth. Kirk tells us that his farthest reading showed they reached as far north 11°44'—about the vicinity of the present day Usisya.* They could see the mountains beyond closing in upon the lake and convinced themselves they were near its further extremity; indeed, to the end of his life Dr. Livingstone believed Nyasa to be one hundred miles shorter than it really is. He only glimpsed the sumptuous scenery of its most beautiful part and the mountains that bear his name today. After turning south they came slowly down the coast again, jeered at by a people even more truculent than before because the white men had been robbed and were said to be retreating before the Angoni. 'The people hereabouts', wrote Kirk furiously in his own journal as though to relieve his feelings, 'are the ugliest I have seen in Africa and the most inhospitable.' Charles for once was in full agreement with him. 'The lake people,' he wrote to Mrs. Fitch, 'are by no means good looking. The women are frightfully ugly.' The white men's irritation was not improved by a mutiny among their Makololo porters whom they abandoned near the mouth of the Lintipe river. They left the lake to the sound of the slavers' distant gunfire echoing round the hills like the muttering of a mounting storm. It was a fitting end to the trip. Dr. Kirk in particular had had his fill of Lake Nyasa and with the memory of his discomfort still lying sharply in his mind, wrote that it had been 'the hardest, most trying, and most disagreeable of all our journeys. It is the only one I have no pleasure in looking back on.'

* In *Narrative* (p. 386) Livingstone writes 'This was the last latitude taken, 11°44' S. The boat had gone about 24' farther to the north . . . but fever prevented the instruments being used.'

6

THE LAKE ABANDONED

One of the peculiarities of the Zambesi expedition was the way it could change abruptly from miserable frustration to extravagant optimism, and from tragedy to farce. So now, only a few weeks after their harrowing experiences on Lake Nyasa, Livingstone and his bemused companions found themselves suddenly plunged into an atmosphere of 'opera bouffe'. We find this new flavour beginning to appear early on the morning of February 1st, 1862, as they steamed towards a brig which bore the absurd name *Hetty Ellen*. She was swinging slowly at anchor just outside the Luabo mouth of the Zambesi. The sun had scarcely appeared above the glassy sea that day before one of the passengers on the brig—the Rev. James Stewart—was up on deck and watching the white silhouette of the *Pioneer* becoming more distinct as it glided towards him. Mrs. Livingstone had been awakened early that morning too, and she was standing beside him on the deck. Suddenly Stewart lowered his glasses to catch her arm, and with an excited 'there he is' pointed to a figure in smart white trousers, frock coat and blue consular cap who was waving to them from the top of the *Pioneer*'s paddle box. Only a few minutes later Dr. Livingstone was embracing his wife, as a thoroughly embarrassed Stewart backed away, murmuring breathless words of greeting, but never for an instant taking his eyes away from the 'great pioneer and Prince of travellers' he had come half-way round the world to see. This reunion of the Doctor with his wife marks the beginning of the last phase of the Zambesi expedition, and, although it began happily enough, from now on his past troubles were to fade into insignificance compared with those that lay ahead.

To the gaunt veterans of the expedition it must have seemed that a miniature armada had gathered off the Zambesi mouth for the rendezvous with the *Pioneer*. Besides the *Hetty Ellen*, two naval cruisers had dropped anchor near by, while a couple of paddle boats fussed around them unloading stores to be carried over the bar. In these days of modern harbours, it is difficult to appreciate just how hazardous it was a century ago to cross the shallow bars that lay outside many of the East African river mouths. It was a common occurrence for boats to capsize in the offshore surf, and for valuable lives to be lost. But the party coming in to join the expedition was fortunate; the good weather held, and by 9 a.m. on the day after their arrival, the *Pioneer* had safely towed the *Hetty Ellen* and the two paddle boats across the bar, and they lay safely at anchor a little way up the Zambesi.

If Livingstone had complained before about his expedition being top-heavy, he had every reason now to deplore the added responsibilities represented by the arrival of so many unlikely recruits for the mission at Magomero. It was as though a whole new troupe of actors had suddenly appeared uninvited on the stage, and there was very little Livingstone could do, but make the best of it and hope he would be rid of them soon. Yet one would dearly love to put the clock back and see the expression on his face as he welcomed his new guests on board the *Pioneer*, and stared unbelievingly at the mountains of luggage piling up on her decks. For they were a strange (and remarkably well provisioned) group of people, stranger than any he had known before, and he must have realised that from now on things were bound to pass out of his control. It had been difficult enough to manage a mere handful of men; now he had to deal with a party which included five women. For a very short time these newcomers dominate the story of the expedition to the lake, and it is as well for us to identify them at once.

One of them, as we have seen, was Mrs. Livingstone, and she at least could be relied on to be a support and comfort to her husband. Seventeen years had gone by since David Livingstone quite dispassionately decided it was time he got married. Mary Moffat was both eligible and one of the few unmarried girls living in sparsely inhabited Bechuanaland and it was natural that she became his choice. Their courtship, as it happened, fitted in rather conveniently with Livingstone's convalescence from his famous encounter with a lion, but even so there was nothing very sentimental about it. It was wholly in character for Livingstone to make no attempt to embellish the charms of his bride and we find him writing with devastating candour to a friend that Mary was 'not romantic but a matter-of-fact lady, a little, thick, black-haired girl, sturdy and all I want'. One has the feeling that Mary on the other hand may have wanted a good deal more from her marriage than she received, and we would very much like to have had a word from her on the subject. For half of Mary's married life was passed in shoddy boarding houses and filled with hard separations, poor health, loneliness, resentment, genteel poverty, the chilling indifference of parents-in-law, and constant anxiety for her husband and brood of wilful children. Yet through it all Mary Livingstone never lost faith in her gruff unsentimental David and one is glad that the few weeks remaining to her after their reunion on board the *Hetty Ellen*, were passed wholly in his company.

But Mary Livingstone was only one of five ladies who climbed aboard the *Pioneer* at Kongone. For Bishop Mackenzie in a moment of incredible folly had begged his two sisters to come out and keep house for him at Magomero. One of them amazed her friends by becoming engaged just before she sailed, and in consequence only Miss Anne Mackenzie had taken passage to the Zambesi. It is difficult to imagine a more unlikely person to meet on the Zambesi in 1862 than Miss Mackenzie. She was elderly, decidedly spinsterish, precise, very stiff, and, according to poor Livingstone, possessed of 'rather a loose tongue'. Yet one cannot help admiring her spirit in venturing into this untamed part of Africa. She was a confirmed invalid and a good deal of her time recently had been spent stretched out on a sofa with blinding headaches. One of the sailors during the voyage depicted her as being 'thin and delicate but awfully tough', and characteristically Miss Mackenzie relished the description. She declined to travel alone, and so, beside a pet donkey and two broken-down old mules she was accompanied by a housekeeper and a maid, as though determined to bring all the trimmings of diocesan comfort to the Shiré highlands. The character of her two white girl companions is glimpsed in the terse description of them given by one of their companions on the boat, who wrote they were 'rather fond of dress but a little steadied by being attached to the mission'.

It is a great pity they never reached Magomero; one can be certain Jessie Lennox and Sarah would have left some happier memories there than the sad ones that haunt the place today.

Then there was the charming Mrs. Burrup whom everybody liked, a girl of twenty-one, straight out from England where she had been married two days before they sailed. Kirk brings her back to life in a few words; she was, he says, 'full of life, talked nautical and jumped about'. Her energy amazed Miss Mackenzie who once took someone aside to inform him incredulously that Mrs. Burrup was 'capable of walking twelve miles'. Mrs. Burrup's husband was an enthusiast if there ever was one. He had set off ahead of his bride to join the missionaries at Magomero, and after persuading the Portuguese to give him a passage up the Zambesi, then made an incredible trip up the Shiré by himself, to be presented by Kirk to the startled Dr. Livingstone as 'Mr. Burrup from Oxford'. The Doctor grudgingly admired his initiative, but typically growled in a letter to his sister Janet that Burrup 'came up this river in a canoe without knowing a word of the language or a bit of the way'.

Captain Wilson of the cruiser *Gorgon*, the ship's surgeon and several other officers also joined the growing congestion on the *Pioneer*; their orders were to do all they could to assist the Doctor, but none of them except a gunner named Young stayed long enough with the expedition to make very much impression. Nor did the unfortunate clergyman who was marooned at the mouth of the Zambesi with instructions to guard the surplus mission stores. A lighthearted naval paymaster named Devereux, on the other hand, was a particularly welcome addition to the company, and a good deal of our knowledge about the next few weeks is owed to the diary he wrote at the time.

But it was the last member of the 'cast' aboard the *Hetty Ellen* who must be accounted the strangest of them all—the Rev. James Stewart. He had come out to Africa to investigate the possibility of establishing a Free Kirk Industrial Mission in the Land of the Lake. Stewart was an unsmiling man with an ear-to-ear beard, prematurely old at thirty-one and so morose and uncommunicative that no one quite knew what to make of him. One implausible (but delicious) morsel of gossip whispered that the newcomer was a philanderer who had enjoyed the favours of Mrs. Livingstone. Rae was convinced he was a 'speculator' or a 'trader in disguise', and here for once he was in agreement with Charles Livingstone who sounds genuinely perplexed when he wrote home: 'What is this Mr. Stewart? None of us like him. Is he a humbug, or does he really mean to be a missionary? Dr. K. says that he was very rude and insulting to his (Dr. K's) mother in Edinburgh before he left. . . . We have no room for these [missionaries]. They eat up all our nice things and we can't get them replaced. They take care of their own boxes as this Stewart tried to do by turning out our boxes into the rain.' The truth was that Stewart was a paranoiac, and tremendously introspective person, who was so absurdly egocentric that he emerges from the pages of his own journal as a fatuous yet somewhat pathetic figure. He is never quite at ease, always suspicious, always doubtful of his acceptance, indulgent only to his own prejudices, and filled with the melancholy of a professional presbyterian pessimist. Although there is a quaint flavour of modernity about his repressions and introversion, one knows at once that, had he been born in an earlier century, the James Stewart of 1862 would have been quite at home in the company of John Knox.

At the time of his arrival at Kongone, Stewart had succumbed to an almost maudlin admiration for David Livingstone. A little more than a year later he was back in Scotland calling him all the bad names he could think of. Perhaps the strangest reading in all the contemporary reports of the expedition is Stewart's account of how he changed from a hero worshipper into one of the Doctor's most peevish critics. He came to believe he had been lured by false information into an unhealthy country and uncongenial company. He was convinced he had then been made an outcast by the 'Puseyite prejudice' of the Anglican missionaries, and he took refuge in sulkiness and carping disparagement of everybody else's efforts. His final gesture before leaving the expedition was particularly absurd but symptomatic of his discrepant emotions at the time. He blamed all his frustration on Livingstone's hyperbolic descriptions in *Missionary Travels*, and as he came down the Zambesi for the last time, he flung his copy of the book into the brown waters of the river with the muttered incantation (which must have often returned to haunt him), 'So perish all that is false in myself and others'. What no one could have foreseen at the time was the way the deaths of two men altered the whole course of Stewart's life. Hostility towards the missionaries at Magomero changed into sympathy and admiration after Bishop Mackenzie's martyrdom, while at Livingstone's funeral Stewart seems to have gone through some form of spiritual resurgence which eventually brought him back to the lake to establish the great mission he himself named Livingstonia.

And now with the advent of this company, which would have looked more at home at a vicarage tea party than on the Zambesi a hundred years ago, the story of the expedition for a little time takes on an atmosphere of pure farce, which only serves to accentuate the coming tragedy and throws it into starker perspective. For there is a quaint, almost an unreal quality about these men and women who joined Livingstone on the overladen *Pioneer* and then wobbled off up river with him. On the way out from England they had formed themselves into high and low church parties, and according to Devereux, had spent most of their time 'fighting like cats and dogs'. But now they seemed to be settling down more amicably. Doctor Livingstone in particular made a brave effort to be cordial. Even Captain Wilson calmed down and (after a little persuasion) gave up his wild scheme of leading fifty bluejackets up river to the support of Bishop Mackenzie. He may have regretted this a little later on for his sailors were released instead to the less exciting pursuit of Portuguese *aqua ardente* (they called it 'hoggydent' and Livingstone 'vile spirit secretly sold') and African women, which set the indignant Stewart breathlessly recording that 'one woman was abused five times'.

After a period of confused activity, while the *Pioneer* loaded up with a prodigious quantity of mission stores (in which someone had thoughtfully included innumerable casks of wine, several polished wardrobes and fifty thousand fish hooks), the ship set off up river, listing so badly that sometimes one paddle wheel was raised clean out of the water. Everyone on board, with the conspicuous exception of Mr. Stewart, was behaving in an almost kittenish sort of way. Livingstone in accordance with the pervading mood was quite prepared to amuse his guests with accounts of his adventures in Africa (the lion story was in particular demand), and one day unbent so far as to join the young naval officers in startling the ladies with imitation lion roars after they had ventured ashore. The antics of Katie, Miss Mackenzie's donkey, never failed to be entertaining, and one day there was a particularly comical scene when the ship's dog fell through a skylight on to the saloon table at dinner time scattering soup and mashed pumpkin in all directions. But the loudest laughter of all occurred when a native chief came on board the *Pioneer*, fell deeply in love with Sarah the maid, and was only persuaded to leave the ship because he had not enough cows and goats to buy her.

In between all the banter, there were more serious conversations about the coming rendezvous with the Bishop. Livingstone's harsh voice could be heard explaining to Miss Mackenzie that he feared his own schedule had fallen far behind time—but no one seemed particularly concerned. He had met the Bishop, he told her, at Chibisa only a few days after getting back from his own unhappy trip on Lake Nyasa, and had discussed with him then the imminent arrival of the *Hetty Ellen* at Kongone. They had agreed, he continued, that he, Livingstone, should take the *Pioneer* down river as soon as possible and bring the mission ladies up as far as the confluence of the Ruo and Shiré to rendezvous there on New Year's Day with the Bishop. The Doctor had made it clear, he said, that he would not be able to bring them all the way up to Chibisa and that Mackenzie would have to make his own arrangements to conduct the ladies across country from the Ruo to Magomero. Next day the two men had parted cordially and Mackenzie seemingly had been quite unconcerned at the prospect of pioneering a road through unknown country to the Ruo (and only a little upset by the bleak intimation that the *Pioneer* was 'not a passenger ship' when he asked his friend whether one of his missionary brethren might travel with him to Kongone). Miss Mackenzie, after hearing Livingstone out, confessed to feeling some anxiety about her brother still, for as she pointed out, it was now the middle of February, and he must have been waiting for them at the Ruo for at least six weeks. Livingstone in his turn was able to assure her that this was unlikely. His own trip down river to meet the *Hetty Ellen*, he told her, had been unavoidably delayed, largely because the *Pioneer* had been marooned for 'five weary weeks' on a sandbank (where, he added thoughtlessly, his ship's carpenter had died of fever). It was not until January 7th, Livingstone went on, that they had reached the Ruo mouth. They had made quite certain then that Mackenzie had not arrived there, so presumably he must have heard of Livingstone's trouble and altered his own plans accordingly. Indeed, the Doctor concluded, it was much more likely that they themselves would have to do the waiting at the Ruo rather than the Bishop.

So the subject was dropped, and no one even dreamt that the pieces of Miss Mackenzie's tragedy had already fallen into their appointed places or that a slower doom at that moment was overtaking Mrs. Burrup's husband. Instead, the conversation turned again to the scraggy chickens and bananas they had bought that day, and to the shifting sandbanks and changing currents that were holding them up in such an exasperating fashion. For as was always the way with the Zambesi expedition, things seemed to be going wrong. Not until the third week in February did the ship creep up to the Portuguese settlement at Shupanga, and amid such a confusion of orders and counter-orders, consultation, and dissension, that we find Devereux lamenting in his diary, 'I never saw such constant vacillations, blunders, delays, and want of common thought and foresight as is displayed on board the *Pioneer*.' It is wonderful that the restless Captain Wilson controlled his patience for as long as he did, but near Shupanga he suddenly exploded and announced his intention of taking Miss Mackenzie and her three lady companions up river in one of the paddle boats, ahead of the slow-moving steamer. He was perhaps moved less by misplaced chivalry than by fretfulness. All attempts to dissuade him were dismissed with the scornful assurance that once he was free from all these incompetent missionaries he would be at the Ruo mouth within four days. Rather helplessly the other passengers watched poor agitated Miss Mackenzie say good-bye to her donkey, sneak another of her boxes into the paddle boat, and then totter into it herself, clutching Mrs. Burrup's arm. It was February 17th, 1862.

The events of the next few weeks are so bizarre that they remind one of a chapter from a novel by Somerset Maugham. The Shiré was in flood; Wilson's progress was agonisingly slow; the boat was open both to the heat of a fierce sun and to soaking rain. Miss Mackenzie went down with such a severe attack of fever that she was unable even to rearrange her pillows as she lay motionless on the hard boards at the bottom of the boat. Eleven pitiless days and nights, not the expected four, dragged by before Wilson and his exhausted party rowed up to the Ruo mouth. Eager enquiries were made at once about the Bishop, but the local chief assured them he had not come there. They anchored that night in mid-stream, only a hundred yards from Mackenzie's freshly dug grave, arguing about what they should do next. In the morning they decided to row on to Chibisa. Six more dreadful days went by before they pulled wearily after nightfall up to the bluff on the top of which the village stood. All the sailors by now were prostrated with malaria and Miss Mackenzie had become so ill it was feared she would die. Food for days had been running short and even Mrs. Burrup had lost her sparkle. It is not difficult for us even now to visualise that benighted scene below Chibisa's village, for it has the impact of a cinema film put into slow motion so that every detail of its action may be appreciated. We see Kirk, who had come with Wilson as his guide, standing up carefully in the boat, with his legs straddling the inert forms of his companions and peering anxiously about. There is no sound to be heard but the murmur of gently splashing water; nothing to be seen except the silhouette of trees standing by the river bank, looking ghostly in the moonlight. Then Kirk catches sight of a man staring down at them from the top of the cliff. There is a shouted question about the Bishop, and a half-heard answer which sounds like 'O Shuile', and Kirk knows at once that Mackenzie is dead. He looks anxiously at Miss Mackenzie's prostrate form—and sees her stirring, for she knows enough Zulu to guess the meaning of the message. She does not speak; there is only a faint sobbing. 'And Mr. Burrup?' Kirk shouts again, and is told that only a short time before he had been carried past in a litter, and on up into the hills. Several days in fact went by before Mrs. Burrup learned that her husband too was dead, and longer still before the forlorn little party on the Shiré could piece the whole harrowing story together. It seemed that after leaving Dr. Livingstone, Mackenzie became engaged in a punitive expedition against some recalcitrant chief, and this had delayed his arrival at the Ruo to meet his sister until January 11th—four fatal days after the *Pioneer* had steamed past. Of all the clergymen at Magomero, only Burrup had been fit enough to accompany the Bishop on this last journey. Finding no one at the Ruo rendezvous, the two men had decided to settle down in a native hut there on Malo Island and await the steamer's return.

They were in one of those predicaments which haunt one's dreams. The local chief was evasive and disinterested; they had no idea where Livingstone might be, but a nagging suspicion grew that he had abandoned them; they were utterly helpless, and tormented by an increasing anxiety about the safety of their womenfolk; and they had lost their precious supply of quinine when their canoe had been upset higher up the river.

Inevitably both men went down with fever; soon they were too weak to leave their hut. We know very little about the way they spent the next three ghastly weeks, except that they tried to pass the time by learning quotations from the 'Epistle to the Romans' in the original Greek. But it is easy to imagine Burrup's despair as he watched his friend sink into a deepening coma. On the last day of January 1862, the first Bishop of the Universities' Mission to Central Africa died. Burrup somehow found the strength to carry the dead body across to the mainland in the silver twilight of the evening, and how moving it must have sounded in that tangled wilderness as he whispered the few words his fevered mind remembered from the funeral service over his grave. Then he stumbled back to Magomero, where he himself died three weeks later.*

It was the middle of March before Wilson (who himself had nearly succumbed to fever) got his afflicted ladies down to the *Pioneer* again. They were carried on board by pairs of silent bluejackets as Livingstone, grieving for his friend the Bishop and the

---

* He was buried there, but James Stewart in his journal notes that his head was later disinterred by the local tribesmen and used as a fetish, in unconscious anticipation of John Chilembwe's action fifty years later.

effect his death would have on his own crusade, crouched in his dimly lit cabin murmuring 'this will hurt us all'. Then he moved across to the table where his journal lay, to tear from his soul his own immortal monument in words: 'I will not swerve a hair's-breadth from my work while life is spared.'

But a greater grief was waiting at Shupanga, which ever afterwards for him would be a name of death and deep shadows. Mary his wife became ill, and before the end of April Livingstone had buried her under the great baobab tree which he had so often pointed out on his way down the river in happier days. 'She was a good wife', he wrote next day to Mrs. Fitch, 'a good mother and a good but often fearful and dejected Christian. I loved her when we were married and the longer I lived with her the more I loved her. . . . Her loss quite takes the heart out of me—everything else I have encountered in life only made the mind rise to overcome but this feels crushing. . . . I have a sore heart.' A little later in his journal we find his final touching *cri de cœur* that has almost the Brontë touch: 'My dear, dear Mary has been this evening a fortnight in heaven—absent from the body, present with the Lord. . . . For the first time in my life I feel ready to die.'

All the members of the Zambesi expedition, except its leader, by this time were exhausted both physically and morally and it was clear to them the whole enterprise was disintegrating. It seemed almost symbolic when Horace Waller, one of the Magomero missionaries, broke Mackenzie's shepherd's crook by hanging his gun on it. What seems surprising to us now is that the expedition managed to struggle on for another futile year before receiving its official notice of recall, and that even then it did not end for another eight months. Yet at the beginning of this, its final phase, after the grieving women and the sailors had slipped away, there were still certain grounds for optimism. A new boat the *Lady Nyassa* had arrived from England to be used as a deterrent against the slavers, and the mourning Livingstone threw himself into the task of building a road past the Shiré cataracts to carry her to the lake. But Kirk and Rae and brother Charles by now were moving in a sort of dream-like trance, hardly aware of what they were doing. And still the expedition's tale of grief and mortality continued. These are the saddest months of all its course. The stricken band at Magomero was reaping the whirl-wind sown by the 'Bishop's War' and soon the mission formed an island of civilisation surrounded by a sea of savagery. The surviving missionaries watched grimly as fifty women and children of their flock died from starvation; then three of the boys liberated by the Bishop sold themselves into slavery again for the price of a meal. After enduring the famine as long as they could, the ailing missionaries and their remaining followers staggered away from the death trap of Magomero, abandoning the land of the lake to the Yao slave hunters and their Arab and Portuguese masters. Their flight was arrested temporarily at Chibisa where they endured another ordeal of useless suffering, and two more of the white men died. The whole Shiré valley by this time in Livingstone's words had been 'converted into the nearest possible resemblance of what we conceive the infernal regions to be'. Bloated corpses floated down the river each day in ghastly procession, and every morning the *Pioneer*'s paddles had to be cleared of their macabre catch. Charles noted gloomily that 'soon there will be nobody left to teach but alligators', and that he was eating 'work house food', while even the spartan Doctor complained 'we have been out of everything save salt junk and bad pork'. Livingstone was tortured by the sight of so much suffering around him and by the growing realisation that unwittingly he was responsible for it. For by now it was obvious that his efforts had opened a way into the interior not for civilisation but for the slavers. Young Thornton died, and if Livingstone's account is true, a Dr. Meller who had come to help, 'got into a mortal funk' and spoke of leaving. Then Charles Livingstone and Dr. Kirk contracted dysentery, and after he had nursed them through it, David Livingstone himself became seriously ill. Towards the end of April, 1863, both Kirk and Charles plucked up courage and asked permission to withdraw from the expedition. 'I let them go willingly', Dr. Livingstone wrote virtuously to a friend, and yet he was unable to find a single gracious word for Kirk before he left. Of the original seven members, only the Doctor and Rae remained, still working on the cataracts road and dismantling the *Lady Nyassa* for its transport to the lake. One day they heard a boat had come up to Chibisa.

It carried a new Bishop to the Universities' Mission. He was called Tozer, and he was an utterly different person from Mackenzie. 'Bishop, a non-resistance man', Livingstone summed him up scornfully after his arrival, 'vegetarian, and inclined to leave the country: prays for their Majesties of Portugal.' Tozer had brought a brusquely worded dispatch from Whitehall with him, which, although paying tribute to Livingstone's efforts over the last six years, also drew attention to the enormous cost of the expedition and came to the point with 'Her Majesty's Government cannot however conceal from themselves that the results to which they had looked from the expedition under your superintendence have not been realised'. It ended with the curt intimation that it would pay no more salaries after the end of the year. Livingstone read it on the day of Gettysburg.

The official notice of recall may not have been unexpected, but the implied rebuke was a bitter blow to Livingstone. A worse one followed; Bishop Tozer announced his intention of evacuating the Universities' Mission first to an isolated mountain top near the sea, and then clean out of the mainland to Zanzibar. This was the end of Livingstone's dream. All his toil, all the suffering, all the deaths, had only resulted in the withdrawal of every glimmer of Christian influence from the land of the lake. But there was nothing the Doctor could do about it but protest, give orders for the reassembly of the *Lady Nyassa* and relieve his feelings by fulminating against Bishop Tozer. He was 'bolting', he wrote, from a 'wretched down-trodden people', and went on to sneer that it was as though St. Augustine had been content to attempt the conversion of England from a safe refuge in the Channel Islands. But it was Waller who summed up his feelings of despair more vividly: 'Why don't the very rocks groan on those beautiful hills?' he cried. 'The lamp is flickering and soon enough it will be dark enough, aye, even for the Portuguese slave trade'.

꿩   ꙫ

Any other man but Livingstone would have conceded defeat at this stage and waited comfortably at Chibisa for the river to rise high enough to float his ships down to the sea and home. But things did not happen like that with David Livingstone. Instead, we see something extraordinarily impressive about the way he rises above his resentment and suddenly begins to accept all his rebuffs without demur, and regards them as the inscrutable will of Providence. He finds his old sense of certitude again, and while waiting for the rains to fall decides to pay a last visit to the lake, and investigate the routes the slavers used. 'I suspect Dr. L. has gone to the lake again, seeing that his only chance is to return with something new in his hand,' mused the disenchanted Kirk when he heard the news in England. But how badly he had underestimated this incredible man. The new journey was not an attempt to pluck something from failure but was impelled by the old clear motive of righting a great wrong. Perhaps because he was virtually on his own once more, Livingstone becomes the man of the trans-African journey again, as he tramps up the silent Shiré valley for the last time. With him on this walk of seven hundred and sixty miles (which is accomplished in fifty-two days) he takes an ailing steward from the ship whose anaemia he thinks might benefit from the change—and strangely enough his rude therapy seems effective. The entries in Livingstone's journal capture his new gusto; they give us the impression of a squire admiring his ancestral domain rather than a frustrated explorer. The natives of the lake shore seem less ugly than they were before, they are even 'well shaped', while the women whose voices previously he had found raucous, now possess a 'merry ringing laugh'. He takes a 'delicious bath' in the clear waters of his lake, gives some patronising attention to the fishing industry at Chia, and then a little farther north comes wearily to seat himself 'down under a magnificent wild fig tree' (which still stands there) while he waits confidently for hospitality from the local Arab chief. Livingstone has reached the great slave emporium of Kota Kota.

Nowhere else in the world does there exist a town so unwholesome or so squalid as Kota Kota; never was there a place so little recovered from all the shocking deeds of its past. Even today its people are surly and suspicious as though mindful of old horrors, and one feels that at any moment and with little provocation they will suddenly resume the savage ways of a century ago. Their huts remain things to be carefully bolted and

barred at night; the place still reeks with the odour of decay, and
death, and freshly dug graves. The wails of driven slaves yet
linger in this town's disquieting air, and every evening come
screaming into life as a whole army of bats go darting by against
the darkening sky like the souls of lost demented spirits. A
tortuous track, hardly broader than an English lane, winds down
to Kota Kota from an open countryside, whose fertility they say
is owed to all the blood that has been spilled upon it. It runs
right through the town to the old dhow harbour on the lake,
where one can still sense a hint of the excitement left behind by all
sorts of strange arrivals and departures. On the way from the
cassava fields outside, the yellow grit which forms the surface of
this haunted path changes imperceptibly into dirty grey sand, and
then, in the centre of the town, into a fine black dust, soiled by the
contaminating dirt of centuries of human habitation, and pulverised by the dragging feet of countless slaves who have passed by
in miserable procession. Here, near the lake, this 'via dolorosa' of
Central Africa is overhung and shaded by two lines of enormous
gloomy trees, some of them mangoes and kapoks planted a
century ago by the Arabs, others set up quite recently by white
administrative officials and so more familiar to northern eyes.
This sombre avenue is thronged with ghosts and woven through
with memories, the most vivid and enduring one of which is that
of David Livingstone turning, as he believed, for the last time
with a gesture of farewell to his beloved lake and then moving
slowly up the narrow road which is part of the old slave trail
from Cazembe's country. His remembered presence has given a
certain iridescence to this evil place; here somehow, even today,
one feels that Livingstone still is very close. It is as though his
spirit has never really gone away and it only requires a puny
effort of imagination to see that familiar figure trudging up the
hill again as it did a century ago. One sees him then as an integral
part of Africa and knows that for the remainder of his journey,
he will travel unmolested.

A few days march westward from Kota Kota in 1863 brought
Livingstone to the watershed overlooking the swamps where he
was destined to die. At that moment he was trembling on the
brink of brilliant discoveries which would indeed have given

him 'something new in his hand', and redeemed all the failures of the Zambesi expedition. But he hesitated, remembering his obligation to take the *Pioneer* down river as soon as possible, and turned away to go back to the Shiré cataracts. A little later Livingstone was carried safely down to Kongone on a Zambesi by now so full that, in bitter-sweet valediction, it had become once more the 'glorious river' of his dreams.

When Livingstone returned to England to write the euphemistic *Narrative* of the Zambesi expedition, he believed he had seen the last of Lake Nyasa. But already it had become as much a part of his life as the very air he breathed, and sooner or later he was bound to come back to it again. He did so in 1866 and it is a little strange to see that he is a very different man from the one we knew before. For he is gentle and ageing now; all his endurance is ebbing away. But he is no longer a person to be pitied; rather he is to be envied, for he is doing what he wants to do more than anything else in the world; he is where he prefers to be above all others. He comes to Nyasa overland by the Rovuma route, leading a motley caravan of sepoys, Zanzibar askari, Comoro porters, mules, Indian buffaloes, and even baggage camels. He is lost, found, and lost again; he sees only a single white man—Stanley—before his wanderings end with his death in the swamps of Bangweulu seven years later. Quite early on this last journey he comes to his 'lake of stars', close to where the Misenya stream trickles into it and there he seems happier than he has ever been before. 'It was', he writes 'as if I had come back to an old home I never expected again to see; and pleasant to bathe in the delicious waters again, hear the roar of the sea, and dash in the rollers.' He passes slowly round the foot of the lake scribbling continuous letters to his friends in a small tremulous script so very different from the bold hand-writing of earlier years, but gradually the messages become fewer and less impelling, like a gentle voice fading in the distance. Sometimes he stops to rebuke a chief for some misdemeanour, or turns a raiding party from their prey, and everywhere he is succoured by those very Arab slavers to whose destruction he has pledged his life. For the amazing paradox of David Livingstone's career already has begun; his enemies the Arabs see him as a man a little mad and therefore to be honoured and assisted. And truly he moves in a dream-like state now rather than with full awareness, obsessed with a terrible determination to discover the sources of the Nile, believing he is passing through the land of the Old Testament. All the old bitterness and irascibility have drained away from him; he is obedient only to those dictates he believes are Heaven sent. And so, as we watch him for the last time at the lake, which already he has endowed with a sparkle of his own lustre, we see him wearing an unworldly aura of predestination scarcely matched since the days of the mediaeval saints. He knows no doubt or dubiety as he moves on towards his apotheosis at Ilala, which somehow will redeem all his earlier failures as leader, liberator, husband, father, and friend. For he has already glimpsed the final truths; now he gazes ahead to where all that yet remains hidden will soon be revealed to him. And he leaves his lake confidently, for now, through his efforts, she lies on England's conscience, a ward to be protected and watched over until that guardian heart-beat, nearly a century later, begins to falter.

Part Three

MORNING

THE APOSTOLIC AGE

Only in the October of 1875 did white men come back to Lake Nyasa intending this time to make it their permanent home. 'It was a lovely morning', Lieutenant E. D. Young recalled later of that triumphant day, 'and with a gentle breeze our beautiful craft rode over the swell as the great blue waters of Nyasa received the first steam-vessel that had ever entered into an African lake. It was a moment of great excitement and of great thankfulness.' Two years had gone by since Dr. Livingstone had died, as he would have wished to die, in the wilds of Central Africa, kneeling beside his bed in prayer. Almost miraculously his servants had succeeded in embalming the corpse and carrying it through a thousand miles of hostile country to the coast whence a respectful ship bore it home for the last time. All England seemed to be waiting at the Abbey when the body was brought to Westminster for burial, and another wave of missionary enthusiasm swept across the country. It set innumerable bright-eyed orators hymning the need to continue the Doctor's work beside the lake, and scores of volunteers clamouring to go out to the Nyasa mission field, but by the symmetry of destiny it fell to James Stewart, the dead man's earlier detractor, to become the moving spirit of an enterprise which in the end accomplished many of the Doctor's most cherished aspirations. For in the clear light of Scotland after his return from the Zambesi, James Stewart's attitude to Dr. Livingstone had undergone another change, and when he went back to Africa in 1867 to take charge of the celebrated Lovedale Mission, Stewart was a very different man from the one who four years earlier had written petulantly, 'I part with Dr. L., and have no wish whatever to meet him again.'

Stewart happened to be home on furlough at the time of Livingstone's funeral on April 18th, 1874, and the emotions of that experience seemed to crystallise his thoughts: after spending a long summer night in meditation he sternly set about the task of

convincing the General Assembly of the Free Church of Scotland
that the best memorial it could raise to the dead hero would be
the establishment of an Industrial Mission bearing his name
beside the lake.

Stewart's suggestion was discussed at length in council and
finally approved, though with the proviso that the enterprise must
be headed in the first instance by someone thoroughly familiar
with Nyasa country. In practice this narrowed the field down to
Lieutenant E. D. Young, who had been Livingstone's 'active and
most trustworthy' captain of the *Pioneer* and had subsequently
led a remarkably business-like expedition to Central Africa to
investigate rumours of Livingstone's death during his last journey.
Accordingly Young was approached and, after a becoming
interval of reticence, he agreed to exchange his comfortable
coastguard duties at Dungeness for less predictable responsibilities as temporary head of the new Livingstonia Mission. At this
stage good fortune smiled again upon the project by producing a
young medical graduate named Robert Laws who was anxious to
join it; unfortunately he 'belonged' to the United Presbyterians,
but lengthy negotiations resulted in his being 'lent' to Young's
expedition as his second-in-command. Soon afterwards several
artisans were recruited for the enterprise in Scotland, and an
English sailor engaged to take charge of the small steamer that
had been purchased for transport in sections to the lake.

Young and Laws had much to do that winter but in a creditably
short time their preparations were complete and the personnel of
the Livingstonia Mission had travelled to the Port of London and
were gathered in the saloon of *Walmer Castle* to say farewell to
their relatives and a few ghost-like survivors of the Zambesi
expedition who had come to see them off. Waller and Captain
Wilson, who were both there, led the others in such fervent prayer
that no one heard the ship's warning bells; luckily the opened
fingers and impious eyes of Young's teen-aged daughter prevented the involuntary return of them all to Africa, and it was
only an undignified stampede and some dexterous manœuvring
with a gang-plank that enabled the visitors to regain the security
of the West India Dock before the first white men to live beside
the lake set off on their great adventure.

The shore of Lake Nyasa

Maples and Johnson, Likoma, 1894

Five months later, to the strains of 'All people that on earth do dwell' rendered by its entire company, the mission steamship *Ilala*, named after the district where Dr. Livingstone had died, steamed out of the Shiré into Lake Nyasa. For the next few days the missionaries cruised along its south-western coast searching for a suitable place to establish their first station and after rounding Cape Maclear they found one in a peaceful bay with a sandy beach sheltered by a semicircle of high wooded hills. The patriotic Union-Jack pattern of gravelled paths which characterised this original Livingstonia was already slanting through Young's mind as they dropped anchor and rowed across the deserted lagoon to begin laying out the station. It was Sunday, October 17th, 1875, and Laws wrote home triumphantly a little later 'Livingstonia is begun', adding with characteristic punctilio, 'though at present a stretch of canvas stretched between two trees is all that stands'. At the time they seemed to have chosen an admirable site: Mponda, the local Yao Chief, had approved of it during one of his few moments of sobriety, the anchorage was well sheltered, and they believed the cool off-shore breeze would discourage mosquitoes; moreover, it was far enough away from established trade routes to avoid precipitating Mackenzie's agonising problem of having to deal with runaway slaves. But Cape Maclear turned out to be alarmingly unhealthy despite the breeze, while the immediate neighbourhood was almost deserted, and even the most zealous evangelists can do little in the absence of potential proselytes. Indeed, five years later Dr. Laws was ruefully noting that his present liabilities were 'five graves' and his assets 'one convert'—and even he came into the class which Laws would later call 'converts to calico'.

But Cape Maclear was never intended as anything more than an experimental site, and only a month after raising the first tent there, Young and Laws, with five other European members of their staff, set out in the *Ilala* to explore the lake, and circumnavigate it for the first time. Beyond Nkata Bay, Livingstone's 'furthest north', everything was rumour and uncertainty, and so this pioneer voyage was a real geographical advance. They took the *Ilala* up the eastern coast first and were delighted by the succession of beautiful sandy bays they saw, but at Losefa, lying

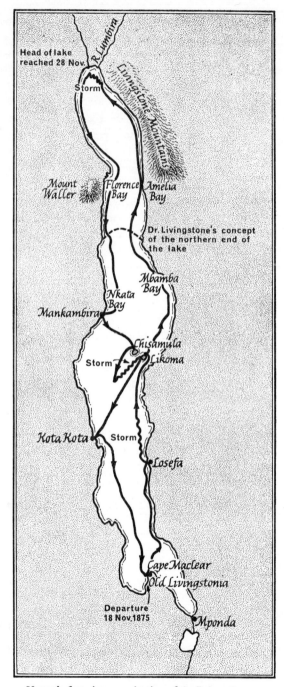

Young's first circumnavigation of the Lake, 1875

almost opposite Kota Kota, they were shocked to come across sinister evidence of the Arab slave trade. A fleet of dhows was anchored in its harbour and Young tells us that in the town 'prosperity was visible on all sides and it was plain that large quantities of beads and calico had been brought thither from the coast'. The Arab slavers of Losefa were reserved and fearful that the white men might threaten their profitable trade, and for the first time we hear of the effective propaganda they put out that the Europeans intended to carry off the natives to eat; one of them, Saedi, let slip that their dhows annually ferried ten thousand slaves across the lake from Kota Kota.

Beyond Losefa the lake shore had been laid waste by the Angoni (whom the missionaries knew as the Ma-Viti). Writing about the country south of Mbamba Bay, Young says 'The Ma-Viti fell upon the villages, and now only ruins are to be seen. Sad indeed it is to look at the broken pottery strewn about . . . but saddest of all to see hundreds of skeletons lying about everywhere.' As they steamed farther north they were astonished to see the Manganja huts wedged into rocky crevices and whole villages built on wooden piles out in the water. The end of November found the *Ilala* at the head of the lake with Young and Laws arguing about whether the Lumbira River flowed into the lake or was a second outlet, and possibly the Rovuma itself.

After surviving a particularly violent storm soon afterwards the two men turned to the congenial task of naming the bays and mountains after their friends and relations. Neither Laws' sister-in-law Amelia nor Stewart's daughter Florence were forgotten, but when they came to the tremendous mountain range that falls into the north-eastern corner of the lake they rightly decided on a more illustrious appellation. These fretted precipices and fantastic pinnacles are so savage and so spectacular that one wonders how long it will be before they take their proper place among the world's most famous landscapes. For a description of them we cannot do better than turn to the original account Young set down in his book *Nyassa: a Journal of Adventures*. 'We were now sailing', he writes, 'along an iron-bound coast. The mountain ranges, which had ever been on our right and left, now assumed in the case of the eastern one an aspect of the most stupendous

magnificence. During many years of service in the Royal Navy it
has fallen to my lot to see nature under these phases best calculated
to impress the mind with wonder, but never in my life did I feel
the spirit of awe and the appreciation of one's own nothingness so
palpably as when the vast chain of mountains hung over the dark
blue depths which we were navigating. The barometer, it is
true, will show one that he has gained a great height on many a
mountain far higher than these of which I speak, but then the
effect is lessened by climbing gradually-ascending slopes and hills
which precede the final ascent of the height which crowns all.
In this instance the mountains come sheer down into the water
like a wall. At a guess I should give them an altitude of eight
thousand feet above the level of the lake, but there are peaks which
must reach ten or twelve thousand feet at the very least. To enhance the beauty of the scene, scores of exquisite waterfalls are in
sight. Too high up for the ear to catch the sound of the falling
torrent, the eye was at no pains to realise motion where all was so
still, and the white skeins hung like floss silk from places which
seemed inaccessible to all but the winds and the mists of the lake.
In memory of my old chief, and in fond recollection of all which
he had done to dispel false assumptions respecting Africa and to
point out to men her real title to beauty and magnificence, I
named this north-east range the "Livingstone Mountains".'

It is a shade disconcerting to find that later Laws always claimed
that, in fact, it was he who gave the Livingstone Mountains their
name, and the same sort of awkwardness recurred after the *Ilala*
had come to another impressive natural feature, which reminded
Laws of 'a grand old fortress' and the more travelled Young of
'some huge monument erected in times when Pharaohs stuck at
nothing'. For Young concludes this part of his account with, 'I
have named this mountain after my friend the Rev. H. Waller',
while we are told by Dr. Laws' biographer that 'the Doctor was
much impressed by this great natural feature and named it
Mount Waller after the editor of *Livingstone's Last Journals*'.

The advent of the Livingstonia pioneers threw a spotlight
again on the Nyasaland mission stage, and now many other
denominations of the Christian Church scrambled to get into the
act. The missionaries, as one observer noted, 'came in droves'

and for the next fifty years their influence dominated the lake country, giving to it an unctuous Victorian flavour that lingered there long after it had vanished from nearly every other part of the world.

Looking back now from the favourable vantage point of hindsight we can see that the impact made on the local Bantu by the immense volume of Christian endeavour poured out so liberally upon them was largely vitiated by the diversity of denominational forms in which it appeared. Sometimes it seemed that the various sects of the Christian Church were more concerned with competing among themselves for converts than with true evangelism, and one can sympathise with the bewildered chief who asked, 'Why are the mission headmen against one another and speak so many hard words?' More perhaps than any other factor, their schisms prevented the missionaries from giving the people of the lake that sense of unity which ultimately was to be provided by African nationalism. That was their tragic, their fundamental error, and posterity may well consider that the greatest contribution they made to the country was material rather than spiritual, for besides the Gospel they introduced education, good husbandry, new fruits and vegetables, and perhaps most important of all they prepared the way for national cohesion by systematising and committing to paper the Chinyanja language.

There is no doubt that it took a very special brand of courage to undertake mission work beside the lake in the days before the establishment of civil government. After all, the men who came there were cutting themselves off indefinitely from civilisation, exposing themselves and their families not only to unknown diseases but often to mortifying humiliation, and sometimes even death, at the hands of savage tribesmen or capricious chiefs. Perhaps it was natural then that many of these early missionaries took refuge in private little worlds of their own, walled about by a prim certainty of the superiority of their faith but all too often enveloped in a cloud of moral gloom. And perhaps it was natural too that they never noticed what bores they had become.

The curious flavour of their lives comes out most clearly in the accounts they sent back to their supporters at home of their endeavours beside the lake. Often they reek with pious hypocrisy. Sir Harry Johnston, the first British Commissioner in Nyasaland, often blazed at 'this awful accumulation of cant' exhibited by certain missionaries, and one cannot entirely blame him for they wrote—and presumably spoke—in an affected mawkish jargon. Invariably in their books they part from each other 'with eyes not dry'; their experiences are always 'the reverse of disappointing'; no opportunity is ever lost to point a moral; they rarely travel as ordinary people do but 'pass by on the Master's business'; and their plans scarcely ever fail to be 'fulfilled to the great advancement of His work'. Native customs that might shock the laity are either ignored or concealed in coyly esoteric Latin in the sea of correspondence that flowed back to Britain, and we are not surprised that their own trousers are termed 'unmentionables'. But the lushest metaphors of all are reserved for the act of dying, and though drooping brethren may have been comforted by contemplating 'the eternal song that ceaseth not' lying in store for them, it may be doubted whether the more rudely healthy welcomed the repeated assurance that 'the fullest ears are taken first'.

And with the missionaries' euphemism went a diminished sense of the congruous. 'Is it not marvellous', gasped one newcomer to Nyasaland in the nineties 'to see elegantly robed men, at some hundreds of pounds yearly cost, preaching a gospel of self-denial to men and women slaves with only a scrap of goat skin round their loins?' And sometimes this detachment led them into an arrogance that would have seemed more familiar to us had it occurred in mediaeval clerics. They saw nothing unusual in claiming the power of life and death over their converts and hangers-on, even after civil government had been established. This attitude was bound to lead to trouble, and it came quite early in the Shiré Highlands. The Established Church of Scotland, which had quickly followed the example of the Free Church of Scotland in despatching a mission to Nyasaland, at least avoided Young's mistake, and set up their station in the most populous part of the country not far from the long evening shadow of Chiradzulu. Since the rival denomination had already appropriated the name of the district where Livingstone had died, they called their settlement Blantyre to commemorate his birthplace.

A strange choice was made for the leader of their mission—the Reverend Duff Macdonald. One tends to visualise him now as a sort of clerical Ivan the Terrible, but in fact Macdonald's only defect was an inability to control what Johnston called the 'unbridled lust and abominable cruelty' of his subordinates. He was one of those odd blends of humility, erudition and ill-directed severity that from time to time is seen in clerics of the Protestant Church, especially in Scotland. For although he made himself an expert on Yao customs and language, and was never so happy as when presiding over the annual picnic treat of his Sunday school classes, yet he was devoid of balance, and countenanced disciplinary measures in his mission that would have made a Captain Bligh wince. The Blantyre mission 'owned' an enormous tract of land in the highlands (and laid claim to the whole of the Mlanje plateau 'because one of our missionaries was the first white man to ascend the mountain') and Macdonald ruled over it in the manner of a despotic Yao chief. Thieving was punished at Blantyre with a hundred lashes; murder by a firing party. One murderer was executed in particularly clumsy circumstances by a squad of mission boys, while about the same time an alleged thief, who confessed his crime after being given a hundred lashes, received two more floggings, one of which was administered by some macabre whim beside the open grave waiting to receive the condemned 'murderer'. Only afterwards did it transpire that the 'thief' had been entirely innocent. But worse was to follow. A second 'thief' was flogged and then locked up in a shed to recover: when the mission servants went to let him out they found him dead. Reports of these pleasantries at the Blantyre mission filtered back to the British newspapers and an ugly scandal blew up. The Assembly of the Established Church, after meeting in pained conclave, dispatched a committee to investigate the charges on the spot, after which a nervous shower of resignations (including that of the mission 'agriculturist', Mr. Buchanan, whom we shall meet later at the receiving end of the whip) almost denuded Blantyre of missionaries until a new start was made under the auspices of the Reverend Clement Scott.

It is only fair to remember that at this time no civil government existed which could ensure order in Nyasa country, and the missionaries were obliged to discipline their stations themselves: and not unnaturally use was made of the harsh punishments customary to the indigenous people. Even Dr. Laws was not entirely convinced that corporal punishment could always be avoided, but after troubled reference to his Bible and particularly to *Deuteronomy* xxv. 3, he decreed that forty lashes should never be exceeded at Livingstonia, and on the one occasion when he found it necessary to order a flogging he stopped the punishment after thirteen strokes had been given.

But then, of course, Robert Laws possessed an unusual flair for getting on with Africans. He measures up perfectly to our idea of what a Victorian missionary should be. To begin with his background is exactly right. He came from humble stock. His father was a cabinet-maker living in Aberdeen, and an Elder of the Kirk; his mother died of consumption when he was two and the little boy's earliest recollection was of being lifted up to see her lying in her coffin. Young Robert grew up in an atmosphere of intense missionary enthusiasm at the time when all Scotland was ringing with the renown of Dr. Livingstone; his nightly prayer was 'O God, send me to the Makololo', and his favourite reading, predictably, was about the lives of the great missionaries. For a second wife his father chose a stern Calvinist who had little affection to spare for the boy. When he was only twelve Robert Laws became an apprentice at the princely salary of 2s. 6d. a week, and we are not astonished to learn that (after resisting the temptation to purchase a greek primer) his first week's earnings were dropped into his stepmother's lap. Things improved after a bursary and 'a little fund for Christ' laboriously collected by his Sunday School teacher translated young Mr. Laws to Aberdeen University, from which presently he emerged as a medical man anxious to work as a missionary in Central Africa. And for the next half century, with the authority of seniority hanging increasingly about him, Laws laboured beside the lake and competes with two other doctors—Livingstone and Banda—for the distinction of being its most potent single human influence.

Despite its obvious disadvantages, Laws was in no particular hurry to move on from Cape Maclear, and five busy years went by before he transferred the station to Bandawe in Tonga territory, half way up the lake. Here he was plunged at once into a situation full of new perils and uncertainties. Mombera's Angoni lived in the hills nearby and came raiding down to the lake shore every year. At first Laws and his family were in considerable danger from the younger hot-headed Angoni warriors, but probably never more so than when Mombera's young son died soon after Mrs. Laws had greeted him with an affectionate pat on his head and a murmured 'such a fine child'. For the local witch doctor gave it out that Mrs. Laws had used instead the ominous words 'so high and never any higher'.

But gradually Laws' relationship with Mombera improved, and in the end they came to regard each other with respect. Laws was eventually allowed to send Mr. Sutherland, the gardener at Bandawe, and later Dr. Elmslie, to live among the Angoni. Even now, across the gulf of eighty years, one still feels awe at the cold-blooded courage displayed by these two men. They were very lonely and often very frightened; Mombera was under continual pressure to kill or at least expel them from his country, and in 1885 Sutherland was so sure he would have to leave that he obtained the chief's permission to stay on as a slave at his court, for as he explained later, if he was not allowed to do a missionary's work, he could at least live a missionary's life in Angoniland; he had actually selected his master when he was reprieved. Fortunately, a little later a timely thunderstorm happened to follow one of Dr. Elmslie's prayers for rain during a prolonged drought and this rocketed the white men's prestige; Mombera was even persuaded to put a stop to his impis' annual raid on the Tonga. From now on mission influence increased among the Angoni and perhaps the corollary occurred, too, for Elmslie sounds almost complacent in his book *Among the Wild Angoni* when he describes the chief's punishment of some 'wild youths' who had disobeyed his orders: 'Mombera', he tells us, 'called them up. He said "You are not chief. I am chief. You went to Bandawe with war. Cut their legs", and they were thereupon hamstrung. "You killed Tonga. Cut their wrists", and the tendons were divided, and the miserable wretches crawled away to hide and die.'

But Bandawe turned out to be even more unhealthy than Cape Maclear even though Laws, who believed malaria was caused by the 'miasma' rising from the lake, took the precaution of facing the mission houses inland, and in 1894 the mission moved for the third time to a high plateau above Mount Waller. There the Livingstonia Mission still flourishes, pouring out a constant stream of teachers, artisans, preachers and young politicians who are destined to become the rulers of the lake.

Six and a half years after Laws first set foot on the beach of Cape Maclear, the Reverend William Percival Johnson appeared on the Nyasa scene, and he must be counted the most remarkable of all its missionaries. He was wearing the long white robes of the Universities' Mission to Central Africa when he walked down the hill to Mtengula with his friend Charles Janson and caught sight of the blue waters of the lake. It had taken them six months to travel there from the coast at Dar-es-Salaam, and it had been a dreadful time. But now in the manner of Xenophon's ten thousand they shouted 'Thalassa' and assured each other excitedly that the distant lake exactly resembled Galilee. Charles Janson, in his companion's words, was 'a remarkably handsome man, full of English life', but that morning, which marked the return of the Anglican mission to the lake, he was only three weeks away from death. 'Will' Johnson, however, lived on to work beside Nyasa for the next forty-six years. He was weirdly tall and lean, lantern-jawed and bird-like in his movements; people were later to call him a 'living saint' and the 'Apostle of the lake'.

After they had rested beside the water and bathed in it, the two men turned northwards and trudged along the beach. For years Lake Nyasa had dominated their thoughts, but now its beauty excelled their expectations; they saw it as 'an earthly paradise' and found a sort of holiness in the air they breathed. That night they celebrated their safe arrival by opening the bottle of champagne carried all the way from Zanzibar—only to find, in Johnson's words that it was 'perfectly rotten'. It seemed a bad omen. For some time Janson had been suffering from dysentery and now he began to sink. The end came at Pachia on February 21st, 1882. Johnson has left us a curiously evocative account of his friend's irascibility in extremis and of his death. 'Once in agony', Johnson wrote, 'he cried out "Maples and I have spoken of how you could not sympathise with other's pain". So', Johnson goes on, 'I lifted up my voice and wept, and he melted and said, "What's the use of making yourself miserable?" Except for this he was perfectly patient, making every now and again an ejaculatory prayer.' He died a short time later. One wonders what the natives of Pachia thought as they watched the strange white man, with the tears running down his face, who tenderly wrapped the body of his companion in coarse matting and buried it beneath a little cairn of stones. For our own part we can sense something of Johnson's misery and loneliness in the words that close this account: 'So Charles Janson left us on Shrove Tuesday 1882, and I went on up the coast alone in that Lenten season.'

For the rest of his long life Will Johnson made the lake his parish and preached the Gospel from a boat along its shores. He seemed to sense the mystery and wonder of Nyasa more than any other man, perhaps because his own enigmatic personality so closely matched the lake's. His years of hand-to-mouth existence and self-denial enabled him to enter very intimately into the feelings of its indigenous people. To them, and indeed to us, Johnson was a man beyond ordinary definition; essentially he was a mystic; there was a fanatical set to his head, his detachment was uncanny and the more one reads about his life the more it seems to have been curiously unreal. He behaved always as though he were living in biblical days; every event was interpreted in scriptural terms. Thus, when armed only with 'Keble's little book on the Eucharist', he faced a gang of savages who were determined to kill him, he saw them not as Angoni but as Philistines. Illnesses that would have prostrated any other man were disregarded by Johnson: when his eyes became infected, he allowed them to scar so badly that he lost his sight. Almost miraculously an operation to construct an artificial pupil restored at least blurred vision to one eye, but always afterwards he was obliged to hold two fingers before it, opening and closing them to regulate the light that entered.

The disability naturally made it difficult for Johnson to continue his itinerant services in the hills around the lake, but he had no thought of giving up. An African deacon has left us a glimpse of him at the age of seventy, tottering down the lake shore preceded by a servant whose 'voice', Johnson would say, 'supplemented my sight'. He goes on to describe how Johnson would approach a native village calling out 'come and hear the words of God', and whereas in the early days of his mission they would have mocked and thrown rotten mealie cobs at him, now the villagers gathered round to hear him preach. We have another description of Johnson six years before he died, given this time by a European visitor who found him 'a bent, very wrinkled old gentleman, very active and with the most courtly manners'. To her he seemed to have outgrown his era; all his friends were dead; Johnson alone seemed to go on forever.

Long before that in the eighteen-eighties, however, Johnson and his friend Chauncy Maples had been the Damon and Pythias of the lake. They had been up at Oxford together when they read a notice calling for volunteers to continue Mackenzie's work in Africa, for, despite Livingstone's gloomy prognostications, the Universities' Mission always intended to return to Lake Nyasa. Soon the two men were at Zanzibar preparing to join the priests sent into the interior to establish a chain of stations reaching towards the lake. The emphasis of their work lay in pure evangelism. They had learnt the lesson of Mackenzie's disastrous militancy, and now they refrained from interference in local politics, and even eschewed self-defence in danger. These celibate men were of the stuff from which martyrs are made; they selected their tombstone epitaphs before they left England, and by 1900 their mission was reporting sadly that of the two hundred missionaries so far sent into the field, fifty-seven had already died on service.

Chauncy Maples was the 'beau sabreur' of the mission; in many ways he reminds us of his predecessor, Mackenzie; certainly he was the ideal foil for Johnson's asceticism since his exuberance and virtuosity were something more than priestly, and if at first they puzzled his colleagues, they very soon delighted and stimulated them. He could turn his hand to anything from cookery to poetry, but, like Johnson, his enduring passion was the lake, and it once inspired him to write the only sonnet that so far has been dedicated to Nyasa:

Cerulean Lake! Let this thy mission be
To speak to us of Him, who in His hand
Thy waters broad uplifts; and so may we,
While lingering on our pilgrimage, a land,
Not bounded by earth's limits, ever see
But far above her mists—the Heavenly strand.

It is almost impossible to conceive two more different men than
the urbane Maples and the unpolished, artless Johnson, yet they
were devoted to each other. From the unpromising material of
Likoma Island they created a tropical Iona and initiated the building there of a cathedral the size of Winchester's, which still stands
like the figure of a knight in prayer beside the lake. Recalling that
their Bishop at Zanzibar had raised his own cathedral with its
altar standing on the site of the whipping post of the old slave
market, they chose to place theirs beside an even more macabre
punishment place; which caused a newcomer to Likoma in 1889
to gasp, 'three or four women had just been burnt alive at Chipyela. . . . Maples had done all he could to prevent it, but had no
power to do more than speak about it. . . .' Chipyela, 'the place of
burning', he adds in explanation, is only 'a few yards from . . . the
great cathedral'. But today Likoma has forgotten these ancient
horrors and its air instead is threaded through with memories of
two dedicated men, so that when the tower bell calls for evensong
across the island, one half expects to see the tall figure of Johnson
stumbling down the rough paths to the cathedral with his hand
on Maples' shoulder.

Maples was a strikingly good-looking man whose bearded face
reminds one of his contemporary, Tsar Nicholas II. A photograph taken at Likoma in 1894 shows him sitting comfortably in
a camp chair, while Johnson gazes at his friend with an expression
of seraphic devotion. Only a year after it had been taken, Maples
was dead.

In 1895 he had gone to London to be consecrated Bishop of
Likoma, and there is something very touching about the way
Chauncy Maples hurried back to his see immediately after the
ceremony in St. Paul's. No one was expecting him, and no boat
was available when he arrived at Fort Johnston at the beginning

of September in a fever of impatience to resume his work. Maples had just made up his mind to journey up the lake shore on foot, when a mission sailing boat—the *Sheriff*—turned up. To him this seemed providential, especially as it carried a bundle of letters full of the problems and difficulties that were confronting the U.M.C.A. missionaries at Kota Kota and Likoma, and despite several warnings about the weather the Bishop at once set off in her for Kota Kota. That afternoon they put in at Nkope to buy food, and Maples had time to conduct a short prayer meeting before sailing again in the evening. It was nearly dark and beginning to blow hard as they came up to Monkey Bay, and the *Sheriff*'s native crew begged Maples to shelter there until morning. But the only concession he would make was to order the mainsail reefed, and the little boat headed through the night across the lake under her fore and mizzen. The Bishop in his voluminous black cassock stood beside the helmsman, Ibrahim, peering through the slanting rain while Joseph Williams, his only European companion, snatched some sleep in a little cabin in the stern. It was very dark and no one saw the black rocks off Mbenji Island until they were almost on them. As the helm was put hard over, the full force of the wind caught the mizzen, and the little boat breached to. The following wave capsized her. There are several variations in the accounts given of the next few minutes but it seems that Williams went down at once without a sound while Maples managed to cling on to a steel box that floated past him in the darkness. He was a strong swimmer, but as his cassock filled with water its weight began to pull him down. Yet the newly-consecrated Bishop, obeying perhaps a subconscious wish to beatify Nyasa with his death, refused to take it off; and suddenly we see him revealed as a self-appointed martyr who was determined to make the lake his Cain. A fantastic conversation between the doomed man and members of the ship's crew floundering beside him in the water followed, and it merged with the howling wind and became a part of it. 'Can you see land near?' the Bishop shouted. 'No, not near, but we can see it', someone shouted in reply. By now Maples was firm in his resolve: 'Never mind me,' they heard him call. 'I feel my hour to die is come'; and then again, 'You swim on shore and tell the Europeans of my death'. He was determined to be left alone, and when Ibrahim swam up to tell him land was only two miles away and he could reach it without much difficulty, Maples would only answer 'Save yourselves' and 'You must not die for me.' Presently all the survivors could hear were prayers and groans and repeated cries of 'I am a miserable sinner'—until, in Ibrahim's words, 'the water choked him and he sank'. After that they struck out for the land and struggled ashore near Lifu in Leopard's Bay. Two weeks went by before Maples' body was washed ashore, recognisable only by his fatal cassock-shroud. He lies today buried in the chancel of Kota Kota church.

As Johnson waited at Likoma for his friend's return, he had an odd presentiment about his fate. But his attention was diverted by another pressing matter: one of the Likoma priests, George Atlay, had gone across to the mainland a few days earlier to hunt, and had not yet come back; and so when Maples was singing his 'liebentod' to the waters of his beloved lake, Johnson, a hundred miles away, was stumbling along its eastern coast in inky darkness with a search party. He came at last on Atlay's body lying face downwards in a stream, clubbed to death by an Angoni war party; beside him lay a loaded rifle which in obedience to the tenets of his mission Atlay had refused to fire. And soon afterwards a third tragedy afflicted the little band of Anglican missionaries beside the lake, for after burying Maples' body, Sim, the priest at Kota Kota, went down with malaria and died there miserably, because in his delirium he found that death was not the beautiful thing he had expected, but something very lonely and very terrifying. Today his agony is part of the atmosphere of that evil place.

But Will Johnson seemed indestructible; he pursued his work beside Nyasa, mystical still in his attitudes, pellucid in his simplicity, patrician in his ways, and sometimes reciting his bemused wonder at finding himself a legend during his own lifetime. He died at last in 1928, and his tomb in the little church of Liuli on the lake shore is still an object of Christian pilgrimage. By that time many other missionaries had followed the two 'grand old men' of the lake, Laws and Johnson, to Nyasaland: one of them—Joseph Booth—was destined to throw a long shadow across it.

But a far worse danger than 'independent' Evangelists threatened to darken the bright morning of the lake's 'Apostolic Age'; only five years after Johnson had buried Janson at Pachia, Arab slavers from Tanganyika bore down on the Wankonde tribe living at its northern extremity, and for a time seemed likely to establish an impregnable slave empire around its shores.

Slave caravan, from a drawing by David Livingstone

Scene on board a slave dhow

8

MLOZI

The early European explorers found the Wankonde by far the most attractive of the people living beside Lake Nyasa, and all their accounts marvel at the exotic, almost polynesian, flavour of their lives. The Nkonde villages were scattered across the enormous fertile plain which extends the Rift Valley northward from the lake, and here they had developed a surprisingly viable economy based on the unusual combination of cattle and bananas. The very name 'Nkonde' means 'banana', and stresses the importance to them of a crop which is virtually labour-free. The fruit, after being ground into porridge, provided the Nkonde people with their basic food; banana leaves served as thatching material and plates as well as fuel and towels; sap from the plants produced an efficient substitute for soap while the tree's fibres were worked into coarse string which was woven into blankets. Scores of tidy Nkonde villages were hidden away at the northern end of the lake among luxuriant banana groves which themselves were interspersed between beautiful sycamore and cotton trees. 'It seemed a perfect Arcadia about which idyllic poets have sung,' gushed the twenty-year old Scottish explorer, Joseph Thomson, after seeing Nkondeland for the first time in 1878, and he goes on, 'I felt as if I had fallen upon some enchanted place'. Even the dour Consul Elton who preceded him was scarcely less enthusiastic when he declared Nkondeland to be 'the finest tract of Africa I have yet seen. There is nothing to equal it either in fertility or grazing land in Natal—the reputed garden of Africa.' For the Nkonde country was not only very productive, it was remarkably beautiful too. Against the dramatic backdrop of the Livingstone mountains fat herds of cattle grazed the plain by day and came trooping back every evening to scrupulously clean byres in villages of neat brick and bamboo huts which Thomson assures us 'were worthy of a place in any nobleman's garden'.

But it was the people themselves rather than their exquisite surroundings who particularly fascinated the early white travellers on Nyasa. Perhaps it was the high proportion of hamitic blood running through their veins which made the Wankonde seem quite different from the other lake people, from whom indeed they held themselves aloof. For they were well-mannered and hospitable—and delightfully unsophisticated too. In the mild climate of the northern lake shore they moved about almost naked, the men with only ornaments of copper wire wound about their waists and tremulous bells tied to their ankles, while the women were content to proclaim their modesty with tiny aprons of bark cloth about nine inches square. And they had been spared the troubles that had overwhelmed the southern lake dwellers. The Angoni had avoided their country and the Yao gangs never penetrated so far north. And so the Wankonde had slowly forgotten their warrior traditions and found their chief excitement in ancient ceremonies with unremembered meanings. Especially picturesque were the evening parades which brought all the young men dancing in a jingling procession between the rows of huts of each lakeside village until they plunged into the warm waters of the lake in a single laughing line for a ritual bathe. For generations they had lived in peace hearing only vague rumours of the monstrous traffic in human flesh that went on beyond the mountains and down the lake shore. Only after the Arab slavers who had set up their petty principalities in Tabora and Ujiji and Kagei in Tanganyika began to look around for new hunting grounds and heard from their native allies that at the northern end of the lake 'the grass is ready for burning', did the slow doom of the Wankonde begin to form; and it came in the shape of a half-caste Arab trader named Mlozi.

Mlozi always assured his friends his name meant 'almond tree', adding that it perfectly suited his mellow character, but he was careful to refrain from reminding them it might also be translated as 'witch' or 'sorcerer'. His faithful enemy, Mr. Fotheringham, has given us this description of Mlozi at the time of his arrival at the lake in 1884: he was, he says, a 'middle-aged man' and 'a sly diplomat' who 'wore a white robe with a muscat sash thrown over his shoulder, and whose shaven head was set off by a small white cap giving effect to his sloping brow and clean-cut features'.

Fotheringham might have gone on to say that although Mlozi's face was invariably wreathed in a benignant smile, his eyes never for a moment lost their cold hangman's stare. Even today a peculiarly evil aura still hangs about Mlozi's name. He is the Tiberius of the lake, a man without pity in his make-up and capable of the most grisly crimes. But no one ever doubted that Mlozi possessed a peculiarly obstinate brand of courage, and it enabled him to challenge British authority in Nyasa for many years. Nor was he lacking in the oriental shrewdness of his ancestors: he always knew when to retreat or compromise, yet he always came up fighting again a little later on. It was this tenacity of spirit which has invested him with a strange and savage dignity, and even now it still compels our reluctant admiration.

We do not know in any detail what circumstances first brought Mlozi to the lake. We hear of him trading in the Luangwa valley during the 1870's, and then he appears as a vassal of the powerful Kabunda whose mercenaries were terrorising the Lofu valley. Seemingly Mlozi then decided to strike out for himself and ventured into Nkondeland. He came on sufferance and was received at first with such hostility that he found it wise to withdraw from the district for a time. But he was back again to trade in 1886, and this time he obtained permission from a petty chief to build a settlement for himself, which he promptly surrounded with a stockade 'for fear of lions', and garrisoned with armed men. Slowly now his real purpose became clear; he intended to carve out a fief for himself at the northern end of the lake and enter into an alliance with other powerful slavers like Jumbe on the western shore, and Makanjira and Mponda in the south. Between them they would be able to dominate the entire lake region and he himself would be favourably placed to open up a promising northern slave route to the sea, far removed from the growing influence of the missionaries in the Shiré highlands.

Recent events had improved his chances of success. By 1886, after the European states had begun to challenge their political power, the Arabs' attitude in Central Africa had hardened towards white men. Then, too, the benign influence of the pro-British Sultan of Zanzibar had been corroded by outside agencies and his distant subjects were weakening in their allegiance to him. Nor were they the more pure-blooded Arabs of Livingstone's time. A new generation of xenophobic half-breeds had taken over from their 'white' Arab fathers, and now even pure Bantu who had successfully adopted the Moslem's religion, clothes and manners, were welcomed into the Moslem fold and called themselves *wazungu*.

Once Mlozi was securely established within his stockade at Mpata and contemplated the virgin slaving ground near by, there did not seem very much standing between the Wankonde and utter annihilation—nothing, that is, except the figure of a single white man who was living not more than twelve miles away in a mud hut beside the lake, near Karonga's village. Unfortunately for Mlozi that white man was a pugnacious character and possessed a tenacity fully equal to his own. His name was Monteith Fotheringham.

Fotheringham at this time had been in the country four years, employed by the African Lakes Company, and only recently had been promoted to manage its new store at Karonga. The company had been formed ten years earlier by a group of philanthropical Scottish businessmen in response to Dr. Livingstone's appeal for legitimate commerce to enter Central Africa and develop communications and trade. Two somewhat flamboyant brothers, John and Frederick Moir, were enrolled as joint managers, and by 1879 they had installed themselves in the Shiré highlands. Appreciating the possibilities of the Nkonde ivory trade, they chartered the mission steamer *Ilala*, and sent Fotheringham up to the 'north end' of the lake to establish a trading station and construct a road—the Stevenson road—to connect Nyasa with Lake Tanganyika. The African Lakes Company, usually known by its native name, 'Mandala', was an extraordinary institution. Even now it is difficult to know quite what to make of it. Although it had been formed primarily for humanitarian reasons, and staffed by men who 'had received the missionary call', its transactions were often so transparently avaricious as to cause it to be openly accused of swindling. Sir Harry Johnston, who usually referred to the company as 'the Vampire', once charged it with buying 140,000 acres of good farming land from a gullible chief for trade goods worth £2 13s. 0d. Then, too, it wobbled uncertainly for many years between its original role of a trading concern and becoming an agency to foster imperial expansion on the lines of Rhodes' powerful Chartered Company, whose subsidiary it did for a time in fact become.

When Monteith Fotheringham first arrived in Karonga he was in his early thirties. He was stockily built with fierce prominent eyes and a rubicund face which was encircled by an immensely aggressive red beard. He was a man of very quick temper and very few words and even these were spoken in such a thick Scottish accent as to be barely comprehensible even to those who knew him well. The Africans nicknamed him 'Thunder and Lightning' (but called him 'Montisi' to his face) and they were certain he had swallowed some medicine to make him immune to bullets. In character 'Montisi' was cut something after the fashion of an Elizabethan buccaneer and now, having been born three hundred years too late for his proper rôle, he must have considered himself fortunate to live in a very wild part of Africa which was one of the few places left in the world where he could develop to his full dimensions. A photograph of Monteith Fotheringham that has survived shows him looking like a fairly successful impersonation of Henry VIII, except that his protruding eyes stare out not from below a Tudor bonnet but from under one of those deer-stalker caps beloved by Sherlock Holmes and a whole generation of African explorers.

For a year or more at Karonga, Montisi got on well with his neighbour Mlozi, and he was able to gratify his directors in Blantyre with the information that he found the Arab 'both attentive and polite'. Between them they indulged in several mutually profitable business transactions, but gradually as the Mpata stockade grew stronger Mlozi's attitude to the white man began to stiffen, and when he built two more forts only seven miles from his station and straddling the Stevenson road, Fotheringham scented danger ahead. They were garrisoned by well-armed native mercenaries called ruga-ruga, under the command of Mlozi's two *wazungu* lieutenants, Msalema and Kopa Kopa, and they controlled the land approaches to Karonga. That summer, when the Queen's loyal subjects in Britain were celebrating her Golden Jubilee, Fotheringham's reports to Blantyre took on a graver tone: he spoke of Arab truculence and provocation, then of isolated acts of violence and retaliation by the tribesmen. It seemed, he warned the Moirs, as though the Arabs were deliberately stirring up trouble in order to fight and enslave the Wankonde, and it might be as well for him to clarify matters with a polite enquiry to Mlozi about his intentions; this, he hoped would warn and perhaps restrain him. The next letter to arrive at Blantyre enclosed Mlozi's reply: it was written in beautiful Arab script and read, 'I mean to put the Wankonde utterly down and bring in the Wahenga'; the Wahenga, Fotheringham explained, being the Arab's allies from whom he recruited many of his mercenaries. Soon afterwards he reported that the tension in the area was increasing, that a Nkonde chief had been murdered and another village pillaged by the ruga-ruga, and that marauding parties had been seen coming back into Mlozi's stockade driving long strings of captives before them. All attempts by Fotheringham to mediate between the Arabs and the Nkonde chiefs were repulsed, increasing numbers of natives were captured and driven down the coast to be sold, and as the hot weather set in before the summer rains, the whole countryside reeled into a crescendo of reprisal and atrocity. From his mud hut at Karonga, Fotheringham watched Arab bands moving about the Nkonde plain, burning village after village, 'slaughtering,' he told the Moirs, 'without stint', and added primly that '. . . those women they did not kill, they put in irons and reserved for a fate still more severe.'

Now that he was in business Mlozi began to derive staggering profits from the two commodities he had for sale; ivory was in great demand at this time in Europe, while a slave seized or perhaps bought for a single bead or a cupful of corn at the lakes, would fetch anything up to £5 in Zanzibar. At this stage one should pause for a moment to consider the nature of the grisly slave trade that was overwhelming the Africans living in the country between Nyasa and Lake Tanganyika long after Livingstone's time, and which now was beginning to afflict the Wankonde. Mlozi had learnt his methods from his Arab friends operating from Zanzibar, who were busily engaged in turning a vast area of the African interior into an anarchistic wilderness. Their methods were unbelievably brutal and yet undeniably efficient, so that in contrast, the Yao forays at the southern end of the lake seem casual and ineffective. Their well-practised operations began with the *chifwamba*—the terrible slave raid in the night—that shattered the lives of so many of the inhabitants of Central Africa. Just before dawn the people of an isolated village would awaken to a sudden flurry of shots and screams. As each sleepy man crept out of his hut calling to his friends, he would be speared or clubbed to death by two ruga-ruga standing beside the door. In the dim light of morning, amid the wild confusion of the raid, the women of the village would be hustled into a trembling line and joined there by their children and a few cowed men. Then they would be submitted to a 'selection' every bit as cruel as that practised by the Nazis in conquered Europe. Those deformed, and those too small or ill to march, were killed at once; only healthy adults and the children old enough to run beside their mothers were spared. The frightened survivors were now stripped naked and tethered by iron necklets to a long chain, or yoked together in *gorees* or 'taming-sticks'—young barked trees cut where they ended in forked branches large enough to accommodate a human neck—and there they were locked in place by an iron staple. Yoked like oxen in these slave sticks, which were then fastened in pairs like Roman furcifers, even 'wild' slaves found it impossible to run away. Indeed, if they wanted to breathe with any semblance of comfort and avoid painful chafing of the neck, they had to move very carefully and in perfect unison with their companion at the other end of the goree. Once they had all been secured, the bewildered captives were ordered to move away from their burning village. The Arab whip, the terrifying *kurbash*, thick enough at one end to be grasped comfortably in the hand and tapering at the other to the fineness of a needle, was the driving force which now controlled them. Hissing through the air on to bare flanks and shoulders it soon taught the dazed captives that orders from the Arabs must be obeyed instantly, and drove them off in the direction of Mlozi's or other slaver's stockade.

There the captives would have to wait until enough slaves had been caught to warrant the dispatch of a caravan to the coast. By then anything up to a thousand men, women and children might have been herded together in the slaver's corral for weeks before the awful march to the coast five hundred miles away could begin. Although we have now become hardened by the brutal sufferings of two world wars, the horror of the death marches from the lakes is still difficult for us to comprehend. All the accounts of European travellers who encountered these processions of the damned last century speak in shocked tones of the appalling contrast between the richly-dressed Arabs who led them, riding muscat donkeys, and the strings of hobbled, naked prisoners whose shoulders and thighs were bleeding from the whip. Elton, the British Consul at Mozambique, writes in his journal of meeting slave caravans almost every day when he trudged down the coast towards Kilwa in 1878. In one such caravan, when he tried to count the slaves, he estimated 'there were about 300 in all, in wretched condition. One gang of lads and women, chained together with iron neck-rings, was in a horrible state, their lower extremities coated with dry mud and their own excrement and torn with thorns, their bodies mere frameworks, and their skeleton limbs tightly stretched over with wrinkled parchment-like skin. One wretched woman had been flung against a tree for slipping her rope, and came screaming up to us for protection, with one eye half out and the side of her face and bosom streaming with blood.' Some travellers speak movingly of the enormous festering ulcers that covered the captives' legs and ankles, while others were horrified by the dumb misery of the slaves, by the stench as they went past, and by the noisome swarms of flies accompanying them. The captives travelled on starvation rations. Hermann von Wissman, a German explorer, in describing another of these caravans, tells us breathlessly that it was made up of 'hundreds of slaves, fastened together with long chains and neck-yokes in sets from ten to twenty. The weaker women and children who were not expected to escape were only tied with ropes. Those who had to be specially watched were walking by twos in the slave-fork in which the neck is fastened. One would scarcely credit the miserable and lamentable condition the unfortunate human chattels were in. Their arms and legs were almost fleshless, their bodies shrivelled up, their looks heavy and their heads bent, while they were marching along eastward into an unknown future, further and further away from their homes, separated from wife and child, from father and mother, who had perhaps escaped into the woods or had been struck down in defending themselves.' 'It was a revolting scene,' he goes on, 'to watch the daily distribution of food in the camp of such a caravan. The hungry creatures, with dilating eyes, were crowding round the spot where one of the overseers was stationed to distribute victuals, now and then using his stick to drive back the crowds that were pressing close around him. A small pot, about the size of a tumbler, was filled with corn, maize or millet and poured into the goat-skin with which they covered their nakedness. Some of them, too tired to rub or pound the corn, simply boiled it in water or roasted it in a saucepan over the fire and then devoured it in order to satisfy their craving hunger. . . .'

Those prisoners who showed the slightest sign of recalcitrance were either killed at once or thrashed into submission with the *kurbash* and then gagged with crude wooden snaffles. Each slave either carried a heavy burden on his head, or a tusk of ivory, the heaviest organic substance in the world, was suspended from each pair of *gorees*. Those who became ill were usually beheaded for that was the quickest way to remove them from their slave sticks or iron collars, but occasionally they would be tied to a tree to starve to death and serve as a grim warning to the caravans that followed. It was their practice, an Arab slaver once informed a scandalised English traveller, in dealing with their ailing captives, to 'spear them at once, for if we did not others would pretend they were ill in order to avoid carrying the loads'. Asked whether any of their sick prisoners were set free he answered: 'No, we never leave them alive on the road; they all know our custom', but he added a kindly assurance to the indignant Mr. Swan that if a mother became concerned because her child was tired and lagged behind, '. . . we spear the child and make her burden lighter.'

However much one racks one's brain trying to discover a reason for the Arab slavers' utter indifference to human suffering, no really satisfactory explanation ever suggests itself. Perhaps they consider their walking merchandise as less than human, and consequently to be held in no more regard than animals. Possibly the enormous profits of their trade—they were estimated at anything between 1,000 and 1,500 per cent—made them careless about a wastage which seemed inevitable and anyway weeded out the unfit. Conceivably they had no pity to waste on pagan unbelievers who were every bit as cruel as they themselves, for as the current saying went: 'If you freed three slaves today, two of them, given the opportunity, would sell the third tomorrow.' Horace Waller, one of the veterans of Magomero, was probably nearest to the mark when he likened the Arabs' attitude to that of a squire in the Home Counties preparing for a banquet, for to them, he wrote, it was like 'sending up to London for a large block of ice in the summer; you know that a certain amount will melt away before it reaches you in the country but that which remains will be quite sufficient for your wants'. What makes the extraordinarily callous behaviour of the Arabs even more fantastic is that they still took considerable pains to conciliate their captives' weird beliefs in magic and witchcraft. W. P. Johnson, who once reluctantly joined a slave caravan because it was the only means he could find of travelling safely from Nyasa to the coast, wrote years afterwards in an account of his experiences: 'I now discovered that there was an elaborate ceremony, akin to baptism, before the caravan started. A large bark canoe was placed near the encampment; this was filled with water so that a man kneeling in it would be nearly covered, and each member of the caravan had to be immersed and to get out at the end of the canoe and pass under some "medicine" (charm)—I think it was an elephant tail.' Johnson also recalled how every night '. . . the charms in the elephant's tail were carried round the encampment and all evil influences were adjured not to hurt us, towards the four points of the compass in succession.'

Johnson tells us, too, that the Arabs made their captives 'eat a herb on the hills going down to the coast which makes them forget everything' (and no doubt rendered them easier to handle). He seems to have been the only observer to report that the slaves sometimes seemed almost cheerful on the march, but later he came to the tentative conclusion that this was due less to courage than to a pathetic attempt to win a little favour from the drivers. And, indeed, during the long daylight hours of marching there was little time for the captives to contemplate their misery. It was in the evening that the caravan became its most pitiable. Then the slaves would crouch in long unhappy lines seeking comfort in close proximity to each other, weeping in their terror of the unknown, moaning for the past, wailing for their dead and swaying together in utter misery until the whole night air throbbed with the despair of enslaved Africa.

But worse than anything else for the captives were the attentions of the ruga-ruga. If the Arabs were cruel, these herders of human flesh must have seemed accursed demons spewed from the bowels of hell. Like fiends from a mediaeval fresco, they dressed in gaudy clothes in which red predominated; they wore their hair in long black greasy ringlets and into it they tied filthy bedraggled feathers: crude paint was daubed across their bodies, and blood upon their faces, while obscene necklaces of human teeth rattled on their chests as they moved about. In one hand the ruga-ruga carried a *kurbash*, in the other a cocked musket. They marched beside the slaves beating tom-toms to keep time with their own continuous lulalooing or playing absurd little trumpets that looked and sounded like penny whistles, all the time lashing their victims on to a faster pace to get them quickly through the arid waterless country. Their duties were limited to catching and herding slaves; their wages consisted of daily rations, a small percentage of the caravan's profits, unlimited opportunity for loot, and the carnal use of all the women slaves and boys at every stopping place. There was not a glimmer of pity or humanity in these monsters; even the Arabs feared the ruga-ruga. They were the real rulers of Central Africa before the advent of the white man.

After a march of three or four months the caravans from Lake Nyasa and the highlands to the north reached the sea at Kilwa. There the captives would be herded into enormous barracoons until April when the south-west monsoon began to blow and the Arab dhows came to ferry them across to Zanzibar. It was during the wait at the coast that the girls from the caravans were graded according to their value in Turkish harems, and the boys subjected to crude surgery (which carried with it an appalling mortality), since eunuchs fetched more money in oriental courts than whole men. When the time came for them to sail, the slaves were given water to drink and a meal of Indian corn before being loaded into the dhows. These boats were always in short supply, the barracoons invariably were crowded, and the slaves were packed together in unbelievably tight congestion. Those first aboard would be made to lie down on the rough deck-boards, alternatively head to foot, and then, somehow, a child would be squeezed in between each adult; temporary bamboo platforms were then raised in successive tiers above each line of captives, allowing them scarcely more than an inch of head room; no space at all could be spared for food and water. And now began perhaps the worst part of the slaves' ordeal. With a favourable wind it might take only twenty-four hours to reach Zanzibar, but more often the voyage lasted three dreadful days and if (as often happened) the dhow was becalmed, its human cargo merely starved to death in the incredibly cramped quarters, where it was impossible for a man even to turn his body round. The stench from these loaded slave dhows was indescribable; sometimes when they were intercepted by ships of the Royal Navy it was impossible to persuade a party of the tough blue-jackets to go on board because of the appalling stink of excrement and corruption. And, if the slavers' discipline during the march to the coast had been rigorous, on the dhows it became inflexible; grumbling was punished by nailing the culprit's hand to the mast or his foot to the deck. The sighting of a cruiser from the anti-slavery patrol would often decide the Arabs to eliminate incriminating evidence by dumping all their manacled merchandise into the sea. Similarly, the outbreak of a disease like smallpox, or the almost inevitable appearance of coprophagia among the starving slaves, was dealt with by wholesale drownings. It is no wonder, then, that the dhows arriving at the cool green island of Zanzibar might have only twelve survivors left from an original cargo of three hundred human beings. Those who were diseased or too weak to stand were left aboard the dhow to die rather than render their captors due for custom fees. Only the healthy were taken ashore at this great slave 'entrepôt' (which the British sailors knew as 'Stinkibar') and there they fattened in cages. When they were considered to have reached their prime they faced the indignities and horrors of the Zanzibar slave market where men and women were squeezed and poked about like animals at a country fair in England, and even trotted out to demonstrate their paces. The more fortunate of the captives from the great lakes ended their travels here in Zanzibar, for the increasing prosperity of the Sultan's clove plantations demanded a continual supply of workers. But for the majority, there still remained another ghastly voyage to the harems of Turkey, to princely courts in India, sometimes to Brazilian plantations, and even to the sumptuous pavilions of China. These were the most terrible ordeals of all and they wrote a new depth into the standards of human misery which makes the horrors of the notorious 'middle passage' of the great American slave route fade into insignificance.

It is impossible even to guess at the numbers of slaves torn by the Arabs from Central Africa during the course of the nineteenth century. For every Nyasa native who reached the coast alive, probably four or five perished during the original attack or the overland march that followed. At Kilwa the majority of the new arrivals were sold to work in the Portuguese plantations at Ibo or in the French sugar islands. Even so, at a conservative estimate some 20,000 captives from Central Africa went on to Zanzibar each year, and of these more than half would be sold to merchants supplying the oriental courts. Theirs was a sterile exodus. Very few natives from Nyasa country spread their genes and blood in their new prison homes, for most of the men had been castrated and the women were adept at preventing breeding. So today there are very few negro enclaves in the Orient like those in the new world and in consequence the ultimate effect of the Arab traffic does not compare in importance with that made by the export of seven million West Africans to America during the great days of the Atlantic trade. But if their numbers were less, the sufferings endured by the inhabitants of the lake country of Central Africa far exceeded that of any other people in history. And because this act of genocide took place during the age of humanism and after Europe's conscience had been awakened to their own enormous guilt in the American trade, it seems now to stand out in even more hideous relief.

In 1887 Mlozi could see that only one tantalising obstacle stood between himself and unbelievable prosperity—just as the fugitive Wankonde realised that only one champion might spare them from the full horrors intended for them by the slavers—and that was the presence of the solitary European at Karonga. It would be absurd to suggest that for his part Fotheringham's appreciation of the situation was dictated entirely by altruism. He was fully aware that Mlozi was threatening his own trading station as well as the Nkonde villages—and a great deal more besides. If the Arab slave empire of Mlozi's dreams was to be built he must first drive Fotheringham from his station and expel the Europeans from the lake. Karonga must have seemed an unlikely little place to become suddenly so strategically important but it was clear by now that the stake there was not the mere possession of a few hundred yards of shore line but the future of all the lake's people. For once Karonga had fallen, the Arabs would unite and inevitably the whole country would pass under their control; then for years to come the bush trails to the coast could be filled with fat slave caravans, while only ashes and a few bleached bones would be left to mark the sites of the old lake villages. And so the dirty little collection of thatched huts at Karonga became a symbol rather than a place, for whoever held it was bound in the end to become master of the lake. Everything depended, of course, on the way Fotheringham reacted to the crisis and, after making a hasty inventory of his resources, and discovering there were eight 'station boys' capable of bearing arms, thirteen old Chassepôt rifles and thirty-four cartridges, he decided that if the Arabs attacked Karonga he would fight back. There was a great deal of quixotic courage in that decision and it was of tremendous importance to the future of Nyasa. He set his men to make a breastwork of bales and boxes beside the company's landing place with an annex to protect the hordes of refugees who came flocking into his 'fort'; then he sent off the *Ilala* for help, and despatched runners to the Rev. J. Bain, a nearby missionary, and to Mr. Nicholl, a company man working on the Stevenson road, with scrawled messages imploring them to join him.

After that all Fotheringham could do was to wait for the

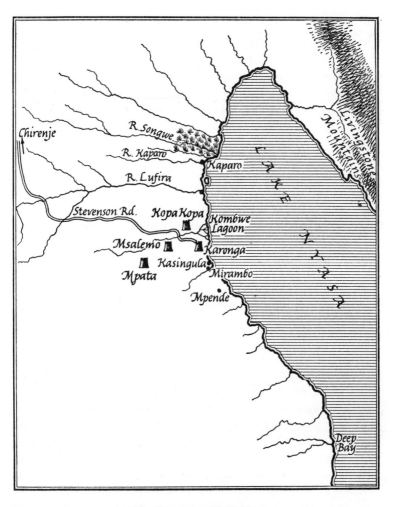

The slave wars of Lake Nyasa

overture of gunfire which would begin the slave war of Lake Nyasa. It was a time of terrible anxiety for him and the tension that gripped Karonga then has never since been quite dispelled; even today, no matter how hot the sun or sultry the air, an uneasy feeling of suspense still persists. But soon the lonely man beside the lake was joined by Bain, and only a little later Nicholl tramped in with half a dozen native fighting men, and eighteen ancient muzzle-loaders. Still the Arabs made no move against Fotheringham's stockade. Mlozi was waiting for reinforcements from across the lake, and to gain time he hinted it might be possible to settle his dispute with the Wankonde peacefully. Even now it is by no means definite who sent off the message telling the tribesmen of Mlozi's new mood; all that is certain is that it brought the Wankonde refugees crowding back towards their plundered villages. The Arabs later put out a story that the Wankonde were obeying a summons from their friend Montisi, whereas Fotheringham himself wrote afterwards that they came 'at the instigation of the wily Wahenga'. At any rate very soon hundreds of people were hanging about among the high bango reeds that fringe the Kombwe lagoon a mile or two north of Karonga, waiting for Mlozi's permission to re-occupy their villages. It was too good a chance to impress the natives with their power for the Arabs to miss, and one afternoon (it was October 27th, 1887) they fell—literally with fire and sword—on the hapless Wankonde. 'About noon,' Fotheringham wrote later of the massacre that followed, 'we heard firing in the direction of the lagoon. The Arabs, through the Wahenga, having drawn the Wankonde into this trap, had now commenced their fiendish brutality. They made the killing of a single Arab the pretext for a general attack. By a stealthy and rapid march they surrounded the lagoon before the natives were well aware of their presence. Immediately a scene of wildest excitement prevailed. The war whoops of the ruga-ruga smote the Wankonde hearts with terror. Armed only with spears they were no match for the Arabs, who, keeping at a safe distance, poured volley upon volley into the reeds, which were soon red with the blood of the dying. Every black who jumped out of the lagoon was shot in the open and not a native escaped who came within range of the Arab

Zanzibar slave market, from a sketch by W. W. Henn

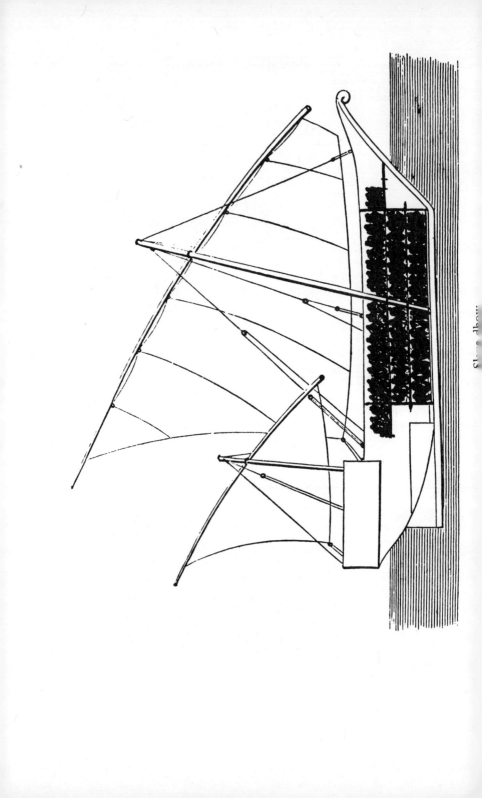

rifles. There was no outlet to the west side, and but small chance of escape on the north. The Arabs gradually moved forward, and the terror-stricken Wankonde were forced into the swamp yard by yard. Maddened by their success, the ruga-ruga rushed upon the natives and drove them farther back, spearing those who stuck fast in the mud.'

'They then fired the reeds, and as the flames rose, the yells of the poor creatures behind might be heard far and near above the steady discharge of the guns. Now another enemy, more dreaded than the Arabs, rose against the natives in their dire extremity. This was the crocodile, who swung his hideous jaws out of the pool and made an easy prey of the bewildered blacks. Those who did not perish by the rifle and the spear were either burned to death or devoured by the innumerable crocodiles that infest the lagoon. Few succeeded in struggling through the slough to the other side. While the attack was in progress, the three Arab leaders, in order to gratify their morbid curiosity, climbed into trees, and with diabolical interest watched and regulated the work of extermination. Darkness only put an end to the slaughter. The native chiefs with the remnant of their people fled to the Songwe river, while the Arabs who had captured a great many women and children, encamped at the lagoon. Surely never was such a cruel massacre as this day had witnessed! It was the butchery of a simple people who had done wrong to no one, who had been compelled to leave their houses owing to the menaces of the intruders, and who had been beguiled into this disaster by professions of friendship and protection.'

'Next day,' Fotheringham goes on, 'the Arabs withdrew from the lagoon, and the Wankonde returned to bury their dead—a rite which is held sacred by the natives. Many of the bodies were past recognition, having either their faces disfigured or heads totally cut off. This was yet another instance of the cold-blooded cruelty of the murderers, who, not content with an afternoon's butchery, had gone round during the night and mutilated the slain.' The Arabs—we hear from another source—reserved a particularly cruel revenge for the chief Nkonde witch-doctor who had offended them by making magic to drive them away. He was tied to a narrow raft of pith wood so that his body, baited with lumps of goat meat, overhung its sides; then he was set adrift in the lake to provide Mlozi and his cronies with an afternoon's entertainment watching a threshing horde of crocodiles slowly tear the wretched man to pieces.

The scattering of the Wankonde was a tremendous moment of opportunity for Mlozi. In the chaos and panic that followed the Kombwe lagoon massacre, a bold rush would easily have carried Fotheringham's flimsy breastwork. But the Arabs were unnerved at the prospect of attacking a white man who was said to be immune to bullets, and for the moment Mlozi was satisfied with sending an insolent message into Karonga to say he had proclaimed himself Mlozi I, Sultan of Nkondeland, and went on to demand tribute from the Company. A postscript ordered Fotheringham to stop working on his half-completed fort.

Fotheringham made a great show of obeying the new Sultan; he was playing for time, and he was more anxious now than ever. Although he knew the *Ilala* was not likely to return to Karonga with reinforcements for at least ten days, each morning he would peer hopefully down the lake for a sight of its smoke stack. 'Already', he wrote afterwards with commendable understatement, 'we began to weary for the return of the steamer.' Then, miraculously, the *Ilala* appeared, six days earlier than he could possibly have anticipated it and she was carrying unexpectedly substantial reinforcements. No less than four heavily armed Europeans waded ashore that day at Karonga. On numbers such as these did the future of the lake depend. There was the British Consul from Mozambique, Henry O'Neill, who happened to be paying a holiday visit up country, his brother-in-law who had come to the lake to collect botanical specimens, a mission worker, and finally Alfred Sharpe, fresh from big game shooting along the southern lake shore, and already possessed of the happy knack of being in the right place at the right time. Now Fotheringham was able to face the Arab threat with rather more confidence. The fortifications round the station were hastily completed, and then the little party of white men settled down to wait for the next move.

It did not take long to find out what that would be. On November 23rd, 1887, an unappetising breakfast of stringy mutton was interrupted by a volley of rifle fire. There was still time before the Arab net closed in to send off Nicholl to seek help from the Mwamba, kinsmen of the Wankonde, who lived beyond the Songwe river; then the others watched the Arabs moving into position for their attack and, in Fotheringham's words, 'prepared to give them a real British welcome'.

Mlozi put in his assault at first light next morning. It was made by five hundred 'Arabs' armed with guns and supported by a cloud of black spearmen. The air was very still that day, the advancing men came on in ominous silence, and for a moment everything on the lake seemed to hang in suspense. But when the six Europeans opened up a murderous rifle-fire the Arabs faltered and fell back into the safe cover of the surrounding forest. The first crisis had been safely (and surprisingly easily) surmounted; as battles go, this original skirmish at Karonga was a very small affair yet it meant that in the end Mlozi was bound to fail in his grand design. But at the time there seemed no reason why the Arabs should not succeed in starving out the little European garrison which was now encumbered by fifteen hundred refugees, and the Arabs settled down to a regular siege, keeping up a heavy fire into Fotheringham's enclosure from the Company's brick store a hundred yards away and from wooden platforms constructed like crows' nests in the surrounding trees. Fortunately their shooting was wildly inaccurate; during the next five days the Arabs killed only one donkey and wounded a couple of natives; it was not the bullets so much as the mental anxiety which most affected the besieged men. The Company 'boys' were notably restless and panicky, while the refugees clamoured incessantly for food that did not exist. By the 28th, O'Neill and Fotheringham were wondering how much longer their provisions and ammunition would hold out when suddenly the firing ceased and silence fell across the plain. Unaccountably, it seemed, the Arabs had raised the siege.

Their reason soon became clear when the white men saw Nicholl and five thousand Mwamba spearmen hurrying down the beach to relieve them. It seemed at that moment that the first round of the slave war had been won by Fotheringham, but it soon turned out that very little had really been accomplished. For, almost immediately, his Mwamba allies, disappointed because they had not indulged in any fighting or looting, melted away to their homes, while the Company natives made it clear they had no intention of facing another siege. The Europeans talked over the situation as calmly as they could and even Fotheringham had to agree it would be suicidal to attempt to defend Karonga by themselves. All they could do was to follow their native allies to the inaccessible swamps of the Songwe and wait there until reinforcements allowed them to attack and destroy the Arab settlements. Next day, after burning all the stores they could, Fotheringham and his companions reluctantly walked out of their little fort leaving behind an immense booty for the Arabs. Mlozi had after all won the first round.

This encounter at Karonga turned out to be a curtain-raiser for a vicious little war that went on beside the lake with fluctuating fortunes for the eight years between 1887 and 1895. One curious aspect of that struggle is that it made hardly any impression on the British people. A reason for this undoubtedly is that not one of its European participants possessed any flair at all for reporting: one has the feeling that had Gordon or even Burton been involved in the lake war, the public's interest would have been caught and held. But the reports that did trickle home read today like a badly written Henty story that has been made practically unintelligible by an absurdly generous sprinkling of respectful parentheses. Thus Lugard is invariably referred to as 'Captain (as he then was, now Sir Frederick) Lugard', or, in later editions, even more splendidly as 'Captain (now Lord) Lugard'. Two other prominent figures turn up repeatedly as 'Mr. (later Sir Harry) Johnston' and 'Mr. (now Sir Alfred) Sharpe', while even clerical preferment is not allowed to pass unnoticed and one missionary name always appears as 'the Rev. (now the Ven. Archdeacon) W. P. Johnson'. Then again, by the eighteen-eighties, the British people had become thoroughly disillusioned and bored with adventures in Africa, which always seemed to end either in humiliating withdrawals as at Majuba, or in an unbearable agony like Khartoum's, and they had no wish to read about any more of them. And there was yet another and perhaps a more creditable reason why the Nyasa slave war failed to attract much public sympathy: although it was continually being represented as a humanitarian Jihad fought by a few white men against a fearful evil, ordinary people began to wonder why local missionary support for it was so far from being unanimous. Indeed, a feeling grew that there was something dubious and disreputable about the fighting and even the jingo press tended to ignore it. And there was a grain of truth in these suspicions; some of the participants in the war without doubt were inspired less by philanthropy than by motives of commercial advantage and political supremacy. Yet many of the men who were to join Fotheringham at Karonga and face unpredictable dangers with him from disease and an unrelenting enemy, were inspired by the very highest motives, and today one cannot help counting it unfair that their remarkable feats of courage and endurance never figured in the imperial anecdotage of Great Britain's golden age.

9

THE REJECTED SUITOR

The six white men hiding in the Songwe swamps did not have to wait very long for reinforcements. On December 9th, 1887, the *Ilala* steamed up again with four passengers: Hawes, the British Consul at Blantyre, John Moir, one of the joint managers of the African Lakes Company, and two other fighting men. Moir immediately assumed command. He was a bespectacled, dry-as-dust looking man who would have looked more at home on the dais of a lecture-room than as leader of a piratical attack against a nest of Arab slavers. Lord Lugard, writing in later years about Moir, says that 'his character was one of the most extraordinary I have ever met with in my life', and he never pretended to understand him, for John Moir was a strange blend of impulsive courage and sudden irresolution. But no one was aware of his failings when he arrived at the Songwe mouth; all they saw was a man bubbling over with enthusiasm at the prospect of expelling Mlozi from Nkondeland. He did not seem particularly impressed by the way Fotheringham and O'Neill had managed things so far, and adopted a rather condescending manner. All they had to do, he explained to his companions, was to enlist the five thousand Mwamba warriors again, get them thoroughly excited about the immense booty they could pillage in Mpata and then lead them to it. He made it all sound easy enough and two days before Christmas 1887, the Mwamba spearsmen were lined up in an immense circle round Mlozi's village and given the word to go. In those early days of the slave war, the stockade at Mpata was not the formidable thing it became later on and it was carried in the first rush with very few casualties. Then the looting began and the fighting stopped. For as soon as the tribesmen had loaded themselves up with all the booty they could carry, they simply disappeared in the direction of their homes. Heavy rain began to fall and a half-hearted attempt to fire the village failed; Sharpe was limping about with a spent bullet in his heel, while Moir, wounded a little more severely in the thigh, was so engrossed in trying to find his spectacles, which had dropped off in the excitement, that he failed to keep in touch with the situation. It came then as an unpleasant surprise to the white men to discover that far from being masters of Mpata, they were stranded in a hostile village, and they withdrew hastily (and with loud recriminations) to their old quarters in the swamp. Very little had been accomplished by their attack. Admittedly Mlozi had lost some property and possibly some prestige, but his power otherwise was undiminished. Indeed, on balance his situation was even improved, for the white men were bitterly divided now about what they should do next. John Moir clearly was fed up with the whole affair and anxious to get away; Hawes was having second thoughts, too, and talking weightily about 'co-existence' and then came out strongly for the evacuation of Karonga. O'Neill on the other hand demanded that they make another attempt to destroy Mlozi, while Fotheringham was inarticulate with fury at any suggestion that not only the Wankonde but their Mwamba allies, too, should be abandoned to the vengeance of the Arabs.

In the end a compromise was agreed upon. Fotheringham and Nicholl were to join Dr. Cross at Chirenje Mission sixty-five miles from Karonga up the Stevenson road; there they would build a stockade and act as a check on Mlozi's reprisals, and as a testimony to the Europeans' intention of returning to renew the war. For his part, Moir undertook to organise a strong relief expedition the moment he got back to Blantyre. There was an awkward scene when Fotheringham, who by this time had come to know his man, insisted that this promise be given in writing, but in the end Moir meekly sat down and wrote out his guarantee that fifteen well-armed Europeans would be back at Karonga before the end of April, and gave a verbal promise that the *Ilala* would return with ammunition within a fortnight. Fotheringham and Nicholl then set off for Chirenje while the *Ilala* steamed south with the two Consuls still engaged in acrimonious argument. Indeed by the time they got to Blantyre, Hawes and O'Neill were finding it very difficult to agree about a single thing, while Moir discovered that his airy promises of a quick relief were much more difficult to fulfil than he had anticipated. In fact ten weeks, not the promised two, went by before the *Ilala* sailed north again. The delay was by no means entirely Moir's fault. For one thing, the Portuguese were being more than usually unco-operative and they impounded some of the arms intended for his relief force. Then he had to wait while one of the recruits disappeared to prospect for gold. But it was Consul Hawes who turned out to be the greatest hindrance of all. We never seem to know very much about Hawes. Contemporary accounts only refer to him briefly, and we are left with the impression of a bad-tempered featureless man who for a few weeks makes a thorough nuisance of himself. Yet one cannot help feeling a certain sympathy for him. He was convinced by now that with the slender resources available, Mlozi could never be evicted from his stronghold at Mpata, and as the British Government's representative on the spot, he felt obliged to advise Whitehall to withhold official recognition from any but a properly equipped expedition. Yet here was his consular colleague O'Neill, far from his own sphere of jurisdiction, not only publicly disagreeing with him, impairing his prestige and suggesting he was dishonouring a solemn pledge, but even going behind his back and imploring London for permission to lead a new attempt on Mpata himself. In the end Hawes washed his hands of the whole affair and took himself off on leave to England, appointing Mr. Buchanan (who had lately been dismissed from the Blantyre mission after revelation of the fierce punishments inflicted there) as his deputy, while poor O'Neill, having been thoroughly deflated by a stiff reprimand from the Foreign Office for his interference, withdrew a little later to his proper duties at Mozambique.

All this time, up at Chirenje, Monteith Fotheringham was hanging about waiting with growing irritation for John Moir's promised reinforcements. This for him must have been the worst time of the whole war. He was almost certain that he had been abandoned; he was suffering from malaria and bored to distraction; all he heard were rumours that Mlozi was on his way up the road to attack him. 'It is too bad to keep me here,' the harassed man wrote indignantly to Blantyre, 'and not to send me the necessaries of life.' He would stare at the written promise of early relief he had extracted from Moir and then fling the scrap of paper away from him with a curse. And in one respect at least he was justified in believing Moir had broken faith with him, for no serious attempt had been made in Blantyre to recruit the fifteen promised men for Karonga, and in the end only five European employees of the Company sailed for the 'north end' in the *Ilala*; they were commanded by the second of the Moir brothers—Frederick.

Buchanan, in his new official capacity, had turned out to be scarcely less a hindrance to Moir's plans than Consul Hawes, insisting that another attempt be made to negotiate a settlement with Mlozi before any more fighting took place. And so, when at last the long-overdue expedition sailed up the lake, the U.M.C.A. mission steamer *Charles Janson* was steaming just behind with Buchanan and the Rev. W. P. Johnson on board. Somehow or other Buchanan managed to obtain an interview with Mlozi on the beach a little below Karonga. 'We shook hands heartily,' he reported afterwards to London, and then recounted how at the end of a long discussion he had managed to persuade the Arabs to pull down their stockades and leave the country. Buchanan, it seems, then went back complacently to Karonga where he found Fotheringham was busily restoring the damaged breast-work. This, he assured him, was quite unnecessary since the crisis was over and Mlozi had agreed to sign a formal treaty with him the next day. But the unhappy gentleman was disappointed when he arrived for the ceremony in the morning. Mlozi, it seemed, had changed his mind and all Buchanan got from him was a cryptic message to say: 'If you want me out of the country, you must come and put me out.'

One cannot help feeling a little sorry for Buchanan at the failure of his first attempt at diplomacy, but the lesson was nothing like so chastening as his next experience. He had convinced himself by now that the Arabs were indeed determined to convert the whole lake area into a Mohammedan slave state and, after giving Frederick Moir his official blessing for a renewed assault on Mpata, he decided to call on the Yao chief, Makanjira, on the way down the lake and advise him not to get involved in the struggle. Makanjira 'of the ears' was a fearsome half-mad creature. He had a great reputation for savagery and once had startled a party of guests by serving up human flesh for dinner, but no thought even of this sort of hospitality was in his mind on the day Buchanan landed below his village with Johnson, six Askari and a large Union Jack. Instead a truculent crowd was waiting for them and presently the white men were mobbed and seized. The saintly Johnson made no resistance but Buchanan fought back and Makanjira promptly had him stripped and flogged with a *kurbash*. Then the two men were locked up for the night in a native hut where, according to Johnson, all Buchanan could do was to repeat incredulously 'and this to an Englishman'. Next morning they were ransomed for two drums of paint which Makanjira wanted for the decoration of his slave dhows. Buchanan's report of the incident created something of a stir in Whitehall, especially as he had used the Swahili spelling 'dau' for dhow, and Lord Salisbury was constrained to denounce Makanjira 'in no uncertain tones', not so much for maltreating British subjects as for his impudence in ransoming them for mere cosmetics intended for his daughter's use.

Meanwhile, the ruined fort at Karonga had been re-occupied in force on March 3rd, 1888, and Frederick Moir found himself in command of ten Europeans and five hundred native soldiers. This younger Moir was a tough, teetotal, fire-and-brimstone Presbyterian, and there was no streak of his brother's unreliability running through his nature. A photograph taken of him some-where about this time may not flatter Frederick Moir but it remains a classic of its kind. We see him in a photographer's studio seated rather nonchalantly on an unconvincing papier mâché rock, looking like a hero from an old 'Western' film who had unaccountably exchanged his stetson for an enormous pith helmet shaped like a coal-scuttle. Moir stares winsomely at a far distant horizon; a magnificent beard reaches halfway down his chest and partly hides a shirt riddled through with pockets and pouches, all tightly fastened with bachelor buttons; what look like smart pin-stripe trousers disappear suddenly into tremendous knee-length boots, one negligent hand rests in a frozen gesture on his hip, the other is clasped tightly (and somewhat rashly) over the muzzles of a double-barrelled rifle. In short, here is the very model of the God-fearing Victorian Empire builder, splendidly prepared to handle truculent natives with exemplary justice and uncompromising severity; and that perhaps is what Frederick Moir wanted to be more than anything else.

Frederick Moir, like his brother, had given a great deal of thought to the problem of reducing Mlozi's forts and as soon as he arrived at Karonga he announced his own rather ingenious recipe for victory. He proposed, it transpired, to set the Arab villages on fire with a shower of primitive incendiary bombs and storm their stockades during the ensuing confusion.

Fotheringham's response was perhaps a shade less enthusiastic than it had been for the older Mr. Moir's plan, and with some dubiety he watched a series of hazardous pyrogenic experiments being conducted on Karonga beach. Frederick, however, was as full of enthusiasm as any schoolboy and many years later recalled fondly how he had 'soon designed a fire-dart to be shot from a 12-bore muzzle-loading rifle. It was made of solid bamboo about twelve inches long. Just behind its point, a hole was bored through it, and from the ends of this, deep spirals to steady its flight were cut down to the base. Through the hole and down the spirals were inserted bark cloth, which protruded for a foot or so beyond the dart. Damp gunpowder was rubbed into the cloth, dried at the end of the tails, so as to make sure it would take fire on discharge. . . . I soon found myself able to fire about 150 yards with very good direction.'

The great 'fire-dart' attack on the slavers took place on April 10th, 1888, and was a thoroughly confused affair. Even after all the accounts about it have been read, it is still difficult to make out exactly what happened and what went wrong. Moir himself tells us that the attack was made on Kopa Kopa's stockade, while Fotheringham is quite definite that Msalema's was the target. The action began in a particularly chivalrous sort of way with Moir firing off his revolver three times as though he was the starter of a race; presumably he meant to warn the Arabs of what was coming and give them a chance to surrender. Then he mounted a convenient ant-hill and began shooting off his incendiaries. Somewhat to everyone's surprise they started an encouraging fire and Moir very confidently then led his men into the attack. But they were met with such a hail of bullets that the A.L.C. 'soldiers' only stopped long enough to fire their muskets before turning tail and vanishing. Although Fotheringham as usual was untouched, Moir's right arm was shattered just above the elbow, almost certainly by a wild shot from one of his own men. That was the end of brother Frederick's attempt to solve the 'north end' deadlock and a few days later, Fotheringham, holed up in Karonga once again, found himself in what was becoming an all-too-familiar posture, as he waved goodbye to yet another assault force withdrawing in the *Ilala*. Poor Moir afterwards had a bad time and was lucky not to lose his arm. After calling in at Bandawe for first-aid treatment, he went straight on to Edinburgh where his fractured elbow joint was excised. In the end he made a good recovery, which he characteristically ascribed not to the surgeon's skill but to 'the great value to health of total abstinence and clean living under the most trying climatic conditions'. Meanwhile, Fotheringham and the five other Europeans who had agreed to remain with him resumed their vigil at Karonga, strengthening its defences and wondering who the *Ilala* would produce on her next trip north. Seven anxious weeks later he was delighted, when the boat returned 'with a party on board which', Fotheringham wrote, 'in point of numbers and equipment far exceeded our most sanguine expectations'. In command was Captain Frederick Dealtry Lugard, D.S.O., of the Norfolk Regiment, the future Lord Lugard of Abinger.

Lugard, even thus early in his career, was a man worth anybody's study. Brought up in the rigid code of English public school, Sandhurst and the 'gentlemen's' army of Queen Victoria's reign, he had already distinguished himself in three campaigns before he was thirty. His friends thought of Captain Lugard as a fox-terrier of a man; he was slight, wiry and full of nervous energy. But there was another quality about him too which comes out in W. P. Johnson's description of his friend as one 'who in all his writings and doings recalls in a real and good sense a Knight of the old time'. Yet when he came to the lake in 1888 Lugard was an unstable, half-demented creature with tick-like gestures and haunted eyes, who had just passed through an intense emotional experience. There was little to suggest he would soon become one of Britain's most famous colonial statesmen.

In his autobiography Lugard tells us that his health at this time had been shattered by the hardships of a Burmese campaign; but here he is being a good deal less than frank. His breakdown was mental rather than physical, and followed events which read more like the opening chapters of a P. C. Wren novel than anything that might have happened in real life. Lugard as a youth had made the army his whole life and until 1886 he was regarded as a confirmed bachelor. Then, while stationed at Lucknow, he fell deeply in love with a remarried divorcée noted for her beauty and wit. The ex-misogynist briefly entered into a dream-world of happiness until an untimely rebellion in Burma separated the two lovers. During the course of the campaign Lugard was horrified to hear that his beloved had been seriously injured in a carriage accident; a kindly Colonel gave him leave to hurry back to India, and finding there that she had already sailed to England, Lugard in a passion of concern followed in the next boat. Arrived in London his whole world suddenly fell apart when he burst in on his goddess making love to another admirer. For a time it seemed doubtful whether the wretched man would emerge from the shock of disillusionment with his reason, and as something dimmed in his mind he determined to cut himself adrift from the life he had known in the past; it was only thanks to the good offices of influential friends that he was persuaded not to resign his commission but to go on sick leave for some months. Rather pathetically, we find him trying to find distraction as a volunteer in the London Fire Brigade but the pursuit of conflagrations in the city proved an inadequate anodyne for his injured feelings and only a little later Lugard took the more conventional escape route of the rejected suitor by going off to Africa, ostensibly to shoot enormous numbers of inoffensive wild animals. But morbid thoughts of suicide, in fact, were running through Lugard's tortured mind at the time, although he was determined to make his death appear accidental. There was rambling talk of joining an expedition to rescue Enim Pasha from Equatoria and he made an attempt to enrol in an Italian army invading Ethiopia. After having been thoroughly snubbed for his pains he took passage down the East African coast in a condition of tremendous physical and mental distress. Only after the shadows had lifted a little did Lugard decide that if he were going to get himself killed, it might as well be for a good cause, and when he sailed for Mozambique and caught sight of a file of miserable slaves boarding his ship he realised he had found one. Only a little later he met that fiery abolitionist, Consul O'Neill. O'Neill had just returned from Karonga and he handed Lugard a copy of the impassioned appeal he had sent to the British Government asking it to support the white men fighting Mlozi. O'Neill was watching Lugard as he read it, and mused aloud: 'You would be a godsend to them', and with those words the outcast realised his duty lay in fighting the Arab slavers at Karonga. 'I can think of no juster cause in which a soldier can draw his sword,' Lugard wrote to his brother a little later from the Shiré highlands in the cliché-laden idiom of the day, adding, 'My chief idea in coming out here was to do my little aid in stopping the slave trade and this would be a blow at its very roots'. The new crusader arrived at Blantyre on May 12th, 1888, the same day as Frederick Moir came in nursing his shattered arm. Although he was calmer now, Lugard must have made a curious impression on the little settlement. His frantic eyes, distraught expression and hollowed cheeks were set off by a drooping moustache which had been allowed to grow so long as to give him the appearance of another Vercingetorix on his way to fight the Roman Legions. But John Moir recognised his high gift for leadership at once and soon persuaded Lugard to supersede him as commander of a third well-equipped expedition for the relief of Karonga which was about to set off. It must be admitted that Consul Buchanan viewed the arrival of a regular soldier on the scene with rather less enthusiasm. One can sympathise with his predicament; only a short time before he had been given precise instructions to do nothing against Mlozi without first obtaining sanction from London, but here was one of the Queen's own officers proposing to become involved in the filibustering war and by his mere presence lending it an impression of official authority. But in the end Buchanan reluctantly gave Lugard his qualified approval to fight the Arabs, although it was understood that if expediency dictated it Lugard's actions, like those of an Elizabethan buccaneer, would be disavowed.

Lugard left for Karonga on May 18th, 1888, gathering up his fighting men on the way. His was a strange little army. It was composed of three tried veterans (John Moir, Dr. Cross and Alfred Sharpe), six pious A.L.C. employees, and nine wild men from Natal—old soldiers, prospectors and decayed gentlemen whose only common traits seemed to be truculence and an inclination to use foul language. Yet somehow as the crowded *Ilala* steamed slowly northwards, Lugard's tact and personality— and perhaps his prestige as a professional soldier—enabled him to maintain discipline among his ill-assorted gang. At Bandawe they stopped long enough for Dr. Laws to bear down on them with a great deal of weighty advice and a little further on, near the dhow ferry at Deep Bay, Lugard decided to 'blood' his men in a foray against a notorious Arab settlement; unfortunately the slavers had been forewarned of the attack, and the white men stormed an empty village, the only casualty in the whole ludicrous episode being poor short-sighted Moir who fell into a pothole.

The end of May saw Lugard's force safely installed in Karonga where Fotheringham gave it a splendid welcome, writing happily in his diary that the total of twenty-four men was 'the largest number I believe ever assembled at any place in Central Africa'. He listened respectfully as the energetic regular officer outlined his plans, for it seemed that like the Moirs before him, Lugard had already made up his mind how to deal with Mlozi. He kept telling Fotheringham that the important thing was to reconnoitre the Arab position in efficient military fashion; after that he explained that he intended to breach the stockades with homemade bangalore torpedoes and rush each village in turn. But, as regular soldiers do, before he could think of beginning the campaign the new commander insisted on tidying up his base, and the fort at Karonga took on a new character as Lugard sternly remedied its deplorable sanitary arrangements and even put a stop to the Company Africans' lucrative practice of selling cartridges to the Arabs. Sharpe, who had been away on a recruiting mission, reached Karonga with nearly two hundred Atonga levies about this time and now the fort began to echo with shouted orders as lines of sweating natives were taught the rudiments of infantry drill as well as the way to load and fire their rifles. Aiming the guns, however, was quite beyond them, for the levies seemed utterly incapable of closing one eye, but at least they learned how to point them in the right direction, and with this Lugard professed himself content. The white men for their part were kept employed in moulding bullets, improvising grenades from jam tins filled with gunpowder, stones and clay, or constructing torpedoes from lengths of brass steamer tubing loaded and fused in the same way. These were Lugard's secret weapons and everything depended on them.

Then, one carefully rehearsed evening, Lugard worked up enthusiasm by appearing in the full glory of his D.S.O. and string of campaign medals to make a fighting speech to his assembled men, and explain his plans to them. But before the attack went in, Lugard and Fotheringham carried out a coldly audacious reconnaissance of the Arab stockades at night and it is interesting to discover that the would-be suicide had made the enlightening discovery that life after all retained some of its sweetness, for on his return Lugard wrote incredulously in his diary: 'Here was I . . . in a regular funk of the unseen danger, with every nerve strained to tension, taking as great care as though my life was of extraordinary value.' He was concerned now by the number of his men who were going down with malaria; one European died and although neither his reconnaissance nor his training programme had been completed, Lugard decided he must make his assault without more delay. Accordingly, on the night of June 15th, after dumbfounding the Atonga with the information that his primary objective was not the capture of women, he moved his men quietly to within two hundred yards of Kopa Kopa's, and ordered them to lie down and wait for his orders. Lugard was still quite new to Africa; he seems to have been dismayed when every one of his native soldiers dropped off to sleep at once, and during the next hour the enthusiast fussed round his men, waking them up and making sure every one knew exactly what he had to do. He was blissfully unaware that his very proper orders prohibiting looting and the seizing of women had already taken most of the

Mlozi, from a sketch by Harry Johnston

The Rev. James Stewart   Monteith Fotheringham

Frederick Moir   Frederick Lugard

fighting spirit out of his Atonga levies. Instead, he seems to have been full of confidence that morning and certain that his ingenious tactics were foolproof; indeed all the white men agreed it only needed a little luck and reasonable discipline among the torpedo carriers for the attack to be successful.

'As the first streak of dawn appeared,' Lugard wrote afterwards of his assault, 'we advanced to within 50 yds and I then raised a cheer and led the charge.' But far from being surprised the Arabs were waiting for the attack, and when the Europeans reached the stockade it turned out to be far more formidable than they had anticipated. A loop-holed mud wall six feet high was surmounted by a thick fourteen-foot fence of stout poles woven through with thorns; on the top it bore a grisly frieze of severed heads. Clearly everything depended on the men with the torpedoes and kegs of gunpowder coming up quickly, and Lugard, having himself arrived safely at the wall, looked round anxiously for them—and made the unpleasant discovery that they had disappeared. 'It was difficult,' he wrote afterwards with typical understatement, 'to know what to do', and then he behaved precisely as one would expect a man of his temperament and courage would do: he tried to scale the stockade alone. As he swung himself up, a musket protruding through one of the loopholes fired at him from point-blank range and Lugard as he fell was certain he had found his mortal wound. Sharpe was near at hand and, 'as a last request', was persuaded to take over command. Then the wounded man staggered off in the general direction of Dr. Cross and Karonga.

Ten hours later a bloodstained figure, wearing an incongruous red tam-o'-shanter given to him by a passing native, tottered into Karonga fort. It was Lugard, barely alive, in excruciating pain, tormented by thirst, bled white, and angry to have survived. As he leant against the gate his defeated 'army' crept in, carrying their dead and wounded with them. For the great assault had ended in a disastrous repulse and the men had withdrawn in confusion to the sounds of jeers and taunts from the Arabs. One of the Europeans, shot through the head, was buried later beside the wall; another named Rolfe had been hit by a bullet which exposed the appetite centre of his brain and turned him temporarily into a morbidly voracious eater; but Lugard's wound was even more remarkable. Indeed, there is a touch of the miraculous in his survival.

'I had received a very singular wound,' he writes. 'The muzzle of the gun must have been placed a few inches from my body, for the coarse grains of 'trade powder' had entered the right arm . . . like a charge of shot, and could not be dislodged, while two big lumps of wadding were extracted from the wound. The bullet had entered the elbow joint (which fortunately escaped fracture, or I should have lost my arm), had struck the main artery, but pushed it aside without cutting it,—or I must inevitably have bled to death; it then struck my chest, apparently in a direct line for the heart, but, glancing off a rib, passed along under the skin, and came out at the top of my breast pocket, making a long tearing wound in its exit. Then it struck the wrist of my left hand, carrying into the wound a portion of some letters which were in my breast-pocket. It "pulverised" the main bone of this arm, cutting also a minor artery.'

The events of the next few weeks have a nightmare quality which lifts them above the level of ordinary human experience. Lugard was in terrible physical agony and the fever-stricken doctor who might have helped him slid into malarial coma. Everyone in the crowded camp was irritable or demoralised with fatigue and disappointment. Most of the white men were shaking with fever, and their old cameraderie had been replaced by private rages and frantic criticism. Jones died, and the Africans verged on mutiny. Two A.L.C. men took the opportunity of 'resigning', although there was not the faintest hope of getting them away for weeks. Young Peter Moore beckoned John Moir aside to explain, as he tells us in his diary, that 'I wanted down, that I was thoroughly sick of the warrior's life, that I hated it . . .'. The Natalians began to talk of desertion and of the raft they were going to build to get away from this hell-hole. Sharpe quarrelled with Moir and, like a sulking Achilles, took himself off to resume his big-game shooting. For that matter, not a single man was prepared to serve under John Moir, while Fotheringham seemed utterly incapable of controlling them. The battered Lugard had no option but to resume command, but for the next month he was unable to stir from the rickety chair into which he had fallen at the end of the battle. His useless arms were held out stiffly on splints so that it was impossible for him to dress properly and he could only cover himself with a rough trade blanket. He could not lie down; proper sleep was denied him. Every morning his wounds were syringed through with Condy's fluid and then roughly dressed by a man shivering with ague 'who had been through an ambulance class'. Unable to feed himself, too weak to attend even to his smallest needs, Lugard depended for everything on his comrades. He was unable even to kick away the countless rats which had invaded the fort, or the snakes that followed them. He was tormented by mosquitoes and quite incapable of brushing them from off his face. All he could do was to sit immobilised in his rough grass hut, often delirious with malaria, utterly helpless if the Arabs attacked and desperately anxious about the white men quarrelling in the fort. During that time Lugard knew much kindness and loyalty, and disillusionment, too, but somehow his sufferings burned the madness out of him and when the hellish month of torture was over, this Orlando Furioso of the lake emerged as a rational man again. The *Ilala* turned up at last early in July and nearly everyone in the fort clamoured to get away. But Lugard, who had first claim to medical attention, was well aware that if he left, the whole enterprise against the slavers would be abandoned. It was a hard decision to make, but he announced that he would stay on at Karonga and renew the assault as soon as his wounds were healed. Only a singular sense of duty made him take this course—but, as he wrote a little later in his diary, if he had gone '. . . how could I expect the half-dozen sick survivors to stay on at Karonga? And if *they* went . . . Lake Nyasa would be lost to us—we should simply be kicked out by the Arabs.' Then there comes a cry from his heart as he adds 'God, who defends the right, prevent this.'

But John Moir had no such scruples and he led most of the other white men on to the *Ilala* as soon as it dropped anchor, and set off down the lake towing a steel boat crammed with departing Atonga levies. Each of these unfortunate men wore a little bag of gunpowder round his neck and by ill luck a spark from the steamer exploded one of them. The steel boat was immediately swept by a devastating fire and rather than be delayed by the accident, Moir in the *Ilala* seems to have ordered it to be cast off, and continued on his way. The boat drifted helplessly back to Karonga carrying a ghastly freight of screaming men, and a wave of bitter anger roared through the camp at Moir's apparent callous unconcern. It is only fair to assume that Moir was unaware of the magnitude of this disaster, but, coming on top of their other disappointments, it lowered the morale of the men remaining in the fort to its lowest ebb. Yet somehow Lugard managed to instil new spirit into the garrison, and he spoke to them about a new plan; Moir was to buy a cannon and send it up to Karonga and this without doubt would flatten Mlozi's defences; the best thing they could do, he added, while waiting for the gun, was to stop quarrelling among themselves and harass the Arabs instead with guerrilla tactics.

The months that followed drifted by very slowly for the men, marooned in Karonga like survivors from a shipwreck, and there is a strange and unreal quality about the lives they led; all the old doubts and suspicions that Moir was double-crossing them were raised, discussed, dismissed, and raised again. And judging by the stores that did arrive he seemed to be making remarkably little effort to send even the necessities of life up to them. Discipline faltered when Lugard went off at last for treatment, but he was back again by December. Yet still there was no sign of the long-awaited gun. Everyone was restless and irritable in the fort. Two of the men quarrelled so bitterly they decided to fight a duel with revolvers and Lugard only narrowly succeeded in separating them. And even he began to despair: 'The white men are quite disheartened by broken promises and the scarcity of food', runs one of the entries in his diary at this time. But then in the new year, as so often happens, the shadows seemed to lighten and Lugard could even find grounds for optimism. For one thing, an envoy from the Sultan of Zanzibar turned up with instructions to negotiate a settlement between the white men and the Arabs, and when he was received respectfully by Mlozi, who bent down to kiss the Sultan's letter, some sort of compromise seemed possible. But after a little time the envoy appeared to be finding himself very much more at home in the Arab camp than with the

Europeans at Karonga, and rumours reached the garrison that he had taken two wives in Mpata. Then one day an insolent letter came into the fort to say he had thrown in his lot with the Arabs and that the negotiations were at an end. But by that time it did not seem to matter very much since the ultimate solution to the problem—the long-awaited cannon—had arrived from Scotland. Admittedly it was so ancient that there was a strong suspicion it had been pilfered from a provincial museum; and it was disappointing to find that most of the ammunition accompanying it was faulty. It was regrettable too that the 'organiser of victory', John Moir, had found business commitments made it impossible for him to come north to help renew the assault on Mpata, and it was quite like old times to find he had engaged only a couple of new recruits for the enterprise instead of the anticipated dozen. Lugard called a council of war to consider the situation and had to use his casting vote before a decision was taken to make another attempt on the stockade. A road was then laboriously hacked out of the bush and the cannon dragged along it to the Arab villages. At last, on February 21st, fire was opened on Msalema's stockade. The result was yet another miserable anti-climax and coming after the previous ones, this one was perhaps the hardest of all to bear. For the shells sent up were mostly duds and the amateur gunners only managed to fire twenty-six rounds in three hours, and even then, as Fotheringham in his book laments, 'The shell simply passed through the woodwork and left an aperture of its own shape' without exploding and breaching the stockade.

This disappointment proved the last straw for Lugard. All the endless misery and uncertainty, the unremitting dangers and gallantry of the last nine months, had accomplished nothing. Mlozi seemed as strongly entrenched as ever at the north end of the lake.

Lugard was certain now that he could do no more, and there were plenty of excellent reasons to be found for going home. For one thing it was plain to him that neither the British nor the Arabs were strong enough to break the deadlock: then again, he had outstayed his leave and might be obliged to give up the army; he alone might be able to bludgeon Moir into sending proper equipment up to Karonga, and it was imperative too that the authorities at home be awakened to the Arab danger in Nyasaland. But the truth was of course that Lugard had folded up, was sick to death of the Karonga war, and could think of nothing else except getting away. Even so it still seems out of character for a man like Lugard to leave a task unfinished, and there remains the impression that with returning sanity he had become aware of the futility of his self-imposed penance and was anxious to resume a normal life. His decision to leave was a bitter blow to Fotheringham but he accepted it with generous understanding. The night before their commander left Karonga the garrison held a queer little ceremony which in its way was as strange as anything that had happened there before. It was a homespun tribute to a brave soldier and the men who offered it were intensely serious about it. Lugard's account of that evening reads like pure *Boys' Own Paper*. He describes a circle of bearded short-sleeved men sitting round an open fire in the moonlight. There is a speech or two and finally Fotheringham stands up to say a few more well-chosen words which are scarcely comprehended by his listeners. Then he makes a presentation of a pair of binoculars and an engraved sword to a thoroughly embarrassed Lugard, who will always afterwards value them above any of his honours. Lugard concludes his reminiscence of the occasion on a rare note of nostalgia: 'The familiar chorus of "Dear Old Pals" died away on the night breeze,' he writes, 'and my last evening at Karonga's was spent and gone.' Next morning he boarded the steamer for the voyage south, leaving Mlozi and Monteith Fotheringham still glaring at each other across the devastated Nkonde plain.

10

THE LITTLE PRANCING PRO-CONSUL

By the middle of 1889 there was a curious air of permanence about Mlozi and Fotheringham. They give us the impression of two veteran prize-fighters engaged in an interminable private bout of their own. From time to time each of them is joined in the ring by a band of eager assistants, but very soon the new-comers slip away again, leaving the two principals back in their corners waiting for the next round to begin. This, of course, is an over-simplification of the situation at the north end of the lake during the eighteen-eighties; throughout the whole course of the slave war Mlozi was ably supported by his two lieutenants Msalema and Kopa Kopa, while for most of the time Fotheringham's efforts were buttressed by Nicholl and Dr. Cross. But especially after Lugard had gone, the sporadic fighting which followed has all the character of a personal feud between the two old contestants, and sometimes, because they are so equally matched, one wonders whether the war will ever end. Then suddenly everything changes and takes on a different character as a fresh champion enters the ring—Harry Hamilton Johnston.

No one less like Lugard could possibly be imagined than the new arrival, and yet the two men for years regarded themselves as rivals in the expanding opportunities of colonial Africa. There is none of Lugard's charm or constraint about Johnston. Instead he exhibits all the bumptious assertiveness of an almost grotesquely little man who is over-sensitive about his stature, and, however much we may admire his energy and achievements, Johnston still remains a thoroughly unlikeable person. According to R. C. F. Maugham who worked under him for years, Harry Johnston lacked 'both presence and, at times, dignity', and Maugham goes on to give us this unflattering description of his former chief: '. . . measuring little more than five feet in his tiny shoes, his fresh-complexioned smiling features, and intensely effeminate manner, added to a rather high-pitched squeaky voice which grew almost caressing when he was trying to get something out of you, savoured rather of the drawing-room or the studio than the rugged surroundings of life in the African wilds. Externally immaculate, his minute articles of clothing were distinguished by a certain eccentricity more perhaps of design than material'—which seems a reasonable criticism when we recall that Johnston's favourite headgear was a remarkable straw hat which hesitated in style between a boater and a blue-jacket's sennet hat and was adorned with a white, yellow and black ribbon intended to symbolise racial co-operation.

Above all else Johnston was a snob. He was never so happy as when consorting with his social superiors, and his books are liberally sprinkled with the names of peers whom he 'ran into', and the great houses whose hospitality he 'enjoyed'. Even in the bush, Johnston would always wear evening dress for dinner (with a hideous yellow waistcoat to go with the 'racial' black jacket and white shirt), and insist that a clean linen tablecloth, silver cutlery and cut glass appear on his rickety camp table. One of his enemies in a moment of exasperation once described Johnston as 'a little prancing pro-consul', and the description fits him very well. Yet it would be wrong to dismiss him as a purely comic figure; behind his veil of exhibitionism, Johnston possessed a remarkably brilliant mind, tremendous vitality and an insatiable curiosity which even in his youth had turned him into a one-man walking encyclopaedia. The trouble was that the little man's erudition had to be displayed continuously even at the risk of indiscretion and bad taste. In consequence Harry Johnston made very few close friends and a multitude of enemies. There seemed to be too much in one man for all of it to be genuine, and people came to regard him as a sort of human kaleidoscope, which if it were twisted about showed in turn botanist, artist, explorer, novelist, scholar, dilettante, anthropologist and statesman, not to mention a philologist capable of easy pleasantries in a dozen different languages. So it does not come as a great surprise to us to discover that when Johnston arrived in Nyasaland he was quite prepared to add soldiering to his other accomplishments; what is more astonishing is that in the end he turns out to be the instrument which brought Mlozi to his death. That triumph has been copiously documented by himself. Indeed, as all his contemporaries agreed, there was no excuse for not knowing everything about Sir Harry, for he wrote a prodigious number of books, and most of them to a greater or lesser degree were autobiographical.

Johnston was in his early thirties when he arrived to relieve O'Neill as British Consul at Mozambique. We have a photograph of him taken at this time which shows a mousy little man with troubled, apprehensive eyes and hands clasped anxiously across his stomach. There is no sign in his curiously elfin face of the rabid imperialist who could write: 'I had but one religion, and that was the extension and development of the British Empire.' Nor in the portrait is there any suggestion that when it was taken Johnston was already a widely-travelled man whose work in the Consular Service had brought him to the kindly notice of the Prime Minister, Lord Salisbury. Indeed, at the time when Mlozi first stood gloating over the slaving prospects round Karonga, young Johnston was an enraptured guest at Hatfield. 'The dinner of that Saturday,' we are assured breathlessly in his autobiography, 'was unforgettable', while 'the evening that followed', he titters, 'was altogether enjoyable. Lady Gwendolen Cecil organised theatricals out of the large company of guests. She, I remember, played Lord Randolph Churchill in a wonderful moustache. I—among other impersonations—was part of a whale, and a Moorish slave-dealer in charge of a crew of very large, unwieldy female slaves', but alas! we never discover what happened to the kittenish guest or to his slaves, for the passage ends in a series of suggestive asterisks. But more serious matters than country house charades demanded Johnston's attention on the very next morning when his host took him strolling through the home park to discuss British policy in Africa, and even dropped a hint that Johnston might be just the man to help the Government with a newspaper article about its legitimate African aspirations. Johnston, immensely flattered, obligingly interrupted work on his first novel (it was entitled *The History of a Slave* and attracted notice only from the few scandalised clergymen and disapproving schoolmasters who deplored in it 'the impropriety of the pictures'), and a little later his dissertation for the instruction of the public in colonial affairs appeared in

The Times above the modest pseudonym of 'an African Explorer'.

This was a good beginning for a budding empire builder and things began to move even faster after Johnston was appointed a full Consul and swam into the wide orbit of Cecil Rhodes to become, briefly, one of his puppets. This was the exciting time when Rhodes was at his most ingratiating and ebullient; he was in London to win approval for the Royal Charter which would secure the Rhodesias for him, and was even prepared to 'square the Mahdi' if it would be of any assistance to the Government. He first met Johnston at the dinner-table of a mutual friend; the two men unblushingly outstayed their welcome and continued their conversation until daybreak by which time Rhodes, having agreed to finance the pacification and occupation of Nyasaland, had scrawled his signature on a cheque for £2,000 in favour of Johnston. This was heady stuff and that very afternoon, after depositing his precious cheque and interviewing someone in the Foreign Office, the 'prancing pro-consul' set off happily on a shopping spree that took him to Liberty's, Silvers in Cornhill, and the Army and Navy Stores to buy presents for the lake's native chiefs. By August 1889 (having barely had time to complete a painted 'Study of a Dead Woman Being Torn to Pieces by Hyenas'), he was on his way up the Shiré, for his consular duties at Mozambique were to take second place to directing imperial expansion in the country round the lake. And there, on the riverbank, even before he had properly entered his new province, he had a stroke of luck; he met Mr. Alfred Sharpe.

Johnston describes the encounter in *The Story of My Life*; '. . . we stopped,' he writes, 'on the outskirts of the Elephant Marsh to take in wood for burning; and I decided to go on shore with a rifle and a sketch-book. I heard distant shots as though some sportsman had preceded me. Presently I almost stumbled over the carcase of a magnificent waterbuck which had just fallen and expired. It had such a splendid head that I put my rifle down and began to sketch it. Presently I heard the dry, burnt stalks of the long reeds snapping and realised someone was standing behind me. I looked round. It was a comparatively young and active man with bright eyes, clad in a blue shirt much blackened about the sleeves with the burnt grass, breeches or knickerbockers tucked into gaiters. He wore a stout felt hat, and although so carelessly costumed one felt from his pleasant voice that he was a gentleman.' After the two men had introduced themselves, Johnston tells us that 'Whilst I mused and sketched he proposed making tea for us at his boat and using the milk of the female waterbuck he had killed. Her udder was full. I consented willingly to have a cup, and over it we talked rapidly and decisively.' The upshot of the unusual 'tête-à-tête' was that Sharpe agreed to take service under Johnston and in due course emerged as his invaluable Vice-Consul, and devoted Abdiel.

By declaring a protectorate over the upper Shiré, very soon after Johnston's arrival on the lake, Britain in effect assumed responsibility for the security of the surrounding country and the Karonga war automatically ceased to be an affair between the Arabs and an obscure trading corporation. It became instead the concern of the British Government and more precisely of its servant, Harry Johnston. But Johnston was well aware that with his inadequate resources he faced formidable difficulties if he was to pacify the lake country, and could do so only by combining force with guile and by showing a different face to each of his opponents in turn. The greatest danger, he realised at once, lay in the conclusion of an effective alliance between the Arabs in the north and the Yao slavers on the southern shores of the lake. If Johnston could push a wedge between them, his task would become far easier. Everything really depended on the attitude of Jumbe in the central, and strategically the most important position in Nyasa, and quite cynically Johnston decided to buy his allegiance. Jumbe was an old man; he had known Livingstone in 1863 and had been a great slaver in his time, but now he was anxious to end his days in peace. So when Johnston arrived with a gift of a bottle of Chartreuse as well as the offer of a subsidy of £300 a year in return for an alliance, submission to the Queen, and a promise to stop slaving, Jumbe was quite prepared to accept his terms, and soon afterwards the Union Jack was run up in Kota Kota. The unlikely friendship was cemented a little later by the bestowal on Jumbe of a full toilet set made to the Queen's order, which was inscribed with her initials in gold letters. The Royal gift was presented to Britain's newest ally in a bizarre little ceremony which tickled even Johnston's sense of humour. 'In the array set forth on his great verandah,' the Consul tells us, 'were two vessels not specially ordered by me but supplied almost mechanically in those days with any complete toilet service. "And what are these for?" said the delighted old man: and then himself supplying the answer: "I know! One for rice and the other for curry." And to that honourable function they were apportioned in the meal that followed.'

At the south end of the lake, Johnston, as he had expected, was received with hostility by Mponda whom he described as 'a very repellent type of Yao robber'. Believing it foolish to push matters at this moment, the Consul, as he stood outside the town stockade which was decorated with an array of the heads of the Yao chief's ex-enemies, made a civil remark about the similar English custom of impaling heads on Temple Bar, and beat a hasty retreat. But with Mlozi, thanks largely to the good offices of one of Jumbe's headmen, Johnston was surprisingly successful. He came up to Karonga in the middle of October, 1889, and found Monteith Fotheringham almost *in extremis*, numbed by all the anxieties and weariness of his long stay in the fort. But there was encouraging information that Mlozi was as tired as he was of the war and seemed anxious to find a way of ending it. Even so, Johnston was taking a considerable risk when he offered to meet the Arabs on neutral ground half-way between Karonga and Mpata. He went to the rendezvous accompanied by only a few Atonga and waited there for some time, in understandable anxiety. Presently there was a stir and half a dozen Arabs followed by a band of musketeers strolled into the clearing and settled themselves down on their rugs opposite the white man's chair. A strained conversation began. Things did not go very smoothly at first, for the Arabs complained that some of their women were being held captive in the Mandala fort. But neither party really wanted the talks to end, and a couple of days later the two men met again. This time Johnston was accompanied by the real heroes of Karonga—Fotheringham, Nicholl and Cross, and he was at his most dulcet and persuasive. Speaking in Swahili, he offered Mlozi a treaty which would in fact establish the status quo; while allowing the A.L.C. to trade peacefully on the lake, the Arabs would be free to resume their slaving. Mlozi, after a show of hesitation, accepted the terms. Peace, it seemed, had come back to Nkondeland. There was a great deal of hand-shaking, a bull was ceremoniously slaughtered, innumerable spears were broken to symbolise the truce and the Europeans felt constrained to hang about while the Arabs faced towards Mecca, prostrated themselves on their rugs and mumbled long prayers of thankfulness for the ending of the war.

As the hands of Johnston and Mlozi followed each other that day in tracing their signatures on the treaty, both men were congratulating themselves on a very neat performance. Each of them had obtained a breathing space, and neither had the slightest intention of keeping to the terms a moment longer than it suited him. Their calm cynicism gives to the little scene in the clearing by Msalema an odd sense of amateur theatre, of a drama where the actors forget their lines. One waits for Fotheringham's angry voice to shout his protests at appeasing a set of bloodthirsty scoundrels, yet he announces he is delighted with the Consul's 'triumph', and even writes, '. . . we secured peace on our own terms'. One suspects here, that perhaps because of his fatigue and apathy, Fotheringham was deliberately deluding himself. Then again one expects Dr. Cross to have something to say about Mlozi's past atrocities, or Nicholl to stamp away in disgust, but both smile and say nothing. Only Lugard reacts as we would have anticipated, but of course he was no longer present on the stage, and his distant voice fulminating against the truce, which he accounted a betrayal of all he and his companions had fought for, was scarcely heard in the polite applause acclaiming it. Probably Lugard would have felt better about the cease-fire if he had been able to see the dispatch Johnston wrote about the situation a little later: the Arabs, he reported to Lord Salisbury on February 1st, 1890, because of the war had lost much property and prestige, and would not 'attempt to tackle us again; at any rate, not for several years, and by that time', he adds soberly, 'if we are not in a position to deal with them effectually we should have no right to abrogate to ourselves the position of rulers in Nyasaland'.

No one really expected the peace terms to be kept for very long, least of all Johnston, but he could fairly claim it was Mlozi who broke them first. What is most surprising about the truce is that it lasted as long as it did—five years—long enough in fact for Johnston to fight a series of costly little wars to subdue the Yao slavers, and bring peace to the rest of the lake which, after all, had been his main reason for signing it.

≫   ≪

It is difficult to keep track of Harry Johnston's movements between 1889 and 1895, the years that followed the signing of his truce with Mlozi. He darts about Nyasaland infuriating the planters, offending the missionaries, defeating a succession of Yao chieftains and running up the Union Jack in innumerable, dusty little kraals in front of a ragged line of sepoys at the present (the only photograph we have of one of these ceremonies shows the flag flying upside down). Twice he takes himself off to India to recruit more soldiers, and to Egypt too, where he had the felicitous experience of being 'arrested' by a Corporal's Guard which carried him off from the hotel where he was staying to be the guest of Kitchener himself.* We get a glimpse of him in England too, presenting Lord Salisbury with a live turtle before going off to investigate the delights of the newly invented safety bicycle. Then he is back again in Africa quarrelling with his former patron, Rhodes, or skirmishing with the slavers up and down the lake. And at the end of it all, the whole of Nyasaland is at peace and lying firmly within his grasp—all of it, that is, except the far north where Mlozi still holds sway. And imperceptibly during these years, a new sense of tranquillity has settled over the lakeshore, and now Nyasa basks in unfamiliar security and hope, neither of them obtrusive, but both discernible. Johnston's own position was changing too: in 1891 the humble Consul blossoms out into the Commissioner of a British Protectorate that comprises the whole of present day Malawi.† Only a little later it

* Kitchener's friendly interest in Sir Harry may have been influenced by his impression that Nyasaland abutted on to the southern border of the Sudan.

† Johnston persuaded Whitehall to name the new Protectorate 'British Central Africa'. Lord Salisbury accepted the suggestion with the comment: 'The region it indicates is anywhere but in the centre of Africa; but that again is a British habit. The Middle Temple is not in the middle.'

becomes clear that Johnston, a shade ungratefully, has thrown off
the all-embracing influence of Cecil Rhodes, who after all had
footed most of the bills for his conquests. By doing so, Johnston
gained an unrelenting enemy who from now on would never miss
an opportunity to damn the new Commissioner's character or
ridicule his stature. 'I am not going to create with my funds an
independent King Johnston over the Zambesi,' an indignant
Rhodes protested one day, while his 'King Johnston' was not
slow in retaliating by informing the world that the historic
phrase 'from Cape to Cairo' had been created not by Rhodes (as
his old patron vociferously claimed), but by himself, and he went
on to make an official explanation to Whitehall that the reason he
had broken with Rhodes was a disinclination 'to truckle somewhat
pitifully to a bunch of speculators'. Other things changed too
during these years. The African Lakes Company gave up its
political aspirations and became transformed into a purely
business concern (the African Lakes Corporation, whose initial
letters happily were the same), while John Moir—also in 1893—
was replaced as manager by Fotheringham who at last left
Karonga for good—and somehow Karonga, after that, was never
quite the same.

For his part, Mlozi prospered during the five years that
followed the signing of his pact with the British. He appeared to
accept the continued presence of white men in Nkondeland with
good grace, and after marrying one of Jumbe's daughters, even
allowed it to be known that he himself would not refuse a
Government subsidy, provided it was as large as the one paid to
his father-in-law. As late as 1891 Buchanan, all optimism again,
was reporting that Mlozi was 'fully prepared to maintain that he is
the best behaved Arab in Nyasaland'. But all the time Sultan
Mlozi was buying arms, extending his influence, and sending out
bands of ruga-ruga into the mountains to lay waste the countryside and bring back ever longer processions of slaves. Dr. Cross,
still at Chirenje, watched with dismay as Mlozi's power increased,
and if the new administration preferred to ignore his anxious
reports about the situation in the north, at least the readers of
the *Free Church Journal* were made aware that 'the Nyasaland
Arab question is assuming more and more gigantic proportions.

Slave-dealing Arabs are predominant all over the country . . . and there never was a time in the history of the lake when so many guns and so much powder were in circulation.'

By 1894 Mpata had become a thriving entrepôt for slaves. It was surrounded by a ring of barracoons. The town itself was a good square mile in extent and strongly defended by a moat and stout bastioned wall with a double row of loopholes. Inside its prisons an uneasy throng of Nkonde hostages stood guarantee for the good behaviour of their people. The Sultan was more truculent than ever and announced that by now he was strong enough not only to storm Karonga but to chase every white man from the lake and that 'after Ramadan' he intended to do so. But if Mlozi's power was increasing, so were the pressures on him. Grim-faced Germans were established by now on the northern shores of Lake Nyasa and were causing such interference with his overland slave route that the Arabs had been compelled to reopen the unprofitable and vulnerable dhow ferry across the lake. Because of this restriction, Mlozi's slave barracoons were crammed to overflowing with merchandise he could not dispose of, and, what was even more serious, the supply of gunpowder which was the indispensable ingredient of Arab power began to diminish as Johnston clamped down on its sale and transport. By 1895 Sultan Mlozi must have realised that a net was slowly closing in around him, and despite the enormity of his crimes it is impossible not to feel a grudging sympathy for him. For we see Mlozi now as an anachronism, as part of a system which, having endured for many centuries, had suddenly become out of date. But he shows no inclination to compromise with the new times and somehow one knows for certain that Mlozi will oppose them to the end of his life. At least in one respect he could count himself better off than before: Fotheringham, his apparently invulnerable enemy, lay dead of fever, and the improvised fort at Karonga which somehow had become symbolic of the white men's threat to his way of life, was now garrisoned by ordinary mortals.

The old ingratiating urbanity which had charmed Johnston in 1889, and which we can still see reflected in the photograph taken of Mlozi at that time, had vanished by 1895, and when

Karonga Fort, 1891

Lugard's shelling of Msalema's stockade

Johnston came up on the *Ilala* to renew their treaty, he was repulsed, and in reply to a message of goodwill received only a curt note which read: 'The British . . . have closed my route to the coast: very well, I will close their road to Tanganyika.' It was in effect a renewed declaration of war, and then, as though his attitude might still be misunderstood, Mlozi seized and severely flogged one of the white missionaries working in Nkondeland.

And so towards the end of 1895 Commissioner Johnston and Sultan Mlozi found themselves in a position where one or other of them would have to give in—and neither was prepared to do so. It is as though an intermission has ended and now the curtain goes up on the final act of a long-drawn-out drama. What makes that last act so very different from all the previous fumbling attempts to subdue Mlozi is the competent swiftness and sense of urgency that attends it. Of course, Johnston was by far the most intelligent of Mlozi's antagonists and he had many more resources than his predecessors in the way of soldiers and guns. Indeed his only real problem was to find a way of concentrating his four hundred disciplined Indian and African troops so rapidly and unexpectedly at Karonga that the Arabs would have no time to call for reinforcements from their allies. It was merely a question of logistics and Johnston went to work on it with quiet efficiency. All the British ships on the lake were commandeered while the Germans were obliging enough to lend him their commodious gunboat, the *Hermann von Wissmann*. By the third week in November, 1895, no less than six steamers lay at their moorings in the Shiré, opposite the newly-named Fort Johnston, waiting for the expeditionary force to march in. As soon as the troops were safely aboard (their officers by now had nicknamed them 'The Ever Victorious Army') the little fleet slipped away in the gathering dusk, heading northwards. It was the evening of November 24th, 1895.

Exactly a week later the 'Ever Victorious Army', drenched by torrential rain and in pitch darkness, began trudging through the mud of the Nkonde plain. One contingent made directly for Mpata; the remaining soldiers quietly took up positions opposite Msalema and Kopa Kopa, and with daylight opened fire on their stockades. Only a few scattered shots were fired in reply. Then the Arabs streamed off in the direction of their final fastness, Mpata. By that afternoon Johnston's entire force had been deployed on the red plain around the town, hardly incommoded by the erratic firing from the ancient muzzle-loading cannons peering out from the loopholes in its bastions. All next day a battery of British guns kept up a continuous drum-fire on Mpata; two sorties the Arabs made were repulsed without much difficulty. On the third day a white flag went up above the stockade, and Johnston, revelling in his martial role of a Commander-in-Chief, breathlessly watched the gate open and a familiar figure step out and stand beneath the wall. It was Mlozi. It is difficult now to be certain what exactly was in his mind; what we do know is that he could be heard shouting for Johnston to come and talk to him.

In his books Johnston assures us that he went off confidently towards the Arab, intending to hold a parley, but someone ran up to warn him that Mlozi had a dagger concealed in his *khanzu* and intended to knife him and drag him as a hostage into the town. Johnston accordingly halted a little short of the wall and began a rather absurd shouted conversation. Mlozi, it seems, asked for terms, and Johnston's high falsetto voice could be heard affirming in Swahili that although the Arabs' lives would be spared, he could promise nothing more. Mlozi then turned on his heel calling out he must consult his friend Kopa Kopa, and re-entered the town; the moment he was inside he took a pot-shot at the group of British officers. Clearly the negotiations were at an end.

Johnston seems to have been more than usually highly-strung that day. He was desperately concerned about reports of the approach of a large Arab relieving force, and persuaded himself that unless he dealt quickly with Mlozi he would be caught in a trap between two Moslem armies. Accordingly his artillery was ordered up to closer range and proceeded to fire no less than three hundred shells over open sights into the town. Soon vivid orange flames were to be seen racing through Mpata and a high column of black and yellow smoke rose over it. Yet still there was no sign of surrender. Then Johnston had another of his strokes of luck; a deserter came in and pointed out a tall stone house which he said was Mlozi's 'palace'. The bombardment was promptly concen-

trated on it and by chance Mlozi himself was wounded. This was
the turning point of the action. The deadlock that had lasted seven
years snapped suddenly. All at once the town gate flew open and
an enormous mob of fighting men surged out and made straight
for Johnston's startled troops. One can be fairly certain that
this was less a counter-attack than the escape from a doomed
town of a panic-stricken mob looking for somebody who would
accept its surrender. But that third day of December, 1895, after
all, was intended to be the glorious climax of Johnston's career
and it would have been less than human (and certainly less than
Johnstonian) to allow posterity believe it had terminated in a tame
capitulation; besides, the Indian troops lost their heads and began
to fire on the disordered rabble before them and their behaviour
had to be excused later in the Commissioner's official reports. And
so the disordered Arab flight from Mpata is usually represented
in contemporary accounts as a dangerous sortie in force that was
beaten back only after stern hand-to-hand fighting in the familiar
Victorian style, while the grisly massacre which followed the
arrival on the scene of a motley crowd of 'friendlies' armed with
spears and old flintlocks is transformed into the tireless pursuit of
a stubborn enemy that only ended after nightfall. Thus Hanna's
authoritative account of the action reads: 'The Arabs in despera-
tion made a furious sortie: the Sikhs drove them back to the
stockade, seized the chance to scramble over it, and mastered the
town.' Johnston's biographer, who must have known the facts,
simply speaks vaguely of 'another sortie' which met the Indians
as they stormed towards a breach in the town wall. Johnston
himself has given us two rather different versions of the affair.
The first, appearing in 1897, is in the true Victorian jargon and
reads: 'A furious sortie took place—a sortie which elicited from us
no pity because it was almost as much an impetuous attack on our
own positions. The bullets simply whistled through the air, and
it was marvellous that we did not meet with more casualties;
but our soldiers fought splendidly, and strange to say the timid
Wankonde also came to the front and between two and three
hundred of Mlozi's men were shot or speared. . . . Our attempts to
repulse the sortie brought the Sikhs close to the walls, and somehow or other . . . they scaled the ramparts.' His other account

appears in the autobiography Johnston published much later in 1923. This reads: 'At last, on the fifth day, hearing rumours of an advance from the south of an Arab relieving force, we decided to finish the business by assaulting the town through the breach our artillery was to make in the double walls. We began by shelling vigorously a portion of the town where Mlozi was reputed to dwell in an Arab house of stone. Then we attacked the stockade on its eastern side with the whole of our force. After we had breached the walls and were on the point of entering, we were almost over-whelmed by an enormous surge of the besieged Arabs, their native soldiers and slaves. The rush was so great and desperate that it not only checked our assault, but held us up. The Sikh soldiers or their officers took it to be an assault in force, and the men lay on the ground while the officers in standing up were almost overwhelmed by the fugitives (as they turned out to be).'

'They were shouting the cry of surrender "Aman! Aman!" but some of them remained armed, and we had to shout to them to surrender their arms or they would be shot. One Arab made straight for me, not dropping his gun, and I had to shoot him through the head with my revolver, as he seemed all "berserk", distraught either with panic or war fury. Hundreds of fugitives, however, were making for our camp, which practically had no defences, as we were throwing the whole of our forces on the attack. However, we could not turn back to see what they were doing, and as a matter of fact they were surrendering to the few of our servants and camp followers who were left behind.'

There it is. One has to make up one's own mind whether the slaughter that followed Johnston's bombardment of Mpata was justified or not. But there is no doubt it was decisive. The 'counter-charge' uncovered the Arab stockade and Johnston's troops stormed into a town which was utterly empty of fighting men. Only cripples and idiots were to be seen, and shackled slaves whimpering, not with relief, but for fear of being eaten by the white men. The sepoys passed charred corpses of cats in the midst of the burnt remains of many rats, and stepped over the mutilated human bodies that lay everywhere about the streets. They probed slowly through a maze of lanes, looting, shooting, killing and kicking shrieking chickens out of their way until they came to the central open space of the town where lay the bodies of seventy Wankonde hostages only recently speared or bludgeoned to death. But of Mlozi there was no sign. Johnston himself, we read, trudged back to his camp in disgust, dejected because without Mlozi his victory was incomplete. Then the sound of distant cheering halted him, and he turned to see a white-robed figure being dragged towards him. It was Mlozi whom someone had found hiding in a cellar below his house. Johnston realised then that he had won after all, and we can imagine him staring almost with elation at the Arab prisoner whose appearance he has depicted in one of his books: '. . . his hands tied behind his back. . . . There is a slight wound on his forehead; his face bears the expression of a caged wolf, his pale yellow skin is livid with pain, fear, and hatred. He has lost his round, white cap or fez, or turban, and his bald head looks mean and out of keeping with his careful clothes, which, though soiled in warfare, are still neat and presentable. Round his neck in a dirty cloth bag hangs a copy of the Koran'.

But even now Johnston was still obsessed with the possibility of the second Arab army attacking him. (When it did arrive it turned out to be a mob of supplicants coming in to surrender or, as they put it, 'to catch the Queen's leg'.) And so his account with Mlozi was settled with indecent haste next day. One feels that Lugard would have managed the affair rather differently and somehow contrived to give it at least a semblance of legality. But Johnston merely summoned a panel of Wankonde chiefs to judge a captive who contemptuously refused to plead his case. 'What is the good?' the Sultan asked. 'These people are resolved that I should die. My hour is come.' And there, outside Mpata, he takes on a strange and moving dignity on this last evening of his life. Inevitably Mlozi was condemned to death and they hanged him from a tree looking toward his smouldering capital. A curious story went the rounds of the London clubs a little later that Johnston had entertained Mlozi to a champagne dinner before his execution. It was untrue, of course, but scarcely more bizarre than the incident which did occur when Johnston, just before he left Mpata, received warm congratulations from the Sultan's brother for having given Mlozi 'such a beautiful hanging'.

The soldiers marched away next morning and the dust settled slowly over the Nkonde plain. Fotheringham's ghost must have applauded the peace and the sight of the neat round huts going up again and the people moving in to hack away at the encroaching bush and lay out the banana groves in their old straight places. Johnston, meanwhile, was hurrying back to Zomba to write his official report about the conclusion of the Arab war (he would have been disheartened to know that Lord Rosebery's only relevant comment on his writing was an unkind 'stupendously long'). On New Year's Day he read that his conquest had been suitably recognised with the bestowal of a K.C.B., and now at last he was 'Sir Harry'. In due course the new knight was summoned to Court and seemed only a little abashed by his reception. 'Soon after reaching London,' he writes in his inimitable style, 'I was directed to proceed to Windsor to be knighted by the Queen, and be given by her the K.C.B. which she had conferred on me at the beginning of 1896. This meant, of course, donning my uniform and proceeding to Paddington to place myself under the direction of Sir Albert Woods of the Heralds' Office.' (Sir Albert, we learn at this point in a withering footnote, was 'very uncertain about his h's. He did not seem to care whether he stuck them on or took them off.') Sir Harry goes on: 'I had the happy accident at Paddington station of meeting Lady Lytton and Lady Loch, and travelling with them to Windsor. I think Lady Lytton by then was a widow, and had been given a place at Court. Not long after reaching Windsor Castle, I was admitted to the Queen's presence. The Duke of Connaught was standing by her to assist in presenting the candidates for decorations. The Queen was seated on a small throne or a high chair in a very tiny cabinet, one, I think, associated with Queen Anne. She held a bare sword in her hand. I knelt and was lightly tapped with the accolade. Unfortunately the Duke of Connaught had become mixed in his account of the candidates for various distinctions, so that he confused me with some military officer, who had been severely wounded in India or the Sudan, and the Queen looked at me with lack-lustre eyes and down-drooping mouth, displaying little or no interest. I did not know what to do, and feared that something untoward might occur if I corrected the Prince in the

Queen's presence and reclaimed my proper personality; so I had to listen to a few words of chilly condolence with regard to the non-existent wound, which, as the Queen said, with a flicker of recognition, seemed to have left no trace in my appearance or my alertness—and then at a given signal withdrew from the Royal presence.'

And on this note of anticlimax the slave war of the lake ended. Thereafter Sir Harry's fortunes began to decline. For there was nothing half-hearted about people's opinion of this little man: either they admired him immensely or they loathed him, and it seemed that most of his contemporaries fell into the second category. After short tours in Tunis and Uganda, no consular or diplomatic post quite suitable to his talents ever seemed to fall vacant, and at the early age of forty-three 'King Johnston' found himself pensioned off with a paltry £500 a year. The remaining twenty-six years of his life were passed in the relatively modest role of an unpopular author of somewhat 'risqué' books. Occasionally he would leap very briefly into public notice as an (invariably unsuccessful) Liberal candidate for parliamentary honours, and he won a little notoriety too in such varied capacities as an exponent of spelling reform (which resulted in the production of a 'fonetic alfabet'), as the designer of a new-style Union Jack (predictably in black, yellow and white), as the discoverer of the okapi and as a promoter of tourism in Ireland (into which he gravely proposed to introduce bears and wolves as an added attraction to the scenery). A martyr to hypochondria, Sir Harry lived through the First World War, into modern times, still writing his interminable books which hardly anybody read, and always talking of the great day when he directed the capture of Sultan Mlozi's impregnable stronghold at Mpata, until during that month when the whole world was applauding a young aviator named Lindbergh, Johnston, who by now no less than Mlozi had become a symbol of a lost and irretrievable age, joined him in death.

Part Four

AFTERNOON AND EVENING

THE *BWANAS*

After the execution of Mlozi, the sound of gunfire died away across the Lake Nyasa, and she turned gratefully to catch the warmth of the midday sun. But the lake was subtly different now; she had been caught up in the scramble for Africa, and as the tattered banners of Moslem slavers came down along its shores, the imperial flags of Germany and Portugal and Britain were run up in their place. On the large wall maps of Europe's Chancelleries the lake now looked like part of an enormous jig-saw puzzle; previously a unifying factor in the lives of the Amaravi, now she was herself divided into three, and the lake people found themselves separated from each other by international boundaries drawn across her shores and water.

Nowadays, when our attitude towards colonialism has changed and Europe is withdrawing with almost indecent haste from Africa, it is difficult to realise that only the span of a single life separates us from the time when half a dozen western states were competing together for a place in the African sun. And whatever may have been the ethics of the way they carved up the continent like a joint of beef, one cannot help being impressed by the speed with which they did it. In 1875 only about a tenth of Africa was ruled by white men, yet at the turn of the century nearly all of it had become a sort of European dependency, and *Bwana* Whiteman was lording it from Cape to Cairo.

Occasionally (and this was the case with Nyasaland) European expansion into Africa was initiated by a passionate desire to form oases of Christian example in that untamed and separate continent. But besides spiritual elevation, the Industrial Revolution released other exuberant energies which found convenient outlets in the 'dark continent'; they included a hankering for 'prestige colonies', a fidgety impatience to occupy strategically important ground (if only to deny it to a rival power), and an eagerness to 'peg out' claims to raw materials and future markets—although most African colonies turned out to be economic liabilities in the end.

But what remains so remarkable about this, the most gigantic land grab in history, is the way that as its jingo frontiers advanced to meet each other in Africa, so it gained an increasing momentum of its own. Sometimes when dusty columns of soldiers, bearing different flags, met in remote and squalid villages with names like Angra Pequena and Fashoda, the repercussions had *The Times* thundering, and set highly-strung Frenchmen singing the *Marseillaise* outside the Chambers, or indignant Germans demonstrating under the Brandenburg Gate. And often they brought Europe to the very brink of war.

The partition of Africa may have been conducted chaotically at first, but with the signing of the Berlin Act in 1885, it was regulated to some extent. For this agreement allowed the frock-coated diplomats of Europe to adjust their respective appetites for slices of African territory with at least a show of co-operation and cordiality; after 1885 instead of angry recriminations round the conference table, there were smiles and gracious bows, while hands which previously had stabbed acrimonious fingers at disputed places on the map, now politely proffered rulers to foreign colleagues to draw their straight frontier lines across the blank spaces of a continent. The cartographers were delighted now to splash their patriotic browns and greens and reds about the maps without fear that they would be erased following some demarche a week later, and the fast-moving pro-consuls could begin those impressive swings through Africa which only halted long enough to induce yet another reluctant chief to scrawl a wavering cross on the papers held before them.

The airy way in which Africa was divided into colonies, protectorates and spheres of interest without the slightest regard for tribal boundaries or the wishes of its people was nowhere better illustrated than in the country round Lake Nyasa. There international frontiers were suddenly clamped down on homogeneous tribes like the Angoni and the Wankonde. But at least Britain's decision to declare a protectorate over the Shiré Highlands and the south-western lake shore as far as the 11th parallel was due to a creditable anxiety to nourish and protect the seeds of

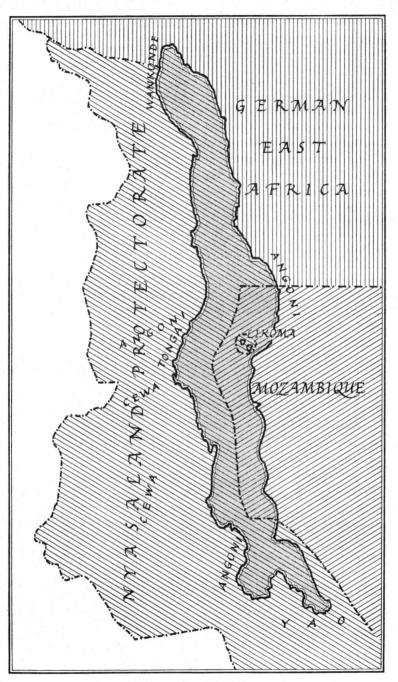

The partition of Lake Nyasa

Christianity already planted there. Even so it was only reached reluctantly and after the markings on Lord Salisbury's map had come to life in the disconcerting forms of indignant mission deputations and apprehensive delegations of planters, which public opinion made it impossible to ignore.

Naked chauvinism, however, induced the Kaiser, who burned with a fateful eagerness to enlarge his empire on the British model, to annex the Nyasa country beyond the 11th parallel. But after England ceded Heligoland to Germany in exchange for Zanzibar, he obligingly withdrew his frontier northwards as far as the Songwe River, and another long stretch of unwanted lake shore fell under England's rule. This still left one hundred and forty miles of the lake's eastern coast unappropriated, and it was conceded by the Powers to Portugal, not without loud protestations from the Universities' Mission whose particular parish it had been, although they were slightly mollified when the offshore islands of the Likoma group were exempted from the award, and remained a watery British enclave in the middle of the lake.

The Portuguese had never occupied any part of the lake shore effectively before, but, conscious of their priority in the local colonial field, they accepted the award as very much less than their due. Nevertheless, three white officers were dispatched at once to rule the new demesne and were promptly clubbed to death for believing that their official duties included raping the more comely local girls. (W. P. Johnson, to whom we owe this morsel of lake scandal, adds drily 'the Portuguese describe them as martyrs'.) Not until 1900 did the Portuguese become firmly established beside the lake, and even then their new subjects did not appear to be particularly impressed for we learn (again from Johnson) that they were known unflatteringly as 'cocks' on account of 'their offensive gallantries with women', and that they also gained a less justified reputation for witchcraft because one pioneer, who had blameless leanings towards anthropology, 'collected the bones of men'.

The German empire-builders, on the other hand, went about their imperial duties with true Teutonic zeal, and by 1892 they were in firm possession of their section of the lake shore. Today they are remembered there with a curious blend of loathing and respect as 'the people of the twenty-five', since that was the minimum number of lashes they imposed for any misdemeanour.* These Herrenvolk of the lake believed in keeping their African subjects in their proper places—which meant either in prison or working as labourers on their estates—and as the Prussian lash imposed Prussian discipline, the lake shore began to groan with its people's misery. Inevitably they erupted in a series of revolts which culminated in the bloody Maji Maji Rising in 1905. Now Lake Nyasa watched strange columns of Sudanese and Polynesian soldiers devastating the surrounding country, and sometimes halting long enough for a few more foreign genes to mingle in Amaravi blood. Predictably the Angoni were the last tribe to submit to the Germans in 1906; by then 120,000 Africans had died in the rising. When at last the survivors returned to their ruined villages and devastated gardens, it seemed to the lake people that of all the horrors they had ever been called on to bear the worst of all was to be ruled by Germans.

It is fashionable nowadays to condemn colonial rule in Africa as a long-drawn-out and unpardonable crime, but there is no doubt that so far as her Nyasa subjects were concerned, Britain did far more good to them than harm. Their interests were always considered to be paramount. As early as 1893 we find that 'arch imperialist', Sir Harry Johnston, assuring Whitehall, 'we do not come here necessarily to subjugate; we come to protect and instruct'. And that was the official attitude in Nyasaland right from the start. Yet although the attainment of self-government was regarded as the ultimate objective, it was generally conceded it would take many many years before the Nyasa people (having in the meantime been transformed into black editions of demo-cratic Britons) would be fit for independence. And without question the British deserve credit for ending tribal warfare and stamping out the slave trade (although it is incredible but true

---

* German East Africa was called a 'flogging colony'. A single magistrate in the capital once imposed 1,800 lashes in one day.

that the last domestic slave was not released until 1956), as well as for having established such security that the native population of the Protectorate trebled during their rule. On the other hand the Government was autocratic and completely failed to provide any legal means for its authority to be criticised, although nearly everyone agreed that this was a modest price for its subjects to pay for release from perpetual fear.

This is all very true and very fine, yet looking back over the seventy-odd years of British rule in the lake country one becomes aware that a splendid opportunity was missed of building up a plural society based on merit instead of race. For though the Government saw a duty before it, it never recognised a challenge, and in consequence poverty was nearly as universal when it abdicated as it had been in the eighteen-nineties, and the Nyasa peasants in the nuclear age still remained tied to a primitive hoe and panga economy. Moreover, the white men, having torn up the ancient texture of tribal life, made no all-out effort to develop the more worthy aspects of Bantu culture and fuse them with their own institutions so that a new nation, drawing its strength from both, might be evolved. Instead the Africans' only path to influence and wealth seemed to lie in the studied mimicry of the white men's way of life.

Perhaps this was inevitable; although modest sums for the country's development were voted by the British Government every year, and the Central African Protectorate grew into Nyasa-land, and the Commissioner was replaced by a plumed Governor, and the Tanganyika coastline of the lake became British after 1914, there was never enough money to provide proper medical services and adequate educational facilities for the lake people. Even so a more enlightened approach might have avoided the acceptance and perpetuation of the enormous gulf that lay between the lake's rulers and their subjects. The Africans, when the white men first arrived in Central Africa, were so dazzled by their fantastic affluence and accomplishments that they accepted them at once as a superior people—and the authorities found it suited them to maintain that impression. It followed that the trim Residents and District Commissioners who governed the Land of the Lake for the next seventy years saw the Africans as a

Mlozi's stockade, from a sketch by Harry Johnston

The Rev. John Chilembwe and family

people who only needed manipulation and protection, and these they provided very well. But few of them made any real attempt to identify their own lives with those of their subjects as Livingstone and Johnson had done. Instead these white officials were essentially birds of passage who looked forward to an eventual perch in the Home Counties with a pension and possibly a C.M.G. That was the trouble; the *Bwanas* were in the country but not really a part of it. Admittedly they ruled it better than it had ever been ruled before, and with a fairness, tolerance and incorruptibility that was the envy of other dependencies, but long after 'outposts of Empire' and 'the white man's burden' had become music hall jokes and the veld had ceased to be a favourite background for European heroism, these Bourbons of modern times still believed their colonial world to be immutable and would continue to provide gentlemanly employment for generations of their kinsmen to come.

These pro-consuls of the lake are now an extinct species, not yet removed far enough from us in time to be seen in clear perspective, nor yet so close as to seem familiar. They remind one of those slightly grotesque fishes seen swimming about behind the thick glass panels of an aquarium, obsolescent and therefore strangely fascinating; tantalisingly close, yet withdrawn and impossible to touch. But because they ruled the lake for two generations, the *Bwanas* of Nyasaland repay a little study.

Their upbringing had made them passionately devoted to animals, outdoor sports, and the protection of backward peoples (roughly in that order). Most of them came from 'good' county families; they obeyed a rigid code of manners, and were punctilious about shaving. They believed quite genuinely that those 'lesser breeds without the law' who had been gathered into the British fold were remarkably lucky, and they even detected a pleasing sense of some divine purpose in the fortuitous way their jewelled lake had been added to the Imperial crown.

When they were not 'on *ulendo*' touring their districts (followed by a procession of porters whose number bore relation to their master's place in the Protectorate's hierarchy), these officials worked with a quite unusual degree of earnestness in government 'Bomas' built at a dignified distance from their subjects' squalid hovels, and still the most impressive architectural features of the lake shore. The earliest Residents pinned up pictures of the Great White Queen on the great white-washed walls of their offices; then they set about taxing their subjects, gaoling those too poor to pay, and sitting in slightly uneasy judgement over the interminable law suits that, with the prohibition of internecine fighting, increasingly absorbed the energies of the lake people. At intervals of approximately twenty years they were replaced by apparently identical figures, and presently a photograph of a bearded king seated before a microphone appeared beside the faded print of his grandmother. Otherwise nothing seemed to change.

The *Bwanas* moved about the lake shore unarmed, unguarded and with Olympian confidence in the superiority of all British institutions. They were studiously genteel and rather pathetically *au fait* with events at 'home'. They discussed the Royal Family with intimacy and invariable respect; no society scandal nor review of the London stage escaped their attention and they were only six weeks behind with *The Times*. They found a peculiar merit in their very immolation from the outside world, and most of them became fanatical in their devotion to the lake. Its charm and protean mysteries engulfed and fascinated them; because the real and the imagined met and mingled about them there to such a high degree, they lost the solid sense of things, and soon they were never really happy far away from Nyasa. Their infatuation was increased by the undoubted bureaucratic advantages of being posted to the lake: they had no contact there with the detribalised native misfits of the towns; instead they saw the African only at his best—as a loyal servant, magnificent hunter, or skilful boatman; they were far removed, too, from the nagging problems of their colleagues in the Shiré Highlands who spent most of their time pacifying white planters or evicting black squatters; moreover, they were comfortably distant from protocol-conscious Zomba where a crotchety Governor penned offensive marginalia on official documents, where unimaginative heads of departments knit brows together over problems of the past and present (though rarely of the future), and where punctilious ladies left cards, played bridge, swapped recipes or got up 'charitable affairs for the natives'.

After a few 'tours' on the lake some of its white votaries became mildly (and some even wildly) eccentric; they behaved like Saki characters who had strayed from Mayfair into the bush and found it suited them. They depended on their servants more perhaps than any other people of modern times, and depended probably even more on the four gallon petrol tins called 'debbies' in which their meals were cooked, and the water heated for the ritual of their evening bath in oval galvanised tubs (whose proper places in more civilised lands is the laundry); in other ubiquitous debbies, too, the euphemistically named 'night-soil' of their domestic establishments was daily borne away through the pre-dawn darkness by a furtive file of prisoners. It seemed perfectly in keeping with the peculiar genre of their lives that each evening was ushered in by the ragged notes of the Boma bugler and the ceremonial lowering of the Union Jack—and usually a polite enquiry from the D.C. or the Doctor as to whether they were free for sundowners (and perhaps poker dice) a little later on.

It was a singular way of life that was at once rewarding, picturesque, delightfully carefree, and yet curiously inaccessible to new ideas. But time which had stood still for so long beside the lake began to roll forwards again during the nineteen-fifties and suddenly it elbowed the white pro-consuls from off the stage and left them in the wings gazing a little bemusedly at their successors. Today only the vast houses they inhabited remain to remind us of this vanished race of men and women in places like Chinteche and Kota Kota, Karonga and Nkata Bay. They look thoroughly out of place, like European fists shaken in the face of Africa, but in them the memory of the *Bwanas* is still warm.

Even now these buildings have not quite lost their small air of condescension and in them one half expects to see their old masters come walking in through the door, throw down a sun-helmet and express surprise at finding the present inmates, their late clerks and black assistants, intruding here. Built with a curious combination of Victorian decorum and the spaciousness of the Deep South, they frown today like historic monuments from small bedraggled gardens where once trim lawns, tended by gangs of convicts, kept the African bush at bay. Around them stretch deep, shady verandahs from which mouldering lines of horned trophies still stare glassily across the lake. From these verandahs—the *khondhes* of Nyasaland—doors lead into small dining-rooms, which even in their hey-day were hideous with their brown granolithic floors and the plain furniture provided by a frugal Government. All the affection (and affectation) of the white exiles was lavished on their lounges. There, leopard skins jostled Persian rugs and bright native mats on the floor; college photographs and an ancestor or two adorned the walls; ormolu shelves groaned under the weight of paper-backs and ivory carvings and silver challenge cups, together with at least one photograph of the 'Dona' in her débutante feathers; low tables stood everywhere, laden with offerings of *Punch* and *Argosy* and *Country Life* until at sundown the magazines were swept away to make room for cut-glass and syphons at the ready, and Haig at less than 10s. a bottle.

But there was one drawback to the lordly lives of the white masters of the lake—the sun. It was a watchful and constant enemy. Every new recruit to Nyasaland was sternly warned against the 'peculiar vibrations' it sent rattling round the white man's brain to its ultimate derangement. And so from early morning until the stroke of four in the afternoon, no one dreamt of venturing out of doors without first clapping an enormous sola topi on their heads. These curious items of headgear were decidedly unbecoming, but somehow they became the totem sign of colonial rule on Lake Nyasa. Many varieties were to be seen. One particularly ugly pudding-basin pattern was favoured by lady missionaries (who wore them horizontal), and senior officials (who wore them jauntily aslant); brown bee-hived affairs were the status-symbol of the Boma clerk, while D.C.'s and big game hunters sported khaki pig-sticking models which somehow managed to bring a touch of Simla to the lake. But most prestigious of all were the puggaried rococo coal-scuttles with feathered hackles that framed the features of Governors and K.A.R. officers, and which carried with them a flavour of Gunga Din and the British square at Abu Klea. Childish necks were considered to be even more vulnerable to the demon sun than adult skulls, and mothers hung them round with ugly squares of red flannel, which luckily was in good supply since prodigious quantities had been imported by the old timers for use as cholera belts and spine pads.

The hot and happy years of the twentieth century drifted away past Lake Nyasa with only the noises of a muddled native rising, two strange battles, and an inexplicable disaster that overtook the largest ship ever to be launched upon her waters, to disturb her afternoon siesta. Then suddenly the sola topi—that very symbol of Empire—vanished from the scene. For sunstroke had joined the vapours, chlorosis, and ptomaine poisoning, as another of those diseases that had never really existed after all. Now rows of unsold 'Bombay Bowlers' gathered dust on the shelves of Indian stores as their proprietors wrung brown hands in shame over stock they could not sell, and up in the *Bwanas'* big white houses the battered companions of a hundred *ulendos* were sadly re-interred in the strange, speckled tin cases from which they had been extracted so many pompous 'tours' ago, and from which they would only emerge again to grace an occasional game of pro-consular charades. And as the *Bwanas* began to move about the lake shore uncovered, they seemed to have been cut down in mystique as well as in size.

Certainly the passing of the sola topi coincided with the withdrawal of European influence from the lake. Neither seemed to be wanted there any longer, and as the sun went down over Nyasa's golden era of colonial rule, the shadows of African nationalism lengthened across the water. But before we listen to the white men singing their *nunc dimittis* beside the lake, we must pause for a moment to consider its singular twentieth-century battles and the tragedy of Florence Bay. Each event was only a small thread in the tapestry of the lake's history, but when they occurred they seemed there to be of almost homeric proportions.

REBELLION

Looking back on it afterwards from the facile vantage point of hindsight, one can see that the first pale dusk of the approaching night began to settle over Nyasa when a Tongan tribesman named Elliott Kamwana returned to his home at Bandawe from the South African goldfields in the September of 1908. At the time no one took very much notice of him. Yet for the lake it was a turning point in its history: Kamwana was the forerunner of nationalism, and the harbinger of *Kwacha*—the 'dawn'.

As a boy, Kamwana had been educated by the Livingstonia missionaries, but in South Africa he had come under the influence of an 'independent' protestant divine, the Rev. Joseph Booth. Booth had been well known in Nyasaland: he set up his first mission station in the Shiré Highlands as early as 1892, and the following year began preaching along the lake shore. He was quite unlike any other of the Nyasa missionaries. Booth was a gaunt-looking man with a trim beard and a severe expression; he had the eyes of an Old Testament prophet, and a pointer's nose for scenting injustices—and a furious insistence on remedying them. He undoubtedly had vision; but he had very little balance. Booth was extravagantly opinionated and absurdly contentious, and perhaps it was these qualities that made him change his religious denomination about as frequently as a modern business executive will change his car. It was inevitable that he should quarrel with all his missionary colleagues—and with the authorities as well; it was inevitable too that he would eventually be deported from Nyasaland, although in fact nearly twelve years passed before he could be induced to leave. This occurred in 1902. Since then every possible epithet has been attached to his name there and every iniquity ascribed to him. But however capricious and unpredictable Booth may have been, he never deviated from one principle, and that can be best summed up by the slogan he was himself fond of using and claimed to have invented—'Africa for the Africans'. When Kamwana swam into his orbit, Booth happened to have become a disciple of 'Pastor' Charles Taze Russell, a Pittsburgh draper whose character was not unlike his own. But there was this difference: although Booth was always short of money, Russell's ventures into evangelism rarely failed to pay him a handsome dividend; indeed his latest foundation, 'The Watch Tower Bible and Tract Society', had proved to be a very profitable business indeed.

Kamwana became an even more enthusiastic convert to the Watch Tower movement than his mentor, and certainly he proved a most effective spokesman for it when he returned to Bandawe in 1908. His fiery style of preaching drew enormous crowds to the open-air services he held up and down the lake shore, and afterwards his congregation would line up in their hundreds for baptism at his hands. Kamwana proclaimed the second advent of the Lord and of a resurrection day when the dead would all be raised. The ungodly, he went on, would be reconsigned to their graves after judgement, but the 'elect' (by whom it was plain he meant his own followers) would enjoy an everlasting messianic heaven. He further prophesied that Christ's second coming was to be expected in the October of 1914, but the exact date, it seemed, depended to some extent on his listeners, for it could only occur after they had sparked off a revolt against the established order in Nyasaland. This eloquent lake-shore Gabriel never failed in his addresses to pander to African atavism by advocating a return to old tribal customs and the rejection of the teachings of the Livingstonia missionaries (especially those concerned with sexual restraint). Usually he ended his sermons by fulminating against the imposition of Government taxes; refusal to pay them he suggested would not involve much risk, since in the new age that was imminent there would be no place for Europeans in the country. We know that on one occasion while preaching at Chinteche he pointed to the D.C.'s house and shouted 'these people you will see no more'. His excited congregations learnt too that although they would enjoy the lives their ancestors had known, they could expect a few agreeable refinements, for Kamwana would go on to explain: 'We shall build our own ships, make our own powder and make or import our guns.' It was a delectable prospect. It was also (in the opinion of the Government) seditious, and Kamwana was abruptly banished from the lake shore until the date of his Resurrection Day had safely passed.

With his disappearance from the scene the momentum of the Watch Tower movement slackened in Nyasaland. This was not entirely due to Kamwana's exile. Booth's convictions had suddenly readapted themselves to the better endowed tenets of the Seventh Day Baptist Church and his support had been withdrawn. And the founder himself was unable to devote all the time he would have wished to his lake-shore following: for, most unfortunately, Mr. Russell had become involved in divorce proceedings on account of alleged misconduct in Pittsburg with ladies of his congregation, and worse followed when an ugly scandal blew up following the exposure of his promotion of a profitable line of 'miracle wheat' seed; these set-backs temporarily deflated Pastor Russell and we hear no more about him in Nyasaland. But Kamwana had already made his mark; 'Ethiopianism' had appeared for the first time beside the lake, and the shadow of 1959 had begun to fall across its waters.

Ethiopianism—the development by Africans of their own independent Churches—was a movement that, although carrying political implications, primarily set itself the task of reconciling Christian and pagan beliefs. Some orthodox rites, like baptism, were retained and even given an exotic emphasis of their own, but there was also a passionate repudiation of the Church's moral discipline. It was a natural reaction to the impact of an alien culture and religion on Africans, and because it was natural it was soon bound to appear again in the lake country. When it did so it came as a far more serious threat to the authorities than Kamwana's apocalyptic prophesies, and by the uncanny harmony of history it erupted at Magomero where the first armed clash between white men and Yao had taken place over fifty years before. And by an even more singular coincidence, the Europeans chiefly affected by it were Dr. Livingstone's own kinsmen and descendants.

Magomero, lying in the shadow of Chiradzulu, is one of those places where almost anything might happen. It became a haunted eerie scene of slow disintegration after 1862 when the missionaries withdrew from the station which Dr. Livingstone had helped them 'set up'. Soon, only a heap of broken sticks remained of the church where Bishop Mackenzie had preached; the defensive stockade beside the river collapsed, and thick bush took over the site of Nyasaland's first Christian mission. Even poor Burrup's grave was desecrated and, in unconscious anticipation of later events, his skull was carried away by a witch doctor to use as magic. The slow horror of the Yao man-hunt then coiled itself round the countryside again, while in 1884 and succeeding years Magomero was pillaged afresh by the Angoni. Robert Cleland who preached in the district four years later has described how his services would be disturbed repeatedly by cries of 'Ngondo'—war—as yet another armed party was sighted in the hills. Even after Johnston had established some semblance of order in Nyasaland, Mount Chiradzulu remained the lair of hold-up men and bandits until a series of punitive expeditions destroyed them.

In 1893, with the establishment of more settled conditions, an enormous tract of land round Magomero was bought by Mr. Bruce, a Scottish businessman who had married Agnes, Dr. Livingstone's favourite daughter. Their son, Alexander Livingstone Bruce, settled at Magomero and worked hard to clear the bush and plant experimental crops of cotton and coffee. Within four years no less than three hundred square miles of Shiré country had been tamed, and another member of the Doctor's clan—Mr. William Jervis Livingstone—was installed as manager of the new estate.

Other planters took up land nearby, but none of them were particularly pleased when an African, the Reverend John Chilembwe, bought ninety-three acres adjoining the A. L. Bruce estate in 1900 and began building mud huts which he announced were to be the nucleus of a mission he had founded himself.

At this time John Chilembwe was nearly thirty years of age and he was already a man worth anybody's study. In him all the themes of the lake's history, both past and future seemed to meet and intermingle. But as with Kamwana and Booth, his character was later to be so besmirched and blackened by an embittered Government that even now it is difficult to form a clear impression of him. For unsuccessful rebels are rarely favoured with flattering obituaries, and there still remains a tendency to dismiss him as yet another African 'prophet' whose inadequate education had filled with absurd pretensions and an embroidery of civilisation that scarcely concealed his underlying barbarism. Indeed what is chiefly remembered today about Chilembwe, at least in European circles, is the voodoo-like manner in which he murdered his neighbour, Mr. Livingstone.

But there was much more to John Chilembwe than this single episode of escapism into savage vengeance, and the more one studies him, the more one's prejudice becomes replaced by a grudging sympathy. Even stranger is the way one observes him with that uneasy sense of precognition which psychiatrists call *déjà vu* and which remains very puzzling until the similarity of his career and Dr. Banda's is appreciated. He was certainly a man born before his time. A recent study of Chilembwe has been discerningly entitled *Independent African*, and those two words probably sum him up as well as any others, for there is a courageously recusant quality about him, and however out of place he may have seemed in Central Africa half a century ago, he would have found himself very much at home there today.

Various accounts have been given of Chilembwe's origins, but there is no reason to doubt the one he gave himself. His father, he states, was a Yao from Mangoche Hill at the southern end of the lake, who 'in the days of Dr. Livingstone' captured a Manganja woman during a slave foray. She fled from him, it seems to the highlands in the south, and his son John was born to her in 1871 at Sangano village near the foot of Mount Chiradzulu. Chilembwe later claimed less convincingly that his mother was of royal Maravi descent, and in America he went so far as to declare himself to be a prince whose name could be translated as 'man of destiny'.

As with Elliott Kamwana, the whole course of Chilembwe's life was changed by Joseph Booth. Soon after establishing his 'independent' mission near Blantyre, Booth had fallen foul not only of the Commissioner, Sir Alfred Sharpe (who summed him up unkindly as a 'shifty, undesirable, dangerous man') but of the neighbouring Scottish missionaries too (who believed he threatened their 'vested interests of the highest kind', by which, of course they meant their comfortable monopoly of Christian teaching in the area). And as he fulfilled his depressing role of the local mission field's *enfant terrible*, Booth, who was very conscious of all their titters and frowns, must have had many despondent moments; perhaps one of them was lightened by the pencilled note he received one morning which read: 'Dear Mr. Booth, You please carry me for God. I like to be your cook boy.' It was signed 'John Chilembwe'.

To such an appeal there could only be one answer: its writer was promptly engaged as a kitchen boy. Very soon he had become Booth's friend rather than his servant, for the youth sparkled with intelligence and had a jaunty eagerness to assume any sort of responsibility. Presently Chilembwe was promoted from the kitchen to the schoolroom, and then to the important dual post of Booth's interpreter and gun-bearer. And only a little later the seal was set on the two men's friendship when Chilembwe became Booth's first convert and received baptism at his hands on July 17th, 1893.

The next four years were busy ones for Chilembwe and his master. In a heady cloud of exaltation they roamed the lake country together, establishing subsidiary mission stations and preaching their slightly unusual brand of Christianity. Then suddenly and typically, the volatile Booth quarrelled with his supporters, abandoned his flocks, and took himself off to America to interest other societies in his schemes for Africa.

And what was more natural for him than to take his closest associate as a travelling companion, since John Chilembwe was not only living proof of the success of Booth's endeavours but later on would be able, at first hand, to deny the persistent Arab propaganda that the European's main object in coming to Africa was to kidnap its natives for food.

After fetching a wide circuit that took him to St. Helena, Liverpool and even Bradford, Chilembwe found himself in Virginia, U.S.A., moving in Negro circles which were highly critical of white men, and where there was a strong tradition of slave insurrection. It was a strange initiation into modern life for a lake Yao who had never left his country before. Very soon he found himself more at home among his new American coloured friends than travelling about the country as a white man's protégé. Rather ungratefully Chilembwe decided to cut himself adrift from Booth and, financed by a Negro church, he entered a seminary in a town with the somewhat ominous name of Lynchburg. The break must have been a painful one, especially for Booth, and perhaps one detects a note of bitterness in the words he used three years later to describe Chilembwe's graduation into 'a full-blown, round-collared, long-coated "Reverend" of the regulation type'. He might have added that Chilembwe had also become a 'full-blown' asthmatic.

In 1900, Chilembwe emerged from Lynchburg seminary and returned to Chiradzulu, clothed in unmistakable European clerical garb and determined to serve his own people. He was a man of consequence now, a Yao peasant who had successfully competed with Europeans on their chosen ground. And he seemed to be in funds; he chose his plot of land at Mbombwe, paid up £25 18s. 0d. for it on the spot, and there among the trees which once had lent their shade to Bishop Mackenzie the first buildings of his own establishment took shape. He called it the Ajawa Providence Industrial Mission. Presently a Mrs. Chilembwe appeared (no one ever seemed to know quite where from) as well as a couple of American Negro assistants. And he was self-supporting, for when financial succour from the States temporarily dried up, Chilembwe was able to eke out mission funds with hunting expeditions in the bush, and cash crops of cotton, coffee and tea as well as pepper and rubber. By 1912 he could boast of eight hundred 'converts' to his creed, while nearly one thousand local children were attending school; four permanent satellite churches had been built, as well as innumerable grass huts where services were held, while at Mbombwe itself an enormous brick church was nearly complete. This edifice which vacillated in design between Scottish Baronial and Byzantine, was a symbol of Chilembwe's success. And indeed it was something of a marvel, for nothing so substantial had ever been created by an African from the lake before. But it did not escape the uneasy notice of Chilembwe's European neighbours that in an emergency it might be used not only as a church but as a fortress too.

In the early years of his ministry at Mbombwe, we see

Chilembwe at his best. He was positively respectable, and if his life was somewhat spartan it was undeniably spiritually rewarding. He revelled in his work and seemed ready to turn his hand to almost anything. Besides preaching and teaching, he would move cheerfully from African Co-operative Society meetings to women's sewing classes, and from the organisation of boycotts on Indian stores to the planning of another building project. And most important of all, he was demonstrating for all the world to see that an African could be a match for the European in energy and imagination. It was a brilliant one-man show.

We possess several photographs of Chilembwe taken towards the end of this fruitful period of his life, and they perhaps reveal him to us better than any words can do. In one of them he appears with his wife and daughter. Mrs. Chilembwe looks the very mirror of the Lady of the Manse while the little girl is a pattern of Victorian childhood propriety. But it is John Chilembwe, with his thickset body crammed into a worsted suit, who rivets our attention, and it is his haunted eyes that particularly catch at our imagination. In them one sees all the puzzled uncertainty and over-sensitivity of the 'marginal man' in Africa. Yet no one would have believed at the time that these were the eyes of a killer.

But there was every reason for Chilembwe to be troubled and disillusioned when this particular photograph was taken. For even in the midst of his remarkable, unbelievable, achievement he possessed no inner peace of mind. He had cultivated the white man's way of life and had even insisted on his followers adopting European clothes and manners, yet now the planters, curiously cool to him before, positively snubbed and avoided him. Perhaps one can understand their attitude even if it cannot be entirely excused. So long as Chilembwe confined himself to proselytism they regarded him as a harmless (though not particularly edifying) example of an African who had done rather well for himself; but the moment he confronted the Europeans in something of the attitude of a black Keir Hardie (and with an exasperating tendency to contradiction), they saw him as a dangerous agitator. For, assiduous in his mission work, Chilembwe was no less assiduous in offering advice (spiced with a wealth of biblical metaphor) to the planters about the way they could improve

relations with their labour force. It even transpired that he was
critical too of certain aspects of Government policy, particularly
the recruitment of Africans to fight in an 'imperial' war against
the Mad Mullah of Somaliland. And so the white men in the
Magomero district turned slowly from suspicion of Chilembwe to
unrelenting animosity. And of them all William Jervis Livingstone made it his business to be as boorish and unpleasant to the
African missionary as he could be.

By the very nature of things these two men were bound to
become antagonists. Livingstone's success as an estate manager
largely depended on his being able to discipline his labourers and
get work out of them at the least possible expense. Inevitably he
resented Chilembwe's influence with his workmen, he instinctively disapproved of their appearing in European clothes, and he
was irritated by the sabbatarianism that denied him their services
on Saturdays. Moreover he regarded the pathetic grass churches
they built on the Bruce estate as impertinent claims to ownership
of ground, and seemed to take pleasure in burning them down.
For his part, Chilembwe began to regard Magomero as a symbol
of the settlers' threat to the ordered progress of his people, and
Livingstone as the worst type of those Europeans whom one of
Chilembwe's friends had once summed up magnificently as
'altogether too cheaty, too thefty and too mockery'. For Mr.
Livingstone was undeniably a bully whose reputation for fair
dealing left much to be desired. Even the Commission that later
enquired into the origins of the Rising (and which no one could
accuse of being over-liberal) found that Livingstone's treatment of
his employees was 'often unduly harsh' and 'in several respects
illegal and oppressive'. So it was small wonder that Chilembwe's
grievances became focused on his Magomero neighbours, and
particularly on the figure of Mr. Livingstone the estate manager.

Indeed Chilembwe became so preoccupied with his hatred for
this man that it began to engross and agonise his brain; every day
his enemy's face would creep through his thoughts to mock him,
and slowly the noble purpose of helping his countrymen and
defending them against injustice degenerated into a less creditable
desire for vengeance on Mr. Livingstone. By 1909 things had
become so bad that this man of God would stand before his

diaconate and swear that he would not rest until his tormentor was dead; it was already a passion on a grand scale, although in fact five long years were to go by before Chilembwe achieved his full and dreadful revenge.

The emotional crisis of Chilembwe's life came after the outbreak of the 1914 war, with the news of African casualties in the Battle of Karonga. He poured out his feelings first to his friends and then in a long rambling letter to the *Nyasaland Times*, and through its imperfect syntax there gleams something of his burning indignation. 'In time of peace,' he writes, 'everything for the Europeans only. And instead of honour we suffer humiliation with names contemptible. But in time of war it has been found that we are needed to share hardships and shed blood in equality.' One can almost hear his indignant pen scratching at the paper as he goes on, 'the poor Africans who have nothing to own in this present world, who in death leave only a long line of widows and orphans in utter want and dire distress are invited to die for a cause which is not theirs'. This, the last public letter of an inveterate public correspondent, splutters to an end on a note of anticlimax with an incoherent prayer that some day the Government will recognise the rights of its Nyasa subjects; it is then signed, rather movingly:

'John Chilembwe
in behalf of his countrymen.'

Even though it trembled on the brink of sedition, the authorities must have been impressed by the sincerity of this effusion for beyond suppressing the issue of the *Nyasaland Times* in which it appeared, no action was taken against its writer. Clearly if his attitude was to be emphasised Chilembwe would have to do it in a more compelling way than by addressing the editor of a newspaper whose circulation scarcely exceeded two hundred. And disdaining the milder methods of persuasion still open to him, he decided to test the untried metal of local African discontent in the fires of armed rebellion.

Weeks of feverish plotting followed. Mbombwe church had been a natural choice for his 'battle headquarters', and as 1915 opened, Chilembwe was to be seen there every evening crouched like a spider in a widening web of conspiracy. And how easy it is for us to visualise the long night vigils he spent in the vestry of the church, with the light of a single hurricane lamp glinting on his gold-rimmed spectacles as he fortifies himself with copious draughts from the 20th Chapter of the Acts of the Apostles, or broods over a well-thumbed military manual, or cajoles a doubtful ally, or issues orders to excited lieutenants who are dabbling in the delicious whirl of cloak and dagger intrigue; and as the sky pales over Chiradzulu we can almost hear his voice again raised to near falsetto, as he stands up to give precise orders about the way Mr. Livingstone is to die.

Yet who knows exactly what he was expecting to accomplish in the weeks ahead? No doubt he hoped a 'servile' rising would trigger off a general insurrection that would set him up as a dog-collared Spartacus, ruling over a black theocracy beside the lake. But the risks admittedly were immense and as his pipe dreams dissolved each morning the 'Reverend' must have had his moments of insight when he realised that all he was likely to achieve was a personal revenge on William Jervis Livingstone, and a John Brown type of martyrdom for himself. And despite all the absurd mismanagement of his revolt, these objectives were at least attained. For Livingstone was executed almost exactly as had been prescribed, and Chilembwe's name today glows in an aureole of adulation while his posthumous reputation, which far exceeds that of his lifetime, gives fire and colour to the aspirations of modern Malawi.

We shall never disentangle all the ramifications of Chilembwe's conspiracy, but the basic plan on which all the rest hinged was simple enough. On the night of January 23rd, 1915, three columns of armed men were to set out from Mbombwe. One was to make directly for Magomero and execute the three white men living there; a smaller party was to deal in the same way with Mwanje, another residential area of the A. L. Bruce estates, while the third force, numbering several hundred men, was to march on Blantyre, raid its arsenal and return with guns and ammunition to Mbombwe in preparation for the next stages of the operation.

The form he intended these to take can only be conjectured. Chilembwe is said to have compiled a list of Europeans who were to be speared through their mosquito nets by their servants at

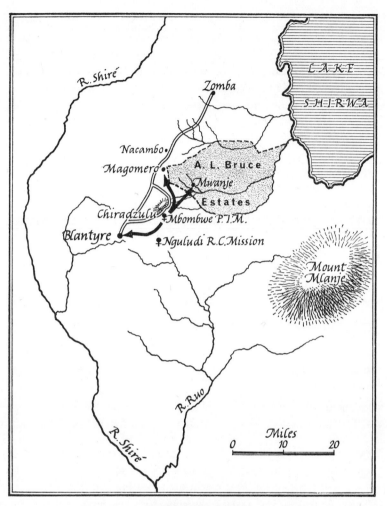

The Chilembwe Rising

dawn on the 24th but proof of this is lacking. It is certain, however, that a section of Gomani's Angoni had promised to rise in Chilembwe's favour, that war drums were to beat in Mlanje whose chiefs had agreed to attack the Boma, and that a number of Zomba headmen had told him they were confident their people would support the insurrection once it had begun. And we know too that Chilembwe was relying on a more powerful ally: the Germans of Tanganyika had been informed of all his plans and had given him a provisional promise of assistance.

About one point Chilembwe was adamant: strict orders went out that no white women or children were to be harmed in any way during the revolt. That injunction shines out like a beacon on a foggy night, and it was implicitly obeyed.

The story of the Chilembwe Rising in Nyasaland is curiously evocative of Mutiny tales from India. We read of faithful servants who spirit their mistresses away from under the very noses of the insurgents, of little pots of plants placed outside doors to indicate those who are to be killed, of dazed survivors capping each other's atrocity stories, and even of the celebrations in the white men's Club which are mistaken by the insurgents for the approach of a punitive expedition. On a small scale it is the same story of mingled hesitation and precipitance as that of 1857, but Chilembwe's initial attack at any rate went very much as he had planned it.

It came as a complete surprise: nothing could have seemed more normal that Saturday night as the ten Europeans at Magomero made their preparations to go to bed, unaware that a mob of spearmen stood outside their houses waiting for the signal to strike. Through the open windows the insurgents could see William Livingstone lying on a bed playing with his infant son, and Mrs. Livingstone in her bath next door, and Mrs. Mac-Donald, her guest, undressing in another room. At 9 o'clock precisely the blow fell, Livingstone fought hard before he was overpowered and then in the presence of his distracted wife he was ceremoniously decapitated. Some accounts say that Mrs. Livingstone was made to hold his head while this was done, and certainly it was afterwards tossed on to her lap. Then she was dragged out into the darkness with her two terrified children while someone impaled the dead man's head on a pole. By some miracle Mrs. MacDonald, helped by her servant, got away through an open window and she stumbled off into the bush and safety. MacCormick, Livingstone's assistant, however, was speared to death as he ran out of his quarters and then the rebels turned their attention to the next house whence two more cowering women and three children were hauled out to join Mrs. Livingstone. Some time was wasted in a fruitless hunt for the third white man they had expected to find there (a fortunate interest in the Belgian Relief Fund had carried him off instead to a jumble sale in Blantyre) and then the rebels drove their bare-footed night-gowned captives through the night to Mbombwe with Livingstone's head borne on its pole before them. Chilembwe was waiting outside the church to receive it.

The attack on Mwanje was rather less successful. One of the two white men living there was quickly killed, but they only wounded the second and somehow or other he slipped away into the darkness with his wife and held the rebels at bay with rifle fire until he made good his escape.

And the attempt on Blantyre armoury was even more sadly bungled. The column tramped dutifully across fifteen miles of difficult country to the town, but discipline during the march was far—even very far—from exemplary and the insurgents had only time to seize a few rifles and 600 rounds of ammunition before they were disturbed by the noise coming from the nearby Gymkhana Club where the annual General Meeting was winding up. The sounds of revelry were taken to be European war cries, and when someone identified the spluttering of a motor cycle engine as a machine gun, blind panic seized the rebels and they streamed off in such disorder that four stragglers were quickly caught, and executed in public next day to discourage other aspiring insurgents.

By the time the survivors of this Blantyre task force had returned to Mbombwe on Sunday morning, Chilembwe's granite mood had passed and he had succumbed to a strange and fatal apathy. It was as though the events of the night had been too big for him. He was, of course, ignorant of the panic that had over-whelmed the local Europeans as reports of wholesale massacre reached out to them. And so when his course should have been to strike at them again and keep on striking, Chilembwe was content to strut around inspecting his frightened captives and to hold his ordinary Sunday service, with Livingstone's head embellishing the high altar.

But by Monday he was a very worried man, listening with growing concern to reports that the Angoni rising had petered out, that at Zomba the planters had rounded up the local rebels without difficulty, and that two German prisoners-of-war at Mlanje had so far misunderstood their proper role as to organise a most successful defence of the Boma. Moreover, Government troops had concentrated with indecent promptitude and by now were closing in on Mbombwe; worst of all the Askaris who had been expected to fraternise with the rebels were firing on them. With the realisation that they were on the losing side, the insurgents' courage evaporated and when darkness fell that Monday evening, Chilembwe's men began to slip away towards the Portuguese border. Their leader watched them go without protest; he merely ordered the white women and children, who might have been invaluable to him as hostages, to be escorted from the village and left where the relieving troops would find them. There was still one more burst of violence before the rebellion spluttered to an end, but it was enough to add greatly to the Europeans' growing fears: one gang's escape route happened to take it past the Roman Catholic Mission at Nguludi, and the retreating men stayed there long enough to spear the Priest, and indulge in an orgy of hymn singing inside the church before burning it down. It was an appropriate ending to the insurrection.

Although none of them realised it at the time, all danger to the Europeans was over then, but as rumours of atrocity multiplied they reacted to the situation with excessive vigour. In plain English they lost their sense of proportion. As one visitor commented later, 'the white population of the Protectorate were thrown into a very great fright over a very little thing', and of course he was perfectly correct. They were fighting shadows, contending with enemies that existed only in their imaginations. The abandoned village of Mbombwe was reconnoitred carefully, after which it was assaulted with tremendous gusto. To make the sense of anticlimax worse an attempt made to fire the great brick church was unsuccessful. A crowd of rebels reported to be massing at Chiradzulu was stealthily surrounded—and turned out to be a gang of convicts weeding the D.C.'s lawn: an impi of spearmen whose approach sent the whites of Fort Johnston scuttling into laager materialised into a party of tourists toting cameras and tripods round the lake shore. Two companies of the King's African Rifles were rushed down the lake from Karonga to deal with the insurrection and dragged their cannons over the eighty-three uphill miles separating Fort Johnston from Zomba in a creditable forty-seven hours. Of course the fighting was over long before they arrived at Magomero but they came in very useful carrying up the dynamite which was used to blow up Mbombwe church, and perhaps they more than anyone else, because of their forced march, deserved the clasp to the African General Service medal which was afterwards very generously distributed.

Many Africans insist that Chilembwe refused to leave Mbombwe with the retreating rebels, but waited in the church as the Government troops approached and then calmly walked out of one door as the soldiers entered by the other; they maintain too that his footsteps were followed for some way until they were replaced by the spoor of a hyena. Others, however, were convinced that Chilembwe turned himself into a bird and flew away to America.

But there was nothing mysterious in fact about Chilembwe's passing, and in the end it may have come as he would have wished it. On February 3rd, 1915, as the military net closed round the last fugitives from Mbombwe, Chilembwe's premature dream of 'Africa for the Africans' faded into the panic of a headlong flight, and the panting distress of a man handicapped by asthma, into a ragged volley of rifle fire and a sprawled body bleeding in the dust with a pair of gold spectacles shining in the sun beside it. They buried him next day in the bush a mile or two from Mlanje Boma.

Can we ever understand all the evolutions that took place in Chilembwe's brain? The most we can hope to do is to glimpse them, and when we do so they make him seem less a person than an attitude of mind, in which the elements of darkness and light are inextricably mixed. Long before his people had ventured into the complex world of a plural society, Chilembwe somehow succeeded in sublimating his pagan inheritance into at least a fair copy of the European culture which he so admired. He had broken through a barrier and had showed that idealism and a social conscience could exist in his race. In him there was at first little of the African's usual preoccupation with the past. He had no thought of using his influence to revive the hegemony of his Yao forebears. He looked into the future rather than retrospectively, thought of his fellow Africans as his 'countrymen' so that one of them later was able to say with perfect truth, 'he was not of one tribe, but for all tribes'. But Chilembwe was suspect by the white men and to their ultimate cost they rejected him. Accordingly as his rankling grievances stripped the layers of acquired rectitude from off his soul like an exercise in geological evacuation, the more barbaric strata of his inheritance became exposed for all the world to see, and Chilembwe's last public act was a repudiation of all he had lived for—the celebration of an obscene church service with the head of his enemy grinning at him from the altar. Circumstances had been too much for this man, and for a moment as he stands in Mbombwe church beside his ghastly trophy, Chilembwe seems to personify all the enigmatic atavism that is such a disturbing feature of emergent Africa today. But the story of *Kwacha* in Nyasaland does not end on that note of appalling consummation. In the same year that Chilembwe died, a youth named Hastings Kamuzu Banda ran away from home. Eventually he was to realise Booth's dream of 'Africa for the Africans' beside the lake which John Chilembwe had so signally failed to do.

13

A NAVAL OCCASION

One morning in the August of 1914, four months before Chilembwe organised his revolt, the British Resident at Karonga sat at his desk deciphering a telegram which had just arrived from Zomba. It told him war had broken out with Germany. After reading it again Mr. Webb walked over to a window that looked out across the Nkonde plain towards the Songwe river twenty miles away and wondered how long it would be before the Germans came swarming across it to attack his Boma. It went through his mind that it might be wise to get away from Karonga while there was still time, for what chance had he, four other white men, and a handful of native police of withstanding a German force known to be concentrating beyond the frontier, and estimated at anything between two thousand and twenty thousand trained soldiers?

His nearest help, he knew, lay a good four hundred miles away at Zomba where two companies of the Kings African Rifles were stationed and the only hope they had of reaching him would be by travelling in the lake flotilla which would certainly be intercepted by the Germans' gunboat, *Hermann von Wissmann*. It was a situation, he realised, that bore a remarkable resemblance to the one which had confronted Monteith Fotheringham thirty years before at this same place; perhaps that precedent served him as an inspiration; at any rate Webb walked out of the Boma a moment later shouting for his sergeant of police to get his men digging defensive trenches and to prepare for a siege.

Meanwhile at Zomba in an atmosphere of hectic improvisation the Governor, Sir George 'Utility' Smith, was studying the local military situation with his staff. Not even the most optimistic among them could pretend it was particularly reassuring. Unless the German invasion force could be stopped at Karonga there seemed little to prevent it occupying the whole Protectorate and gaining command of the lake. Clearly, as first priority,

Karonga must be reinforced without delay, and a rain of orders suddenly began to descend on the Governor's stunned subordinates. The emphasis was on speed; every ship on the lake was to be requisitioned and concentrated with all haste at Fort Johnston ready to sail north with a relieving force; the K.A.R. were to march at once to 'the Fort' prepared for immediate embarkation; three ancient muzzle-loading cannons in the Zomba armoury were to be handed over to the O.C., K.A.R.; all available white men of military age and not in key positions were to be armed with rifles, given shoulder tabs with N.V.R. stencilled on them and enrolled in the Nyasaland Volunteer Reserve; and finally, Commander Rhoades, the Senior Naval Officer on the lake, was to bring the *Hermann von Wissmann* to action without delay. At last the successive orders came to an end, and when someone enquired rather nervously how the last message was to be framed, Sir George, at his most bellicose, picked up a pencil and wrote that Rhoades was to 'sink, burn or otherwise destroy the *Wissmann*'—then he spoilt that authentic Nelson touch by adding a stern warning that, at the same time, Rhoades was on no account to risk the only British gunboat on the lake—H.M.S. *Gwendolen*.

The 350-ton *Gwen* (as everyone called her in Nyasaland) was rather larger than her German adversary and boasted a heavier armament, a single 3-pounder Hotchkiss gun, but it was mounted on her main deck and because of its restricted field of fire was generally considered to be less than a match for the quick-firer the *Wissmann* carried on her foredeck.

But far more formidable than the *Gwen*'s solitary gun was her captain, Commander E. L. Rhoades, R.N.V.R. It would be hard to imagine Rhoades as anything but a sailor. He combined the wit of Sam Weller with the resolution of Horatio Hornblower and the appearance of Captain Kettle. Dr. Sanderson, the Principal (and only) Medical Officer of the Nyasa 'fleet' has described Rhoades as being 'short and spare, with red hair and a pointed beard', and adds in two other (presumably unrelated) items of information that 'he was a product of Rugby' and 'his wit was Rabelaisian'. No one appreciated Rhoades' stories better than his close friend, Herr Berndt, the captain of the *Wissmann* and the two men often arranged their annual training cruises to allow their ships to rendezvous in one or other of the little lake ports where they could spend a bacchanalian evening together. These parties were particularly convivial when one of them was able to celebrate a surprise approach on the rival ship and a successful mock attack.

Rhoades, after receiving the Governor's pugnacious telegram, understandably felt a little ruffled, for no one in the *Gwen* had the faintest idea how to serve his Hotchkiss gun. Anxious enquiries in Fort Johnston, however, tracked down a salesman in the A.L.C. store who had learned the rudiments of gunnery years before in the R.N.V.R. His name was Jock, and although he confessed that his knowledge of gun-laying had become a trifle rusty, he was quite prepared to be helpful. Accordingly he was welcomed on board before he could change his mind, and given half a dozen men to train as gun crew. Rhoades' other problem concerned the total absence of ammunition for his gun, but happily someone rummaging about in the Government sheds on the wharf unearthed several crates labelled 'spares' and they turned out to be filled with Hotchkiss ammunition. It was obsolete, but Jock professed himself satisfied with it.

Then it occurred to Rhoades that it might be a good idea to obtain the services of a few marines in case a landing party was needed to winkle out the enemy ship from harbour, and the local military commander at Fort Johnston was startled to receive an order to produce some. The demand lacked pre-cedence in Nyasaland, but in due course a section of the K.A.R. was persuaded to risk themselves on board the *Gwen*. They were commanded by a Lieutenant Beaumont, who only a few days previously had exchanged a comfortable post with the Public Works Department for military duties, which now to his dis-composure appeared to include sea warfare. Beaumont was one of the more colourful personalities in a European community of 'characters'. Because of his gambling inclinations everyone knew him as 'Champagne Charlie'; he wore a monocle and was rumoured to be well-connected.

Feeling a good deal happier now, Rhoades cast off on August 8th, 1914 to begin his search for the *Wissmann*. The sheer size of the lake complicated his task, and he knew that the German ship, if it was not 'at sea', might be sheltering in one of at least four ports, two at the extreme northern end of Nyasa and two— Wiedhaven and Sphinxhaven—on the east coast where they threatened British shipping passing up and down the lake. Rhoades decided to make first for Nkata Bay, half-way up the lake, in the hope that the fisherman there might have some information about the German boat. The voyage north was uneventful, diversified only by Jock's fretful attempts to armour the more vulnerable parts of the ship's superstructure, and Dr. Sanderson's grisly arrangements with surgical instruments and a pile of protective rice sacks round a camp bed which he announced would do duty as an operating table. And at Nkata Bay there was indeed news of the *Wissmann*: she had been seen at Sphinxhaven three weeks before, hauled on to a slipway for repairs. This sounded promising, and that evening—it was August 12th, 1914 —Rhoades set course for Sphinxhaven, thirty-six miles away across the lake. He timed his arrival there for first light.

Sphinxhaven, now known more prosaically as Liuli, is situated on a rocky indented part of the Nyasa shore. A native village looks out on to an anchorage formed by two promontories of enormous boulders, in one of which a romantic Teutonic eye had detected a resemblance to the Sphinx, and this had given the place its name. A small slipway had been constructed on the beach some time before 1914, and a few scattered repair sheds and huts for the *Wissmann*'s crew were set up too. Behind them the ground gathered itself up quite sharply into a ridge which the efficient Germans had fortified, but inexcusably they had never got round to connecting the place by telegraph to their administrative centre at Songea, only eighty miles away. This fact, however, was unknown to Commander Rhoades at the time.

The *Gwen* made her landfall according to plan just south of the 'sphinx' as the sun came up over the distant hills on August 13th. Rhoades took her close inshore and then turned to port and crept round the promontory, expecting to come under rifle fire from it at any moment. But the only sign of life to be seen was an excited mob of lepers scuttling about the island in the bay where they had been marooned by the Germans some time before.

As he came round the point Rhoades saw with relief that the *Wissmann* was still high and dry on the beach a mile away. The official history of the war tells us that he then chivalrously 'summonsed her to surrender', but in point of fact Rhoades was unconcerned with such niceties at the time and merely bellowed at Jock to open fire. One cannot help feeling very sorry for Jock at the awkwardness that followed: for days he had been practising his gun crew and waiting for this moment, but after passing the promontory the *Gwen*, now in open water, began to roll so badly in the swell that the small proportion of shells passed up to him which were not dud all chanced to be fired as the boat heeled away from his target. As a result they screamed off, far above the *Wissmann* and over the ridge, to explode miles away in the bush to the consternation of the local Africans. But suddenly, after fifteen minutes spirited bombardment, Jock's elevation happened to be right when he pulled the trigger, and he scored a bull's eye on his target. It came as such a surprise that the *Gwen*'s crew desisted from the wearing task of dumping unexploded shells overboard to give him a hearty cheer.

So far there had been no reaction from the shore to the erratic cannonade, but now a furious figure dressed in white shorts and a singlet was seen to jump into a dinghy and pull frantically towards the *Gwen*. His face was purple with indignation and he was shouting as he rowed. At the foot of the *Gwen*'s companion ladder he threw down his oars with an oath and clambered up. It was the captain of the *Wissmann* and he was roaring 'Gott for damn, Rrrrhoades' in the voice of a man who has stood a joke for a long time and now felt it had gone too far. 'Gott for damn: vos you dronk?' he screamed again as he came aboard. Clearly no one had bothered to tell him that war had been declared.

Captain Berndt's shouting changed into guttural spluttering as Rhoades gently explained the situation to him. He was understood, if interpreted correctly, to desire a strong drink and to sit down—and a chair and a glass of neat whisky were hurriedly produced for him. Then the unhappy Prussian gentleman was led away to an empty cabin loudly intimating to his captors his opinion of the German officials in Songea.

Historians have claimed that the *Gwen* fired the first naval shots of the Great War; certainly she won its first naval victory, and her company thoroughly deserved the happy time they now enjoyed looting the German ship. Only a very resentful 'Champagne Charlie' was obliged to absent himself from this pleasant duty in obedience to precise orders to picket the ridge above the beach in case the enemy mounted a counter-attack. Rhoades, meanwhile, was finding difficulty in scuttling a ship on dry land, and he was content that morning to immobilise the *Wissmann* by removing her essential parts. Long afterwards she was towed away to Fort Johnston, whence presently she emerged, splendidly renamed H.M.S. *King George*.

Rhoades had the *Gwen* back safely in Nkata Bay on the evening of his 'battle' and a cable about his success by then was already speeding to Whitehall. Next morning, as puzzled officers in the Admiralty muttered together over maps of Central Africa, the newsboys in the square below were shouting out the good news. It could scarcely have come at a better time; seen against the sombre background offered by the retreat from Mons, Rhoades' enterprise commended itself to the nation, for it carried a splendidly reminiscent flavour of similar cutting-out expeditions made by Drake and Hawkins. The Secretary of State for the Colonies was particularly pleased to steal Mr. Churchill's thunder with a manly telegram to Zomba which read 'Well done *Gwen*', and even the sober *Times* appeared with larger headlines than usual proclaiming 'Naval Victory on Lake Nyasa'.

Meanwhile, the lake's Trafalgar fought and won, H.M.S. *Gwen* was carrying her distinguished prisoner down the lake to his long captivity, and sometimes, when Rhoades joined him in his cabin, it seemed quite like old times. It is sad to have to record that Rhoades had little time to celebrate his victory at Fort Johnston: categoric orders awaited him there to escort the Nyasaland Field Force to Karonga without delay. For the German army had not yet moved across the Songwe and there might still be time to get the K.A.R. up to Karonga before it did.

LAKE SHORE VICTORY

During the same week of 1914 that saw the German invasion of France turned back on the river Marne, something rather similar, although on a vastly different scale, occurred at Karonga. But it was of the highest moment for the lake; in a scattered action fought just north of the town, a German invasion force was routed and its survivors driven back across the frontier. As battles of the First World War go, of course, it was hardly more than a skirmish—only about four hundred men were engaged on either side—but it was the heaviest fighting ever seen on the lake shore and the casualties suffered were out of all proportion to the numbers engaged. And not only did it repel an invasion, it also discouraged any later German participation in the Chilembwe Rising, and it so boosted morale in Nyasaland as to become a prime factor in producing the hundreds of thousands of carriers from the lake shore who later played such an important part in the East African campaign.

But what gives this action its own peculiar quality is the way both commanders involved consistently disregarded the reports their spies brought in to them, and somehow managed to blunder past each other in the bush so that when they fought their battle, they had both been caught off balance and were facing in precisely opposite directions from those they had intended.

The Nkonde plain lying between Karonga and the Songwe is a wilderness of thick bush interspersed with swamps and tangled patches of forest. Through it a succession of rivers run on parallel courses to the lake. Apart from several minor streams, these are the Songwe and Lufira in the north, then come the Kasoa, the Marungu and finally the Rukuru which opens into the Kombwe lagoon a little to the north of Karonga.

Even today communications across the plain are primitive enough, and in 1914 they were, of course, far worse. It was wild untamed country then, and the fighting that took place there that

September has something of the horror and ferocity of the jungle warfare of the Burmese campaign in the Second World War. The plain was traversed by only one properly constructed road, which lay about a mile inland from the lake and reached from the Songwe frontier to Karonga after passing through the villages of Kaparo and Kirapula. A second less well-defined track led inland from Kaparo to another village named Mambande about four miles from the lake before turning south to Karonga; a third track, which was really nothing more than a path, left the main road a little farther south at the Kasoa river and ran down beside the lake as far as the Kombwe lagoon.

Mr. Webb and the four anxious Englishmen stationed at Karonga when the war broke out were soon joined by several other district officials, as well as by three ladies. They could take some comfort from the very impenetrability of the bush that separated them from the Germans, for it was bound to impede any attack. But it also distorted and exaggerated the information trickling down to them about enemy movements beyond the Songwe, and during the long August days of waiting their imaginations not unnaturally became over-active and morbid as they discussed the blow they knew was bound to fall on them soon.

Mr. Webb, the Resident, would have been relieved to know that his opposite number, Herr Stier, the German Imperial Administrator of Neu Langenburg (the present Tukuyu), sixty miles away, was still more in the dark about events than he. For, as at Sphinxhaven, no one had told him war had been declared; all Stier heard were rumours of a German task force concentrating somewhere near Mbeya which could shortly be expected to move down to his station, but for all he knew it might be manœuvring or merely taking precautionary measures. His plaintive requests to Mbeya for information were all ignored, and in the end Stier naïvely decided to ask his friend Mr. Webb if he knew what was going on. On August 17th, therefore, a runner came into Karonga with the message Stier had written two days before; it began: 'I am not clear whether England is at war with Germany or not,' and went on to ask for news. Mr. Webb was a considerate man and he answered (with what appears to have been unnecessary chivalry) that war had indeed broken out; but in the event this helpful information hardly mattered, for by the time his reply reached Neu Langenburg, Herr Stier was only too well aware of the real situation as he struggled to find billets for twenty-two white officers not to mention eight hundred askari and spearmen who had descended on his station to regroup before setting out on the great adventure of invading Nyasaland.

And by then, too, with the uncanny symmetry of events that characterises this forgotten campaign, British troops were already moving into Karonga. Rhoades having safely disposed of the *Wissmann*, four hundred askari from Fort Johnston commanded by a Captain Barton, were disembarked unobtrusively at Vua, and they marched into the Karonga perimeter on August 22nd. Meanwhile, Webb's strange correspondence with the enemy resumed: another letter was brought in, this time from the German military commander, Captain von Langenn Steinkeller, in which he courteously announced his imminent arrival in Karonga with an expeditionary force and went on to advise Webb to evacuate his Europeans at once, 'to avert a massacre' by the German askari. It was clear the enemy was not yet aware that Karonga had been reinforced.

Von Langenn had already been inexcusably dilatory in preparing his offensive, and even now, when he must have realised that his paramount need was for haste, he allowed still more time to slip through his fingers. Admittedly towards the end of August he sent an advance guard across the border to Kaparo to eject a police posse and occupy the village, but the British were still allowed two weeks grace before the invasion proper was launched.

Barton made good use of the time, enlarging and strengthening the Karonga perimeter and reconnoitring its approaches. Not until September 7th did von Langenn get his column moving across the frontier. His immediate plan—such as it was—had little finesse about it. He intended to march down the main road on the 8th, camp near the Rukuru mouth that night and surprise Karonga at dawn on the 9th. He did not expect to meet much opposition but he did take the precaution of detaching a flank guard of thirty askari and five hundred irregulars under Lieutenant Aumann who had orders to approach Karónga down the Mambande track and make sure no one escaped when the main attack went in.

We can now only guess at what von Langenn intended to do after capturing Karonga. That alone of course would have been a propaganda victory of a sort, and if it could have been followed up by an advance down the lake shore and the incitement of dissatisfied tribes into rebellion against the British, he might well have gained control of the lake. But it is much more likely that von Langenn at the time was scarcely concerned about his next moves and what really drove him into Nyasaland was an anxiety to win a little glory before the fighting was over.

On the same day that von Langenn moved south from Kaparo, Barton, satisfied at last with his defences, issuing orders for a reconnaissance to be made in force towards the frontier. That very afternoon his troops were to march up the Mambande track for a few miles and then turn off through the bush and bivouac at the Lufira river. Next morning he intended to approach Kaparo from the west and recapture it. The plan admittedly meant hard marching for his troops, but they were to travel light, since their thoughtful commander had arranged for all their heavy equipment to be brought up to Kaparo by a tug which happened to be sheltering at Karonga and whose skipper had orders to sail with his cargo just before dawn on the 9th. A scratch force numbering seventy rifles under the command of a Lieutenant Bishop was to garrison Karonga in Barton's absence.

There were of course, obvious flaws in Barton's otherwise excellent scheme: for one thing it was based on inaccurate information and he had no idea when he started off that two columns of German troops were already approaching Karonga.

It was close on two that afternoon when Barton's four hundred men marched out of the Boma perimeter. At that moment Aumann's spearmen were half-way down the Mambande track bound on a 'collision course' with him, while von Langenn with the main German column had reached the Kasoa river. There the German Commander ordered a halt while he listened to an excited scout who had just come up with the information that Karonga had been heavily reinforced. Von Langenn simply did not believe him: as he said to his officers, the British could hardly have got

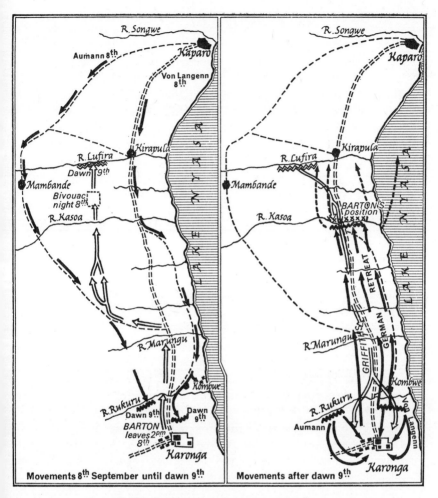

The Battle of Karonga, September 8th–9th, 1914

many troops up the lake so quickly, especially in the face of opposition from the *Hermann von Wissmann* which as far as he knew was still afloat. But he was still a little flustered by the information. It was one of those situations which are constantly recurring in war; should he as a commander discard all his careful plans on the strength of one probably inaccurate message, or should he ignore it? In the end von Langenn decided to continue his advance, but he made one small compromise: instead of marching down the main road, he shouted to his leading file to take the lake shore path which he knew was much less likely to be patrolled.

Only an hour later Barton was confronted by a similar problem: a runner arrived with a report that enemy troops had been seen in Mambande that morning. Like von Langenn, he found the information very difficult to believe, but he was worried enough to hustle his men into the cover of the bush on his right, and to detach a company to cover Mambande, while he moved on towards the Lufira.

At 5 p.m. he received even more disturbing information: an enemy force was reported marching on Karonga down the main road. Nearly any other commander would have hurried his men back to protect his base at once, but Barton had been taught the virtue of imperturbability. Not only did he again doubt the accuracy of the information but for some incomprehensible reason he now convinced himself that the report about the enemy being in Mambande was untrue as well, and after ordering his flank detachment to rejoin him, he continued his advance. Only a little later Barton's men marched slowly through the gap between the two German columns moving in the opposite direction and separated from each other by less than three miles: neither commander had the faintest idea of the other's presence; only their capricious changes of plan had contrived to prevent a clash.

Nothing can be more gruelling than a long hot march through African bush, and Barton's men found it extremely hard going. Thorns pulled at their hands and faces, endless tree roots tripped them up, they were obliged to make repeated diversions to avoid swamps and tangled undergrowth and impenetrable thickets. Darkness was on them before they had even reached the Kasoa,

248

and from then on their progress became still slower. No one was certain if they were going in the right direction; men kept getting lost, and everyone was uneasy about ambushes ahead. Thirty years later the memory of the night's ordeal still haunted its survivors. At ten o'clock, a mile short of the Lufira, the soldiers could go no farther, and when Barton called for a routine halt they dropped to the ground and slept where they lay. They looked like men who had been defeated before the battle had even begun, and with the enemy between them and their base they were indeed in a highly precarious situation; no one would have thought there was enough left in them to fight a battle next day, let alone win it.

The Germans were in far better condition that night: they had moved along good tracks and had rested during the heat of the day: von Langenn was full of confidence as he snatched some sleep only a mile short of Karonga Boma.

So the night passed, with Barton's exhausted soldiers stretched out near the Lufira, von Langenn's men poised near the swamp where years before Mlozi's Arabs had slaughtered the Wankonde, and Aumann only a mile or two away hidden in the mopane bush just off the Mambande track. In the Karonga perimeter a few sentries made their usual rounds and the unsuspecting garrison slept without thought of the blow that had been prepared for them next day.

But just before daybreak the unpredictable, as so often in war, began to rule events. The German officers at Kombwe were fussing round their men getting them into line when they heard the spluttering of a motor engine nearby, and through the faint livid-green of a Nyasa sunrise they saw a tug floundering past them up the coast. It was the boat carrying Barton's heavy equipment to Kaparo, and it was too tempting a target to be ignored. While his men were left standing in their lines, von Langenn's two field guns were hastily unlimbered to open fire on the tug—and the vital element of surprise was lost. Bishop's incredulous garrison was alerted. Worse still, the German gunners became so occupied in shelling the British boat, looting it when it drifted ashore and capturing its skipper, that they never got their guns into action against Karonga Boma, whose wall they would have breached with their first round. Indeed it was not until 7.45 a.m. that von Langenn even persuaded his men to leave the excitement of the small drama of the sinking boat and was able to put in his attack. To his horror it ran straight into a wall of fire. Now this was the old Fotheringham situation all over again, with von Langenn playing the part of Mlozi, and like the Arabs his men were pinned to the ground 600 yards from the perimeter, shouting vainly for artillery support.

The noise of the firing reached right back to the Lufira, and Captain Barton was hardly less appalled by it than von Langenn. Only an hour or so earlier he had managed to get his men to their feet again, and almost immediately became engaged with an enemy patrol on the farther bank of the Lufira. The unmistakable sound of rifle fire coming up the wind from Karonga told him that somehow or other the enemy had got behind him and were attacking his base, and he knew that if Karonga fell it would be almost impossible to extricate his own force. But his spirits rose as the noise of firing continued; provided Bishop held out, he realised that the situation, although still full of danger, was full of possibilities too. So far we have only seen Barton as a very conventional regular soldier who, in twenty-four hours, has managed to make every possible mistake, but nothing could have been more admirable than the way he reacted now. It is not difficult to visualise him standing there in the russet brown dappling of the lake shore's bush thinking of the opportunity that lay before him, if only he could grasp it, and then ordering his second-in-command, Captain Griffiths, to make a forced march back to Karonga with two companies of the K.A.R. while he himself took the more exhausted of his men as far as the Kasoa river to dig themselves in across the line of the enemy's retreat.

Griffiths was no time waster. The troops had taken eight hours to cover the eight miles of rough going to the Lufira the day before, but this time he risked marching straight down the main road and he drove his men relentlessly. He was in sight of the Boma well before eleven o'clock that morning and was relieved to see that Bishop was doing even better than he could have hoped; the Germans were already badly mauled; von Langenn himself was wounded and the soldiers were wavering when, in the words of the official war history, Griffiths' men 'fell on them with a will' from the rear. Caught off balance, the German troops streamed away in defeat, leaving forty-two dead behind them. Two hours later they ran straight into the ambush Barton had prepared on the Kasoa. He had chosen an admirable defensive position; the cover was good and it commanded a clear field of fire. There were several flurries of vicious bayonet fighting when the German askaris broke into the line but it held firm, and by that evening nineteen of the twenty-two German officers engaged were casualties and they had lost over a hundred askaris, a high percentage for any fight, while the irregulars had suffered even more severely. In the fading light a few stragglers succeeded in plodding through the bush to Kaparo, while one fortunate party came across a canoe in which they escaped across the lake. The British casualties had been much lighter, but they were far too weary to pursue the enemy.

Next morning as the bandaged figures of Barton and Webb stood watching the dead being laid beside Lugard's old fighters in the quiet cemetry of Karonga, they were able to congratulate themselves on a very neat performance. They had been extremely lucky of course, but in the years ahead Barton's little victory seemed to shine all the more brightly as disappointments and humiliating defeats mounted up in the campaign against von Lettow-Vorbeck in East Africa. And the lake was never seriously threatened by the Germans again; instead it became an important and secure line of communication to the front, although very occasionally it was regaled by the sight of a small party of the enemy hurrying along its Tanganyika shore with a larger British force blundering along behind it in pursuit. Enormous base camps and field hospitals sprang up at Fort Johnston, and Bandawe, and Mbamba Bay, to serve the quarter of a million troops engaged against von Lettow-Vorbeck, and more men travelled on her waters than she had ever known before. The Germans were still fighting on November 13th, 1918, not far from where Barton and von Langenn had begun the campaign, when the belated news reached them of the Kaiser's surrender, and it fell to Nyasa troops marching up from the lake to fire the last shots of the First Great War.

And as time went on the battle of Karonga assumed a new significance because of two consequences that sprang from it. There, for the first time, Africans from the lake had seen that white men suffered from the same fears and uncertainties that they did, and met the same bloody and undignified deaths, and the realisation shattered the myth of the European's mysterious innate superiority. And the deaths of so many Africans in a battle that was no real concern of theirs, lit a flame of resentment as we have seen in the breast of Pastor John Chilembwe labouring in the Shiré Highlands. Both factors turned out to be feeding fires of African nationalism beside the lake.

15

THE *VIPYA* AFFAIR

Shipwrecks are about the last thing one expects to come across in Central Africa, but Lake Nyasa has had her fill; she has always possessed an evil reputation for storms and no one knows how many anonymous canoes and loaded slave dhows have foundered in her waters. The south-east trade wind—locally called the *mwera* —is funnelled up the Rift Valley and blows for days on end, and when it meets squalls coming through gaps in the eastern mountain wall the sky splits open and tremendous tempests result. As soon as the recorded history of Nyasa began, everyone who went there seems to have had something to say about the dangerous unpredictability of the lake.

The first to do so was Charles Livingstone. How one particular storm looked to him in 1861 is set forth in a letter he sent to a friend soon afterwards. 'At times when sailing pleasantly over the clear blue water,' he wrote, 'with a gentle breeze, and under a cloudless sky, suddenly, without any warning would be heard the sound of an approaching gale as it came roaring on bringing myriads of crested and excited waves in its wake. We got caught one morn, in a frightful gale. As a forlorn hope we anchored in 7 fathoms about a mile from shore with the sea breaking even far out beyond us . . . a dark cloud had come from the mountains and hung directly over our heads'. Dr. Livingstone's account of this same experience was so similarly worded that we can be sure the two brothers often compared their feelings about it. And they had every reason to do so, for the fresh waters of Nyasa during a hurricane are more frightening than the sea; short steep waves are whipped up to heights of fifteen feet, and they advance with a peculiar triple rhythm. Charles Livingstone was again the first to record this odd characteristic, for in his letter he goes on, 'the seas we most dreaded rushed upon us in threes, one after the other in rapid succession. Then a few minutes of comparative calm, and another charge of three of . . . these perpendicular-sided and

253

enraged masses,' and he adds that on this occasion 'for six mortal hours we faced the furious charges of these terrible trios.'

The more experienced Lieutenant Young who followed the Livingstones to the lake had this to say about one of its storms: 'The sea was past all conception: it is the peculiar nature of this lake to raise a sea that could only be found off the Agulhas Bank or in the Atlantic. . . . It is impossible to describe the awful combinations of whirlwinds, thunderclouds and lightning that seemed to throw the lake into the wildest fury.' Bishop Maples, as we have seen, perished in a storm off Salima in 1895 and after that disaster the lake was always treated with vast respect. Then in 1946 the worst of all its tragedies occurred.

For years previously an elderly motor-vessel named the *Mpasa* had been the mainstay of the lake's shipping services, but she was far too uncomfortable to satisfy the tourists who were beginning to visit Nyasaland, and shortly before the outbreak of World War II an order was placed in England for a more suitable ship. Somehow, during the Battle of the Atlantic, space was found to bring her out in sections to Beira for reassembly at Monkey Bay, near Fort Johnston. It was a great occasion when the Governor's wife came down to launch and christen her *Vipya*. She was completed towards the end of 1945 and was by far the largest ship ever to have sailed the waters of Nyasa, for she could accommodate three hundred and fifty steerage and deck passengers, as well as eleven in the first-class quarters, whose comfort approximated to that of an ocean-going boat.

The command of the *Vipya* was shared between two captains, who were to take her out on alternate voyages. The senior of them was a Commander Keith Farquharson, D.S.C., and he probably knew more about the lake than any other man alive. After serving with distinction in the Royal Navy for over twenty years, Farquharson had been appointed Commodore of the lake transport services eight years previously. Commander Farquharson looked exactly right for the part: he was heavily built and rubicund of face, bluff, crusty and sometimes even a trifle difficult. Like so many exiled seamen he managed to create a little seafaring England around him wherever he went, and Fort Johnston vibrated with his personality. He had his eccentricities, of course, but his worst enemies could never accuse him of being prudish or a bad host; indeed he was so popular on the lake that even today people there are reticent about his shortcomings and contradict any suggestion that they may have something to do with the loss of his ship.

Before going into regular service the *Vipya* was taken out on several shake-down cruises, and even the Governor found time to sail with his family on one of them. Like Farquharson he pronounced himself perfectly satisfied with the ship's performance. But it must be admitted that this opinion was not shared by everybody, for one passenger, a Major Hargreaves, when he disembarked, had something to say about the neglect of life-boat drill, and his fear that the *Vipya*'s high superstructure (which had already led her to be nicknamed the *Llangibby Castle*) might make her top-heavy, and he was hardly reassured by her captain's assertion that she was a 'fine seaworthy boat'.

And Hargreaves, it soon turned out, was not the only person who felt uneasy about the ship's stability. At Karonga on her second trip, the *Vipya*, afloat in dead calm water, was seen to be heavily down by the stern. Farquharson when questioned about this, was understood to say that the plates in the African heads were perhaps too heavy, but he hastened to add that this could easily be rectified by shifting his ballast, which consisted of forty-four-gallon drums filled with water. Even more ominously, Captain Flint, who shared command of the *Vipya* later reported that the ship had a very small angle of heel, and that this together with her light draught might make her dangerous in a high sea. But it is only fair to add that no one expected the ship to be taken out in bad weather; her captains were not tied down to a rigid schedule; certain ports were designated as 'weather permitting calls', and it was understood too, that at their discretion Farquharson and Flint could run before a storm or seek shelter when one blew up.

The *Vipya* set out on her fourth scheduled voyage round the lake on July 26th, 1946, with Farquharson in command, and a Mr. Underwood, a newcomer to Nyasaland, acting as First Officer. The ship's engineer was an Indian named Daud Sheik Ali. The African crew numbered over fifty; most of them were veterans in the service and Che Tine, the boatswain, was a particularly reliable and experienced man. No one was certain later exactly how many African passengers were carried on the voyage, but this perhaps is hardly surprising, for even the most honest and efficient clerks would have found difficulty in keeping a proper tally on the hordes of third-class passengers who embarked and disembarked at every port with riotous abandon; probably the figure of 137 third-class passengers given at the enquiry was just about correct, and certainly there was never any suggestion that the *Vipya* on her last voyage was overloaded. The first-class cabins, however, were full; certainly six European passengers were on board and a newspaper report suggests that there were some Indians too; among the former was a prominent local politician, who had brought his wife and parents-in-law along with him for the trip, while a young Customs Officer and a Miss Gough from Tanganyika were also taking holiday cruises. Of the two hundred or more persons on the *Vipya* when she sailed across the lake on July 30th, 1946, five days out from Fort Johnston, only forty-nine were alive that evening, and all of them, with the single exception of the Engineer Daud, were Africans.

The first few days of the *Vipya*'s voyage passed uneventfully enough and on July 28th she sailed into Nkata Bay on schedule and tied up there for the night. Punctually at 9.30 next morning she set out for Mbamba Bay on the other side of the lake. The south-easterly wind which had risen the day before was blowing more strongly now, and once in the open lake, the *Vipya* began to ship water and to roll badly enough to alarm several members of the African crew. Presently they approached Che Tine and it soon turned out that he too was worried about the way the ship was behaving. Some time between 11 and 12 that morning, when they were about half-way across the lake, Tine went below to have a word with Daud. According to the evidence that Daud gave later, a high gale was blowing that morning, the ship was rolling and water was coming in on both sides of the deck. He was sufficiently impressed by the boatswain's anxiety that he agreed they ought to report to the Captain and suggest as tactfully as they could that it might be wise to omit the double crossing of the lake and run with the wind instead directly to Florence Bay.

Farquharson without doubt was a very formidable man, and Daud and Tine must have been feeling somewhat apprehensive as they climbed up to his bridge that morning. Even so they were not prepared for the vituperation that greeted their well-meant proposal. For Farquharson flew into a rage, 'Are you mad?' he shouted at them, and when they told him again of the men's fears all he could bellow was, 'Don't listen to the words of the crew'. One cannot altogether blame Farquharson for his reaction; no one very much relishes being offered unsolicited advice— especially when it is good advice—and in this case it carried with it a suggestion of criticism for his seamanship. But after demolishing the cowering Daud with a final, 'Don't be a bloody fool', Farquharson quietened down, explained that there was only room for one Captain on a ship, and dismissed them with the reminder that he had far more experience at sea and on the lake than the two of them put together. All this time Underwood had been standing beside the Commander on the bridge wondering if he ought to say something; and no doubt he was very glad he had held his tongue when the *Vipya* sailed safely and on schedule into Mbamba Bay two hours later.

Farquharson had originally intended to cross the lake again that same day but in view of the worsening weather he was content to shelter where he was for the night. For the storm was fiercer now and raging across the whole lake. A hundred miles away from where the *Vipya* was berthed, a Mr. Sharpe was standing on the beach at Salima, congratulating himself on not having taken a boat out that day. Sharpe was the son of Sir Harry Johnston's old friend, and as a keen yachtsman he had known the lake since childhood, but the rain and lightning beating down on its waters that afternoon were different from anything he had seen before, and he knew that farther north, where squalls were likely to blow in through mountain gaps, the weather might be even worse.

Next morning, if the evidence given at the Court of Enquiry is to be believed, the storm was as fierce as ever. But Farquharson was determined to waste no more time. Presumably he must have considered omitting his next scheduled call at Florence Bay, which was a 'weather permitting' port, and running instead with the wind to Deep Bay and Karonga, but, perhaps because he was anxious to make another gesture to the faint hearts in his crew, he decided in the end to adhere to the normal itinerary, and at dawn set course for Florence Bay. Once again as soon as she came into open water the *Vipya* began to labour badly and to ship sea over her main deck bulwarks. Daud, whose experience of the lake went back ten years, has told us that the weather that morning was very nearly the worst he had ever seen, yet at 8 a.m. Farquharson altered course directly to the west. If, as was stated in court, the wind was southerly at the time, this could only have made things worse, but it is only fair to add that later on in an Appeal Court evidence was led that the wind that morning was not on the ship's beam but easterly, and if this was so Farquharson's change of course became explicable.

But without doubt he was a very worried man by now, and at 10 a.m. Daud was called to the bridge to report on the amount of water in the ship. The Engineer's account of conditions below was anything but reassuring, and he was dismissed with strict instructions to secure the engine-room doors and keep the pumps going until they reached Florence Bay which by now was less than fifteen miles away. But forty minutes later, when the distance had narrowed down to eight miles, Farquharson on the bridge must have concluded that his troubles were over, for he allowed the deck hands to uncover the main cargo hatch on the deck in preparation for unloading the luggage consigned to Florence Bay. And a little later he altered course again to north and the *Vipya* turned to head directly towards the little port.

It is possible from the accounts given later by the survivors to visualise something of the scene at this time in the ship. The *Vipya* was being tossed about like a cork in the water directly below the shadowy mass of Mount Waller, and she was rolling so badly that the deck-hands were finding it very difficult to stand upright. But two of them—Alia and Sailes—were working on the cargo hatch in obedience to the Captain's orders, and having loosened the tarpaulin, began to move the planks that covered it. Lines, another deck-hand, who should have been there to help them, was below, prostrated with sea-sickness, and soon only Alia remained at work, for Sailes, who had become badly scared because, in his own words, the boat was at a 'slant', went off to find a better sanctuary. Mise, another member of the crew, who was off duty at the time, however had decided it might be safer up on deck and he joined one of the little knots of African passengers holding on to the rails and gaping with dismay at the boiling water; nearby his friend Mbana, who was made of sterner stuff, was unconcernedly swabbing out the latrines and scrubbing the deck. But the majority of the third-class passengers remained huddled together in the passenger hold utterly miserable and with water lapping at their feet. In the engine-room Daud too was staring at the water swilling about across the floor, while his five assistants, including Sani and Yohane who both later escaped, attended to the pumps. All the first-class passengers were below, either in their cabins or fortifying themselves in the saloon, with the single exception of Miss Gough who, having put on a thick coat, was climbing up on deck to see what was going on. Just as she emerged from the companion way she heard Mise shouting; he was pointing at an enormous wave racing towards the *Vipya*. It burst across the deck and as the water poured through the open hatch, the ship rolled far over to starboard; when the second of the 'terrible trios' hit her, the *Vipya* capsized. A few minutes later she was lying on the lake bed in sixty fathoms of water. It was a little before 11 o'clock in the morning.

No one ever saw what happened to Farquharson and Underwood on the bridge, and most of the passengers were trapped below and went down with the ship. Of the Europeans only Miss Gough seems to have remained alive for any length of time, for when her body was washed ashore next day, she had not long been dead. Fortune, however, smiled on Daud that morning; he managed to climb through one of the engine-room windows as the ship turned turtle, and then, followed by Yohane and Sani, scrambled on to the keel. There was a great deal of wreckage floating around and all three got ashore by hanging on to boxes and chairs and planks. No life jackets had been issued, and there was no time to launch the lifeboats, but even so thirteen other members of the crew and thirty-three African passengers, who had wisely come on deck before the end, managed to struggle ashore that afternoon.

A few of them climbed up to Livingstonia in the evening for help, and the Mission staff came down to do what they could for the survivors during the night. Then for the next ten days they were engaged in the grisly task of burying the scores of corpses strewn along the lake shore opposite the oil slick which marked the *Vipya*'s grave. Very few of the bodies could be identified; their skin had peeled away in the water, while crocodiles and the cannibal chamba fish had further mutilated them.

Within a month of the disaster a Court of Enquiry was assembled to investigate its cause. One after another the survivors came up to give their evidence about the weather and the way, just before the ship capsized, the cargo hatch had been opened instead of being kept firmly battened down. Daud came out of the investigation very well, and Farquharson very badly. Predictably the dead man was censured for leaving Mbamba Bay before the weather had moderated, for not treating the boat gently until he was sure of its performance, for having made no attempt to render the ship's deck watertight, and for compounding that omission by opening the main cargo hatch 'at a very critical moment'. The Court also pointed out that no proper tally had been kept of the passengers travelling in the ship, nor had any attempt been made to issue them with life jackets. Not quite all the blame, however, was attached to Commander Farquharson. For one thing it was allowed that on the morning of the sinking the weather had been exceptional, while the owners of the *Vipya*— the Nyasaland Railways—together with its designers were criticised for not having provided a simple method of rendering the ship's main deck watertight.

Reading between the lines of the record of the Proceedings of the Court of Enquiry one cannot help feeling that sometimes the Court despaired of making sense out of the evidence given by a succession of thoroughly bewildered Africans. But if some people suspected that not all the truth about the sinking had come out, at least Daud's evidence seemed incontrovertible, while the Court's findings appeared to be balanced and straightforward.

Yet these findings without doubt were embarrassing to the owners, if only because they presented an open invitation for claims to be pressed in respect of loss of life and property. So no one was particularly surprised when the Railways appealed against the findings. When they did so the final chapters of the *Vipya* story changed abruptly from tragedy to something perilously near to farce.

For in the Appeal Court, Daud, who was recalled as a witness, solemnly disavowed his earlier evidence. Although he had previously testified that on the day of the disaster, 'I told the Captain when I went up to see him at 10 o'clock that there was plenty of water down below', he now swore that what he had really meant to say was, 'I told the Captain that the water was on deck and not at any other place.' This rather lame explanation proved acceptable to the Court. Another remarkable contradiction concerned Daud's original testimony that, 'water was coming into the crews' places and the African passengers' places', when he left Farquharson an hour or two before the ship went down: now he stood up in the Appeal Court with hand-on-Bible assurances that, 'No, I did not say, "water was coming into the crews' places",' and 'No, I did not say, "water was coming into the African passengers' places".' These naïve denials were accepted. Even more incredibly, Daud now discounted the suggestion that a significant amount of water had entered the engine-room, although when questioned in the first Court about conditions 'on the day of the accident' he had stated that 'there was two feet of water in the engine-room'. This last *volte face* was accompanied by the bland explanation that in his previous testimony, 'I was referring to 29th July', and not to the fatal 30th.

Interested parties could not help wondering what had made Daud change his evidence in a way that was so opportune for the owners. Did he perhaps suffer from amnesia? Was he anxious to conform with what other witnesses had said? Had he been persuaded that it might be awkward to account for water in his engine-room when he had been instructed previously to pump it out? Could he (they almost shrank from the suggestion) have been intimidated? Or (and this seemed the most likely explanation) was Daud merely a frightened man whose only concern in the Appeal Court was to say what he considered the Judge most wanted to hear? It was anybody's guess.

The important thing was that the Court accepted his revised

testimony, reversed the original finding that a considerable quantity of water had accumulated below the *Vipya*'s deck before she sank, and exonerated the Nyasaland Railways from responsibility for the disaster.

This was astonishing enough, but a still more astonishing sequel followed. Poor Farquharson had been left now to bear all the blame—and being dead he seemed the perfect scapegoat. But he had resourceful relatives, and in a second Appeal Court they triumphantly produced a Mr. Joseph Oldridge, who proceeded to convince its presiding Judge that the previous evidence given about the wind and weather conditions on the morning of the disaster had been wrong. On the face of it, this must be considered something of a marvel; after all Flint, Daud, and Sani had each separately testified that the weather 'was very bad' on the 30th; and Flint, Daud, Mbana, Sailes, and Mise had all agreed the wind that morning was blowing from the south. Yet here was Mr. Oldridge prepared to swear that they were all mistaken. And Mr. Oldridge could be considered an expert witness: at the time of the sinking he was employed by the Tanganyikan Government to keep meteorological records at Liuli, not far from Mbamba Bay. He informed the second Appeal Court that at 6.30 a.m. on the 30th July he had seen the *Vipya* on the lake 'making steady headway in a steady sea'. He added that 'there was no freshness' at the time, and that 'the force of the wind was about force 4'. An hour later he remembered that the ship was still in sight: it was about half-way to Florence Bay by then, the wind was easterly and everything appeared perfectly normal. The witness was able to recall too that at 8.30 a.m., there had been still 'only little cloud. The weather was overcast, but not threatening.'

Several reversals of evidence had been heard in this case already, but this seemed the most astonishing of them all. Here was a man asserting that Farquharson had left Mbamba Bay in good weather instead of in a gale. And it completely demolished the original finding that the Commander had 'set out in extremely bad weather when he should have remained in shelter until the weather moderated sufficiently for him to proceed with safety'.

Farquharson was accordingly formally exonerated from any blame.

Old Livingstonia, Lake Nyasa

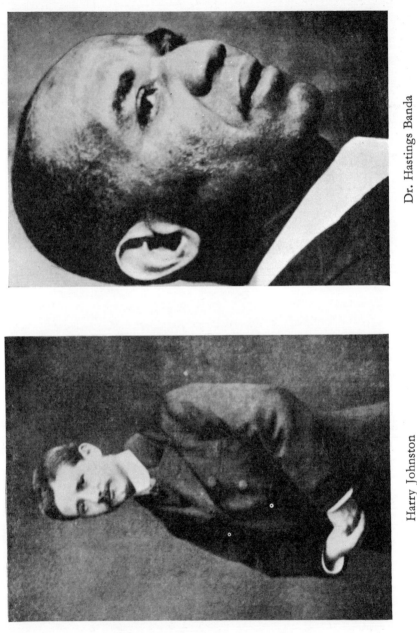

Dr. Hastings Banda

Harry Johnston

This was all very well in its way, but somehow a feeling persisted that the whole truth about the cause of the disaster had not been told. For officially a perfectly seaworthy boat had foundered in fair weather for no reason at all. It did not seem to make much sense. And now it is most unlikely that we shall ever know what really happened to the *Vipya* that morning when one hundred and fifty people lost their lives, since the authorities seem reluctant to discuss the affair. Questions about the exact place where the ship went down have been met with bleak intimations that 'the *Vipya* file is closed'; a plan of the boat is never forthcoming despite repeated requests; suggestions that divers should attempt to recover the bullion the *Vipya* was rumoured to be carrying have come to nothing. Inevitably such studied reticence suggested that some important facts about the sinking have never been brought out.

But in those twilight days of colonial rule it was considered bad form to do anything which might embarrass the local 'Establishment' or shake its tenet of *laissez-faire*, and slowly the *Vipya* incident became effaced from the Lake's memory as though it had been no more than an oppressive dream which had disturbed its afternoon nap.

Part Five

KWACHA

LAKE MALAWI

Among the many tantalising 'ifs' in the story of Lake Nyasa is the question of how long the fires of African nationalism would have remained slaked there after Chilembwe's failure if they had not been kindled afresh by the imposition on Nyasaland of federation with the two Rhodesias in 1953.

For although association with these vastly richer neighbours would undoubtedly have been in the economic interests of the lake people, the more politically conscious of them saw federation only as a threat to the Protectorate's ordered advance towards independence and (what was more important) to the attainment of power for themselves. In consequence they opposed it passionately. Their animosity spread to other European institutions, and by the judicious use of oratory and intimidation they proceeded to project it on to the masses. Suddenly the whole lake was sounding to a hymn of anti-white hate.

Polemics were replaced by physical violence in the August of 1953 when disturbances broke out at Cholo near Chiradzulu, and they were put down only after eleven Africans had been killed. For the next few years an uneasy quiet reigned beside Nyasa, and nationalism (which differs from patriotism because it is xenophobic) was reduced to the conspiratorial mutterings of a few angry young black men (someone aptly nicknamed them 'the Young Turks') who were prominent members of a political group called the Nyasaland African Congress.

Their deliberations were all haunted by the bespectacled Banquo of John Chilembwe, and although violence was never far from their thoughts, no one was certain how it could be best applied to break up the Federation. About one thing, however, they were all agreed; they required a prestigious father-figure uninhibited by tribal jealousies to sweep the masses into the ranks of Congress. 'What was needed', as one of them, Henry Masauko Chipembere, put it later, 'was a kind of saviour.' He might with more accuracy have said what they really wanted was 'a prophet to prepare our way'.

Unfortunately their choice was limited; very few Nyasas measured up to their requirements. But they remembered that sympathetic noises about their cause had been coming recently from a London suburb, where a certain Dr. Hastings Banda was engaged in general practice, and after some deliberation a letter was despatched asking him to assume leadership of Congress, in the happy expectation that he would prove of suitably malleable material. Little did they know their man; they required a 'front': they obtained a master.

This they might have anticipated had they given the matter a little more thought. For there was already a touch of fantasy about Dr. Banda's career. Born in 1902,* of humble Cewa parents who claimed relationship with Chief Mwase, he had been christened Hastings after one of the Livingstonia missionaries, but fortunately the second name chosen for him—Kamuzu—had the more authentic African ring required of a future nationalist leader. He learned to read and write while employed as a domestic by another missionary, Dr. Prentice, and showed such promise that when he was only thirteen years old Hastings went off to Livingstonia for training as a teacher. Then, as now, he was slightly built and this turned out to be awkward a little later when he was entered for a teacher's examination and found himself in a large hall crowded with other candidates. He had been placed towards the back of the hall and directly behind a particularly burly student. It was difficult for him to make out the questions written on the blackboard and Banda stood up to read them over the shoulder of the youth in front. His action was misinterpreted by the invigilator and he was promptly expelled from the examination. It was an event that passed almost unnoticed at the time, but it changed the history of the lake.

Banda felt himself an outcast in a hostile world, and with a vague intention of continuing his studies at Lovedale, he ran away from home. He was barefoot and almost penniless and his funds gave out by the time he got to Hartley in Southern

* 1902 is the date generally accepted for Dr. Banda's birth, but it is given as 1905 in the most recent edition of *Who's Who*.

Rhodesia. Banda was obliged to take a job as an Orderly in the local hospital. Finding conditions there distasteful, he soon moved on to the Reef where he obtained employment as a clerk-interpreter. The Doctor has always been very reticent about his life in South Africa, but it is still possible to build up a blurred portrait of him in Johannesburg, hating the country's racial policy (yet not omitting to learn nationalism from the Afrikaaners), working conscientiously at his job, trudging off each evening to night classes, and augmenting his income by teaching in a Sunday School. His studies may have been intermittent but there was no doubt about his energy and aptitude. Presently a group of American missionaries began to take an interest in the promising young man, and eventually they provided funds for him to enter a high school in Ohio. That was the turning point; in 1931 Mr. Banda emerged from Xenia College as a Bachelor of Philosophy. But the focus of his interests had altered now. Mindful, perhaps, of the crude conditions he had known at Hartley, he announced his intention of studying medicine, and thanks to the continued generosity of his American friends, Banda enrolled at Meharry College in Tennessee. And in 1937 the small boy who had run away from the lake twenty-two years before qualified as a doctor. It was an impressive achievement.

One cannot help being struck by the similarity of Banda's career up to this point and Chilembwe's; in both there is the same humble origin, the employment as a white missionary's servant, the seizing of every opportunity to improve themselves and the liberal education in America. But from now on the pattern changes. Banda still required a British qualification before he could work in Nyasaland and just before Hitler's war broke out, he took himself off to Edinburgh to obtain one. Admittedly this meant cutting himself off from his American benefactors, but, following the happy inspiration of seeking help from the Nyasaland Government as well as from his old friends of the Church of Scotland (who unbeknownst to each other both contributed regular cheques), Banda was able to live in circumstances consistent with his new dignity as an Elder of the Kirk. Both missionaries and the Government naturally assumed that their protégé would return to Africa to work under their auspices as soon as he

felt properly qualified to do so. This turned out to be a time consuming process, and both were to be disappointed.

For after he obtained his British diploma in 1941 Dr. Banda,
who had been badly shaken by the course the war was taking,
seemed disinclined to risk himself on a voyage to Africa, and he
embarked instead on an extensive series of post-graduate studies.
His new attitude resulted in Zomba angrily withdrawing its
support, but this scarcely worried him, for the new doctor was
enjoying his work in England, and besides he had little wish to
become the patron of a crowd of indignant relatives, which as he
explained to a friend, might happen if he returned home.

After working for some time at Tyneside, Dr. Banda drifted
into the comfortable prosperity of a Harlesden practice. He was
forty now. His tastes seemed formed. It seemed that the attractions
of middle-class England had triumphed over emancipatory zeal.
But if his ambitions had become distinctly London suburban, they
were spiced as time went on by contact with a coterie of ex-
patriate rebels from all parts of Africa. Indeed there was sometimes a faintly conspiratorial air about his cosy house at No. 8
Aylestone Avenue, Kilburn, when friends like Kenyatta and
Kwame Nkrumah dropped in, and perhaps it was due to their
prompting that when the federation of his country with the
Rhodesias was mooted, Banda felt obliged to favour the Secretary
of State with his views upon the matter in a well-composed
memorandum.

That was a beginning, and Dr. Banda now found himself
increasingly intrigued by the mounting buzz of African nationalist talk around him. Soon the physician's brow was knit more
often over the situation in Central Africa than over the mundane
problems of influenza and infant feeding, while the cajoling
letters that were reaching him from the 'Young Turks' of Nyasaland were inclined to be more carefully studied. Suddenly Dr.
Banda made up his mind to return to Africa, admittedly not to his
own country, but to Ghana. Probably his decision was prompted
as much by an anxiety to play a part in the building of an independent black state as by his growing interest in political power.
Accra's gain was Harlesden's loss, for that depressing suburb
genuinely regretted the departure of the gnomish little Doctor

with the foppish clothes and black Anthony Eden hat. In particular his panel patients missed the kindly coloured man with the thinning hair and the nervous tick of the jaw that reminded them of a cow chewing the cud, who gave them advice in the slightly imperfect English of an Indian babu. But he was happy to be in Africa again, sniffing the political wind, studying the steps that had led Nkrumah to his throne, and establishing a flourishing medical practice. Presently he was able to devote more time than he intended to Nkrumah's generous coaching as the tantalising vision of himself as an emancipator interfered with his work to the sad detriment of his income. But this was not really of much concern, for the letters from Zomba painting a picture of a whole people waiting for his return were growing more persuasive, and in July 1958, Hastings Kamuzu Banda took the plunge and returned to his own country. He had left it forty years before as an almost penniless student; he came back now as a Messiah.

For the kingmakers had not misled him. They had instead performed something of a propaganda miracle on behalf of a man whose physical appearance seemed singularly unsuited for their intended role of a national hero, and Banda found himself greeted at the airport with loud cries of 'Kamuzu is a lion'; his hands (and even his car) were fervently kissed, and his immaculate suit was swathed in animal skins. He found the adulation unexpectedly congenial; few experiences taste sweeter than being regarded as a *Deus ex machina*. And when it turned out he had brought a slogan —'To Hell with Federation'—with him, the cheering rose to a crescendo and his ambitions soared on the updraught of public acclaim. It only then began to dawn on his dismayed creators that their Frankenstein might insist on monopolising the stage longer than they had intended.

It turned out that Dr. Banda had a lively style of oratory, as well as a flair for expressing what his audiences most wanted to hear, so that as he rattled off the familiar litany of anti-Federation grievances, he seemed to give coherence to their aspirations. It did not seem to matter that his harangues were delivered in English (since he knew very little Chinyanja, a fact that later malice maintained gave the lie to his assertion that he had learned the vernacular at his mother's knee); it merely seemed to add to his prestige. Indeed the Doctor appeared to grow in stature as he came into closer contact with the masses; and no doubt his sympathy reached out ever more strongly to the inarticulate multitudes who seemed to depend on him.

His contributions to the anti-Federation cause continued for some time to be entirely verbal, but occasionally his orations gave the impression of condoning thuggery, and the officials in the Secretariat who had welcomed him as a moderating (if slightly droll) influence now began to look on him with sharp disfavour. The Doctor seemed tireless as he travelled up and down the lake shore pouring out streams of highly emotional oratory, which always began with a shrill screech of *Kwacha* repeated three times, and ended with a long-drawn out *Ufulu* screamed at the top of his voice. For he had quickly learnt the arts of demagoguery, and his tirades never failed to leave each audience shouting itself hoarse as he drove off in his grey Land-Rover to address another gathering.

The ranting pilgrimages became less frequent, and tension slackened, when the fly whisk (which Dr. Banda had added to the rich 'personalia' of African nationalist leaders) was put aside for a brass plate and a stethoscope in Blantyre. But it was a short respite. Few men could have failed to become addicted to all the fulsome adulation lavished on him, and although he would talk sometimes of self-exile in St. Helena (made fashionable by an earlier hero) those threats alternated with more spirited avowals that, 'I hope soon to set the whole of Nyasaland on fire'. The Christmas of 1958 came in with events moving towards a climax. Banda had been reproached for lack of revolutionary ardour during a short visit to Accra, and he returned spoiling for a fight. His followers caught his mood. Murder was in the air when a mass meeting of Congress supporters held secretly in the bush discussed the best way of eliminating 'quislings' and Government officials (together with their families); indeed the crowd abandoned itself to a flurry of wild threats and exhortations until it began to pour with rain and the chief delegates found it was time for them to attend a dance arranged in their honour.

But memories had reached back to the days of the Chilembwe Rising and as Banda drew on his rich store of invective to castigate the authorities afresh, a rash of disturbances broke out all over the country. Violence first flared up (predictably) at Karonga and soon afterwards even the missionaries at Livingstonia were stoned. The situation then deteriorated so quickly that the alternatives for the Government became plain; it must either act or abdicate. It decided to act. In a *coup* (which someone in unconscious parody of *Kwacha* christened 'Operation Sunrise') mounted at dawn on March 3rd, 1959, hundreds of Congress members were arrested. Despite all the heady talk and brave threats, resistance was remarkably slight. Even Dr. Banda's bodyguard melted away into the night as the 'Great Kamuzu' was hustled off in his pyjamas to detention in Gwelo gaol. Only at Nkata Bay did 'Operation Sunrise' run into serious trouble.

Nkata Bay possesses something of the tinkling creole charm of the Caribbean, and many people consider it the prettiest place on the whole lake. The bay itself is divided by a small promontory into two bights, both of which provide good deep-water anchorages. A semicircle of wooded hills lies behind the little port; they are the Vipya foothills in which almost exactly a hundred years before 'Operation Sunrise' was launched, Dr. Livingstone was lost and nearly died. To the south these hills end sharply in Europa Point overlooking the smaller of the two bights, and here the homes of the white community have been set up. Half a mile away the houses of the little town are clustered on a narrow plain beside the lake. The main road from Mzimba approaches them from the north, curving and zig-zagging steeply down the hills; after passing through the town it terminates in a dock area which is enclosed by a security fence; the wharf can only be entered through the double swing gate made of heavy wire mesh which gives on to a twenty-foot wide approach road cut into the steep grassy bank that falls down to the water. After about sixty feet this road opens out into the wharf itself, from which a section of Bailey bridge leads to a floating jetty where lake steamers and motor vessels can tie up.

In 1959, Nkata Bay was known to be a stronghold of the

African Congress, and nine of its local members had been ear-marked for arrest during 'Operation Sunrise'. The precaution had already been taken of reinforcing the town's normal police complement of one white Inspector and fourteen native constables with eight askaris of the K.A.R., but it was appreciated that this force might still be inadequate once news of the arrests became public. Accordingly orders had gone out to a Major Morrison at Mzimba, one hundred and twenty miles from Nkata Bay, to place himself and two platoons of the Royal Rhodesia Regiment—a white territorial unit—at the disposal of the District Commissioner, Nkata Bay, early on the morning of 'D Day'. His instructions were to leave Mzimba at one o'clock that morning: he was expected to pass through Mzuzu half-way down the road soon after daybreak and arrive at Nkata Bay about nine. No one has ever explained why he did not in fact turn up there until three that afternoon. Out of that delay came tragedy.

The D.C. at Nkata Bay had received secret instructions to carry out the arrests at dawn on March 3rd, and to hold his prisoners in the local gaol until the M.V. *Mpasa* arrived at 6.30 that same morning to pick them up. The *Mpasa* was then to sail on to Karonga, collect more detainees and return a little later to Nkata Bay for another batch being brought down from Mzimba, before transporting them all to railhead at Chipoka. A sergeant and eleven young territorials of the R.R.R. had been temporarily posted to the ship to guard the expected seventy-odd detainees.

Everything went to plan to begin with; the arrests were quickly and unobtrusively carried out at first light, and when the *Mpasa* tied up punctually at 6.30 the prisoners were driven down from the gaol to be battened down in her hold.

But soon afterwards news of the arrests became public, and little groups of men and women gathered in the town's dusty streets to discuss them. As their numbers grew, agitators appeared and harangued them; there was a slow drift towards the prison and men were shouting to each other they must release their friends. They were not aware as yet that the detainees were already securely held in the *Mpasa*. Meanwhile, from the deck of that boat the sergeant of the R.R.R. had been watching the crowds gathering and presently, realising they meant trouble, he went ashore and posted four of his eleven men to guard the Boma and two more to reinforce the K.A.R. askaris at the Post Office.

The gaol at Nkata Bay adjoins the Post Office where an uneasy line of policemen armed with truncheons were standing on guard. Soon they were confronted by a mob of men and women numbering about six hundred and it was becoming more excited with every moment that passed. Presently the D.C., who was well known to them all, appeared, but the rabble refused to be pacified. He himself was gripped by a terrible fear that once the demonstrators realised their friends had been spirited away from the gaol they would run amok and revenge themselves on the white women and children sheltering in the houses on Europa Point. He was comforted, however, by the thought that Morrison's men would arrive soon to restore the situation, and at about 8.45 a.m. he slipped away to contact his opposite number at Mzuzu by wireless and enquire when they might be expected. To his great distress he learned that Morrison had not even reached Mzuzu. But when he went on to describe the ugly situation developing at Nkata Bay, the authorities decided to dispatch Lieutenant Southey's platoon of K.A.R., available then at Mzuzu, to his help immediately.

Back in town the D.C. found the crowd by now had increased to a thousand and was more hostile than ever. And presently the word went round that the prisoners were in the *Mpasa*; after a shouted discussion, the mob surged down towards the wharf carrying the protesting D.C. with it. Although this new development promised to be dangerous for him personally, he was relieved that attention was still diverted from Europa Point, and he was confident too that there was no danger of the mob effecting the prisoners' release for he had ordered the master of the *Mpasa* to leave the wharf at the first sign of trouble.

But the D.C. had not reckoned with the calibre of the R.R.R. sergeant who all this time had been studying the situation developing in the town. When he saw the rabble swarming towards him chanting 'to the ship' and carrying the D.C. in its midst he refused point blank to allow the master of the *Mpasa* to cast off, for as he explained afterwards he had no intention of abandoning the six men he had already posted on shore. Instead, leaving a single soldier to guard the prisoners, he hurried his remaining four men on to the wharf, intending to prevent anyone entering the dock area. They reached the gate just ahead of the mob. Hoping that the D.C. would be able to slip through to join him, the sergeant decided not to lock it.

Perhaps that decision was a mistake; a moment later the rabble had surged through the gate and were pressing against the four soldiers who had lined up across the approach road. The sergeant quickly took stock of the situation; he saw that the road widened out some sixty feet behind him, and knew that once pushed past that point nothing could stop the mob from fanning out and overwhelming his men. He shouted to the four young soldiers to stand fast.

For the next hour a crowd of shouting, sweating men and women, a thousand strong, stood jeering and shouting obscenities at the four Rhodesians, spat at them, wriggled naked bellies against their bayonets, daring them to draw blood and threatening to tear them to pieces; there was even an angry argument about who was to have the ring they had seen on one soldier's finger once he had been killed. As the sun rose higher in the sky and a damnable heat was added to the charged atmosphere on the quayside, with infinite slowness the crowd moved forwards; by infinite degrees the soldiers were forced back. One still wonders how those young recruits stood the strain of that hour, how the line held. To them it must have seemed a miniature eternity, a horror without ending. From the *Mpasa* a few yards away its master thought that the whole scene might have been stage-managed for theatrical effect, and wondered what would occur to break the unbearable tension. In its way this was one of the strangest hours the lake had ever known. If one of the soldiers had so much as flinched all four would have been engulfed in an instant; as it was they were remarkably fortunate that no one in all that sea of faces before them thought of scrambling on to the grassed ramp beside the road, to reach the wharf beyond.

All this time the sergeant with a sten gun under his arm moved easily and confidently behind his men, hiding his fears, steadying them now and then with a word, encouraging them with the news that Southey's askaris would be appearing very soon. At the first opportunity the D.C. managed to push through the throng to join him, and three times the sergeant implored him to allow his men to disperse the mob with a few shots; it would save much greater bloodshed in the end, he said; and three times he was refused.

The crisis came that morning at about 11.30. The line of bayonets had been forced back at last to where the road opened out on to the wharf, and no one had any illusions about what would happen if they went back any farther. Wearily the D.C. formally handed over his powers to the military, and a sharp command rang out: the four soldiers took fifteen paces to the rear and on the order 'at the crowd, present', their rifles went up smartly to their shoulders. A dreadful silence fell upon the crowd, but it still came on in a slow, ominous movement.

The sergeant called to his men to stand at ease, and immediately the mob began howling for their blood again. He decided to try his luck another notch; his men were withdrawn again, presented their rifles, stood at ease and retired for the third time. And still the mob advanced; he could do no more; nothing but shooting would stop it now. The sergeant's voice could be heard above the din calling for independent fire. A few moments later the road was empty—but it was not quite empty; forty sprawled bodies lay on the dark asphalt. The sound of the firing echoed round the hills and then there was silence, broken only by a few moans. And at that moment Southey's lorries drove up to the gate.

The four young Rhodesian soldiers still stood in their line across the wharf, but they were swaying a little now and one of them was being sick. The Amritsar of the lake was over; Malawi had her martyrs; and things there between black men and white would never be quite the same again.

❧   ❧

The New Year came in with Dr. Banda still in prison, and it seemed that 1959 would join 1915 and 1953 as just another date in the calendar when an unsuccessful attempt had been made to oust European influence from the lake. But the winds of change were already blowing hard through Africa and within five years he would be dictator of an independent Malawi. For having won a war against Fascism, the British had taken stock of their Empire and decided it was wrong for them to govern people without their consent. The attempt to deal with Nyasaland by fobbing her off on the Rhodesias had not been a success, and so while Banda languished in Gwelo, Whitehall with dignified deliberation adopted a policy of 'scuttle' from Livingstone's 'lake of stars'.

For Britain it was not a particularly heartbreaking or ruinous decision; after all, in the new rocket age, the Protectorate was of little strategic value; it was not on the way to anywhere, it possessed neither oil nor gold, and there seemed to be no question of abandoning Christian missions to savagery, for was not the nation's chosen leader an Elder of the Kirk?

But he could hardly be expected to run a country from Gwelo gaol, and presently (it was All Fools' Day, 1960) Dr. Banda emerged from prison, and took over the active leadership of the Malawi Congress Party which had grown from the ashes of his old African Congress. There was an unexpected sound about its name, but ever since someone rummaging about in the British Museum had come across a map with Ghana written across it, it had become fashionable to resuscitate old native names for African states and political parties; indeed the officers of the new nationalist party in Nyasaland had merely followed a trend when they incorporated in its title a variant of Maravi.

It was a shade disconcerting for the pundits of Whitehall to discover that Dr. Banda's political demands (as political demands are so apt to do) had improved with keeping. There could apparently be no question now of a period of apprenticeship. The Federation was to be broken up without delay. He insisted, moreover, on a brand new constitution for his country, and after London had been treated to the spectacle of yet another bewildered delegation of black freedom fighters enquiring the way to Lancaster House, he got it. The Doctor plunged at once into the excitement of a general election (it is chiefly remembered today because of the sinister implications seen in the popularity of pepsi-cola on the lake shore, for their bottle tops were painted

Waiting for M.V. *Ilala*, Nkata Bay

Likoma Cathedral today

in the colours of the rival political party), and when the results
were announced, it was clear that Dr. Banda controlled the
Assembly.

As he and his 'boys' gathered up the reins—and sweets—of
office, the familiar pattern of a one-party dictatorship impressed
itself on a country which had been opened up by 'commerce and
Christianity,' and the new Prime Minister began to enjoy himself.
He found it delightful to put in a word for a friend with distinguished foreigners, to drop a hint to a respectful diplomat, to
hob-nob with fellow premiers (and even with Royalty) and to
accept election to honorary membership of the Mark Twain
Society of Kirkwood, Mis. And Dr. Banda, who always relished
flattery, could scarcely complain of the quality and quantity that
was lavished on him. He was known now among his followers as
the *Ngwazi* (the peerless one), the *Kamukwala* (great saviour)
and the 'Messenger of God'. In the Assembly he presided (in an
attitude which combined those of *Le Roi Soleil* on his *lit de justice*
and a cheer-leader at an American football game) over debates
that seemed to border on lunacy. During them the 'peerless one'
found it possible to incline his head graciously when a back-
bencher offered to eat a disrespectful political opponent alive,
and even when another assured the House that 'between our
Ngwazi, Dr. Kamuzu Banda, and the God above, there is nothing
but the atmosphere'. But he raised a deprecating hand to the
applause that greeted one member's stern query: 'which one of
you knew that Kamuzu had a toothache in Gwelo and refused to
take an aspro? He preferred death in order to save us.'

In 1964 secession from the Federation was accomplished and
followed by the formal grant of Independence; after a little
persuasion the Duke of Edinburgh flew in to give decent form to
Britain's abdication and watched the Union Jack, that for
seventy-three years had given protection to the lake, make way
for the black green and red tricolor of the sovereign state of
Malawi. *Ufulu* was a reality now, the lake was 'free' at last, except
for that small portion governed by the Portuguese, and no one
expected them to remain there much longer. The *Ngwazi* terminated the celebrations by regaling his radio audiences with five
verses of 'Bringing in the sheaves'. It was an engaging climax to

exactly six years of personal struggle, and somehow that rendering of the old Scots hymn seemed to sum him up as well as anything else could do. For Dr. Banda was a product of the West as well as of Africa. Even if he was a dictator and relished the part, he was also a moderate and a realist at heart, and he preferred phased transition to revolution. Unfortunately moderates did not seem to survive very long in the new political climate of Africa; he was not cast in the proper atavistic mould for a really successful African nationalist. Moreover, he was already uncomfortably aware that, following some assiduous practice in the wings, other voices (they sounded suspiciously like those of the 'kingmakers') were preparing to break in upon his solo. Nor was it so easy to propitiate them with hysterical abuse of the politicos in Salisbury, now that federation, which had always provided such a convenient face when he wanted one to shake his fist in, had been dissolved. He almost missed it.

A little wearily the Doctor (he was well in his sixties now) turned to the problem of ruling a country which combined a rapidly increasing population with a rapidly decreasing soil fertility. Other nations would have to help him feed his people even though their policies might have been previously denounced as anathema; after all he had always said: 'I would even have the devil as my ally.' And as the obedient lake occasionally pivoted sharply to face the north and east with wild swings back to the west again, the sounds of drum beats coming up the wind were throbbing with the discords of communism, and they sounded ominously like the rumblings of a distant storm.

The lake had always been a testing ground for good and evil; now destiny had placed her squarely on the frontier of the two contending philosophies 'scrambling' for the soul of Africa. No one could tell which way that struggle would go, but today there is about Lake Malawi a strange sensation that a full circle had been turned, of a 'this is where we came in' feeling, and that the old saying 'when you play the flute at Zanzibar, all Africa as far as the lakes dances' may become as true there soon as it was on that morning just over one hundred years ago when Livingstone first saw its gleaming waters.

EPILOGUE

If any traveller was so hard pressed for time that he could spare only nine days for a tour of Central Africa, he could do no better than spend them in the modern motor vessel *Ilala II* which sails round Lake Nyasa twice every month. During an unsophisticated 'package tour' (which nevertheless lasts twice as long as an Atlantic crossing) he can watch the enchanted world of tropical Africa drifting by from the comfort of a deck chair, and see the lake shore almost exactly as Dr. Livingstone saw it over a hundred years ago. And he will learn more in those nine days about the fascination and problems of authentic Africa than all the libraries of Europe could teach him in a year.

Ilala II is more like a yacht than a ship, and all sense of time is lost during the sunlit idyll of her voyage. The days dissolve into a kaleidoscopic blur of gold and blue and green; the tourist guesses the time by his appetite, and recalls the date only by scheduled calls at out-of-the-way places that have the most tenuous connections with the outside world. The lake ports have more the atmosphere of the South Sea islands than of Africa; their surroundings are still largely *terra incognita*.

Sir Harry Johnston's *British Central Africa*, published in 1897, even now is the best guide-book to the region. In these ports nothing seems to matter very much except the fortnightly calls of the *Ilala*, and their entire populations are content to spend a whole morning sheltering from the wheeling sun under palms and spreading mango trees watching the ship come slowly up the lake.

Each day on board, amid the excited bell ringing, siren shrieks, and hooting that seem inseparable from all maritime arrivals and departures, laughing crowds of Africans line up on the *Ilala*'s deck to disembark, cluttered up with baggage that includes bicycles, cages filled with squawking fowls, sewing machines and even tethered goats. They are ferried ashore in lighters which return an hour or so later crammed with another batch of passengers who quickly settle down in their cramped quarters to cards and singing and sleeping and the preparation of meals in

281

little cooking pots. It all looks and sounds like a cross between Hampstead Heath on Bank Holiday and an Eastern market, but when the ship weighs anchor again the noise dies down and the first-class passengers—most of whom are white—resume their novels, their deck chairs and their worship of the sun.

The wise tourists plan their lake trips between April and September. Usually they join the *Ilala* at Monkey Bay, one of the scenic gems of Nyasa, and not far distant from Fort Johnston, where they will have been shown Jock's Hotchkiss gun and other relics of the *Gwen*. Most of them still have time before embarking to visit Old Livingstonia a few miles away across the neck of Cape Maclear. A great baobab tree which surely dates from pygmy times marks the site of the first European settlement on the lake. Today the silence there is absolute and all traces of the buildings set up by Laws have long since been consumed by the unrelenting bush. Indeed the only reality about Old Livingstonia now seems to lie in faded mission records, and the five crosses on the mountainside half a mile away which mark the graves of the Free Church Mission's lakeside pioneers.

On the first morning out of Monkey Bay, *Ilala* clears the peninsula which Livingstone somewhat grandiloquently described as a 'grand mountainous promontory' and named after his friend Maclear. Then the boat sets course for Chipoka to embark freight and more passengers from the railhead. Although the fretted scarp of the Great Rift, and the Dedza mountains ahead are impressive enough, and particularly beautiful in September when the trees on their slopes put out the scarlet leaves of spring, the coast line here is flat and swampy, and only interesting because the Akafula fought their last battle among the palms nodding and rustling beside the water. The lake is at its narrowest beyond Chipoka; Makanjira's village can be seen quite easily twelve miles away on the eastern shore where that cannibal chief once seized and whipped Acting-Consul Buchanan. Passing to the lee of the lovely Maleri islands which are feathered with tall trees, the *Ilala* comes close in-shore and passes the rambling tourist hotels of Salima, close enough indeed for her passengers to make out groups of black girls washing their colourful wraps beside clusters of white rocks in the shallow water. The bay beyond is the one in which Bishop Maples was drowned. From now on the whole lake shore is saturated with memories of Dr. Livingstone. Out in deep water for instance stands Mbenji Island which unaccountably reminded him of a thatched house, while to port lies the beach where he and his companions were robbed as they lay sleeping on its sands. A short run north takes the *Ilala* past the zig-zag sand spit which gave Kota Kota its name, and the boat heaves-to there in its wide anchorage amongst a throng of dug-out canoes and dhows whose pattern is identical with those used by the slavers a century ago.

The moment the tourist steps ashore at Kota Kota he becomes aware of a curious feeling of hostility about him—invisible, but menacing and ubiquitous. Nearly all the town's inhabitants are Moslem, and impressive religious ceremonies are to be seen here during Ramadan. A long avenue of gloomy trees runs right through the place, and leads in about half a mile to the 'magnificent wild fig-tree with leaves ten inches long, by five broad' under which Dr. Livingstone preached in 1863, and then sat sadly watching 'gangs of stout young men slaves . . . waiting for exportation'. Close by stands the long thatched church built by the Anglicans at the turn of the century. It is pervaded today by pungent *bouquet d'Afrique* and the ancient evil stench of bats, but it is a moving experience to go inside and peer through the mediaeval gloom at Maples' grave and listen to a familiar hymn being sung by a ragged group of Christians in unfamiliar Chinyanja. The town itself has altered very little since the time it was the chief slave emporium of the lake shore; it is still famous for ivory carvings which are hawked assiduously to tourists. Wandering through the labyrinth of sandy paths that separate its huts, one catches a glimpse here and there of a beautifully worked Arab door which once led into the establishment of some slaving magnate. A hundred years ago an important slave ferry ran from Kota Kota to the village of Losefa, which on a clear day can be seen across the lake. This is the place where Roscher (who called it Nusewa) lived for months in 1859, and whose prosperity sixteen years later shocked Laws and Young.

Immediately after leaving Kota Kota, the *Ilala* passes the Kaombe river mouth where one can still enjoy with Livingstone the spectacle of schools of hippopotomi wallowing in the shallows. A few miles farther on the Dwangwa river opens into the bay which 'was filled with breakers' when the Doctor's party rode out the 'terrible trios' that so nearly put a premature end to the Zambesi expedition. *Ilala* now steers more north-easterly, and comes in close to the Mozambique shore. This is W. P. Johnson country, and someone will point out the 'earthly paradise' of Pachia where he buried his friend Charles Janson one Shrove Tuesday. The boat soon comes up to Likoma Island and anchors off the sandy bay where witches were burned even after the land had been given to missionaries. Likoma today is a saddening place to visit: one of the towers of the great cathedral has already fallen, while the crumbling away of the remaining structure seems to emphasise the spiritual decay of the islanders, who, despite three-quarters of a century of concentrated proselytism, recently summoned a celebrated witch-doctor from the western lake shore to exorcise them of their demons.

The straits between Likoma and her sister island of Chisamula are ruffled by a half knot current; this Charybdis of the lake is widely believed to be the home of the marine monsters which have been seen as far away as Cape Maclear. Leaving it to port, a leisurely afternoon's run takes the *Ilala* straight across the lake to Nkata Bay. This is an enchanting spot; it is delightful to go ashore here for a bathe in the clear surf of Chikwala Beach. Passengers disembark on the wharf which was the scene of the worst blood-letting of the anti-federation disturbances of 1959, and those so disposed may visit the overgrown graveyard where seventeen victims of that tragedy were buried, if only to see a neglected Pantheon which will surely become a place of pilgrimage in the future.

Nkata Bay was the furthest north ever reached by Livingstone during his explorations of the lake, and although he believed it ended only a few miles further north, he left the place a very irritated and disappointed man, because, as he grumbled in a letter sent to Sir Roderick Murchison, 'this is the first time I ever returned without accomplishing all I set out to do'. It is difficult to believe now that only a century ago the peaceful hills above the town were ravaged every year by the Angoni. In them Livingstone trudged for days on end along 'paths purposely destructed', appalled as he went by a grisly succession of 'ruined villages, broken utensils and human skeletons'.

The coast line from Nkata Bay to Karonga is the most picturesque of all the lake. A long wooded ridge, festooned with lacy waterfalls, runs northward beside it, gathering itself up on one side into the splendid cloud-capped Vipya, while on the other a succession of lateral spurs reach down into the water like the gnarled and groping fingers of a gigantic witch. The shore itself is lined with rocks and boulders, which every mile or so give way to perfect half moons of yellow sand bathed in warm transparent water of an unbelievably brilliant blue. They are lined at the water's edge by tall trees standing in their ranks with almost military exactitude. Neat mud huts are perched along the coastal ridge in every glade where they can find a patch of level earth, and at the larger bays they thicken into villages that from the distance look like primitive paradises. Time seems to have stood still in Usisya, and Ruarwe and Mlowi, and it is interesting to go ashore at these places and watch the people living in conditions that have hardly changed since their forebears came to the lake five hundred years ago. The air is filled with the rancid smell of cassava and dried fish; the water laps right up to the doors of huts from whose thatched roofs thin blue veils of smoke drift up endlessly from the fires kept burning inside. Innumerable shouting naked children play in the shallow water, women stand in threes round wooden mortars pounding their grain with long practised rhythm, while groups of their men-folk sit patching home-made fishing nets in preparation for the evening's work.

Beyond Mlowi, the lake's accompanying ridge swells into the great angular mass of Mount Waller, well over 8,000 feet high. On a neighbouring plateau the windows of Livingstonia can be seen sparkling in the sun. Further on the scenery takes on an even greater grandeur as the mountains rear themselves up still higher into the purple heights of the Nyika above Florence Bay. It is here that her course takes the *Ilala* over the rusting hulk of the *Vipya*. At the end of a day's run, whose varied beauty can be surpassed by very few places in the world, she drops anchor as the dying sun begins to streak the blue sky with faint bands of green and rose, in that quiet corner of the lake called Deep Bay which exhales a breathless sense of stillness and peace.

Early next morning the ship anchors off Kombwe Lagoon where the Wankonde were massacred by the Arabs at the beginning of the slave wars. A winding path beside the water leads to Karonga Boma and the little graveyard where Lugard's fighting men lie beside the English and Germans of the 1914 battle. It can be very hot and very oppressive in Karonga; even now a feeling of tension remains there like an enveloping mist too heavy for any wind to lift, and one comes across old men who speak about the times when the ruga-ruga came raiding down the hills. The thought of Lugard's agony in this, the most remote of all the lakeside ports, catches at our sympathy, but it is chiefly Monteith Fotheringham whom one remembers here. Hardly anything remains of Mlozi's old stronghold seven miles away: only the initiated will recognise in a shallow fosse and a few undulations on the plain the Mpata where Sir Harry Johnston earned his knighthood.

Soon after leaving Karonga, the ship enters Tanganyikan waters. So accustomed by now have her passengers become to the clear sea horizons to the north that it comes almost as a shock for them to see that the lake after all has an end. A call is made near its northern tip at Itungi, which having been founded by the Moir brothers was for many years known as Mwaya—the nearest the lake people could get to pronouncing their name. A short drive inland past the scattered banana plantations which so delighted the early visitors to Nkondeland, takes the *Ilala*'s passengers to Kiyela where the Germans concentrated for the invasion of Nyasaland in 1914. This northern extension of the Nkonde plain is a region that is neither land nor water, and even its air has a damp greenish tinge; to the north, however, the ground rises gently to the ridge of the Nyasa-Tanganyika watershed, from which the Akafula and the Bantu who followed them first saw the lake's glistening waters. The lagoon here at Itungi is a favourite refuge for the hippopotomus, and quite obviously it is situated on one of the great routes of avian migration, for the bird-life is particularly vivid, and one recognises visitors that have come here—incredibly—from the Arctic Circle.

286

The *Ilala* turns about at Itungi and after calling in again at Deep Bay follows the course of Mlozi's old slave ferry to Manda on the eastern coast. It is the most exhilarating part of the whole trip; tremendous views are obtained of the blue and silver precipices of the Livingstone mountains plunging straight down into this the deepest part of the lake. The water here is 2,000 feet in depth, and the lake bed lies far below sea-level. This section of the lake shore is still comparatively untamed; one hears stories of witches being burned in the hinterland and some of the African passengers who disembark at Manda are likely to bear marks on their faces which have been scratched there with a chicken claw by an *Nganga* from the western shore in some weird ceremony of exorcism. After passing Liuli, where Johnson's grave broods over his watery parish and a rusted ship's boiler lying in the shallows is all that remains to commemorate Captain Rhoades' old victory, the *Ilala* anchors at Mbamba Bay. In 1875 Young reported seeing 'hundreds of skeletons lying about everywhere' at this bay. Lions still visit its beach at night, but today it is best known for its splendid bathing.

Recrossing the lake to Nkata Bay, the *Ilala* stays there long enough to allow the more active of her passengers to travel through Tonga country to Bandawe where Dr. Laws built his second mission station in the early eighteen-eighties. A haunted graveyard shows how wrong was his aetiological theory that malaria could be avoided by turning his staff houses away from the lake; entire missionary families lie here among many white soldiers from the First World War. It is a peaceful place: the air is woven through with such repose that it is difficult to believe that within living memory this ground was strewn each year with corpses and pock-marked with burnt-out huts after the Angoni raiders had passed by.

After a second call at Kota Kota, the *Ilala* returns down the outgoing course to her home port of Monkey Bay. But no visitor should leave the lake without making a pilgrimage to its southern extremity where it overflows into the Shiré.

In its own way the combination here of spreading blue lake and green river makes this one of the most beautiful scenes of all Nyasa, although there is a feeling something is odd about it, which is not dispelled until one realises that instead of a river feeding into a lake, the reverse takes place and the lake spills out its waters into a drifting stream.

In doing so Lake Nyasa reveals something of her massive power, which a hungry continent cannot long allow to go unharnessed. But whatever may disfigure this unusual river source in the future, the scene today is almost precisely as it was that September morning in 1859 when Dr. Livingstone trudged up a riverside path and gazed at the broad waters stretching away as far as his eye could see. This was then a gateway to an unknown darkness, something of whose horror was revealed that same evening when the explorers met 'a large east-coast slaving party coming from Cazembe's country, having an immense number of slaves and elephant tusks'. For the slave trails of the interior converged upon the Shiré ferry here, before continuing to Kilwa and the sea. Little is left now at the Shiré source to remind us of the routes taken by 'this trade of Hell'—only a few mango trees planted along their course by the Arabs. Nor does one see today the 'banian tree . . . whose pendant branches' according to Charles Livingstone 'resembled a gigantic arm-chair, of course without a seat' under which 'all of us, Drs. L. & K., Rae and myself had our beds spread' on that night of the lake's rediscovery.

Until recently nearly all the men and women who fashioned the story of Lake Nyasa came to it past this Shiré source, and it is a rewarding experience to sit down on the river bank, thinking of all the scenes the place had witnessed, although the bright-winged activity all about continuously disturbs that soliloquy and gives one the sensation of being a spectator at a technicolour production whose *dramatis personae* is composed entirely of birds. Kingfishers plummet like trapeze artists into the river, and rise a moment later spattering jewelled spangles of water into the sluggish Shiré; a troupe of white expectant egrets stands nearby like a supporting chorus waiting for its cue; the quick snake-like heads of cormorants raised to inspect the intruders remind one irresistibly of a nervous producer studying the 'house', and at intervals the great fish eagles, whose particular domain this is, scream out their bursts of raucous applause.

One could never be lonely in this place, if only for its human memories, and of them all Dr. Livingstone's predominate. He came here again almost exactly two years after his original visit, this time by boat and, anticipating every other visitor's experience wrote that he sailed into Lake Nyasa and 'felt refreshed by the greater coolness of the air off this large body of water'. He was here once more in 1866 when he was already drifting into that semi-mystical trance which characterised the last phase of his life, and was distressed to find his discoveries had merely opened up fresh fields to the slavers and that the ferry was in greater use than ever. We know that he sat here on this river bank, brooding over all the place had meant to him, and then turned to set down his reflections in that last journal which he was never to complete. 'Many hopes have been disappointed here,' he wrote. 'Far down on the right bank of the Zambesi lies the dust of her whose death changed all my future prospects; and now, instead of a check being given to the slave-trade by lawful commerce on the lake, slave-dhows prosper! . . . It is impossible not to regret the loss of good Bishop Mackenzie, who sleeps far down the Shiré, and with him all hope of the Gospel being introduced into Central Africa. The silly abandonment of all the advantages of the Shiré route by the Bishop's successor I shall ever bitterly deplore, but all will come right some day, though I may not live to participate in the joy, or even see the commencement of better times.'

How much less despondent he would have felt had he known that only nine years later this river source would hear the triumphant strains of *The Old Hundredth* and see the first *Ilala* steaming into the lake carrying all the bright blessings of Christian civilisation. But Livingstone's melancholy still seems to linger along the river bank, and somehow it communicates itself to everyone who comes here, for they turn away a little sadly when the time comes for them to go, wondering how much longer tolerance and brotherhood can endure beside the lake today, and whether a new darkness even now may not be gathering over these lovely waters.

AIDE MEMOIRE

to the History of Lake Nyasa

c. 5000 B.C. Dessication of Sahara began.

c. 2000 Negro multiplication began.

c. 500 Akafula appeared on Lake shore.

c. 104 A.D. Diogenes reported existence of Great Lakes in Africa.

150 Ptolemy's *Geography* recorded Great Lakes.

c. 400 Bantu appeared on East Coast of Africa.

622 Hegira.

c. 900 Bantu reached Zambesi.

c. 1300 Bantu appeared on Lake shore.

1415 Portuguese captured Ceuta.

c. 1500 Bantu drove Akafula from Lake shore.

1513 Authentic news of Great Lakes reached Portuguese explorers.

1546 Lake Maravi appears on Portuguese maps.

1616 Bocarro visits Lake Maravi.

1722 Correct shape of Lake recorded.

1787 Shaka born.

1796 Pereira journeys past Maravi to Cazembe.

1798 Lacerda visits Cazembe.

1802–10 Pombeiros traverse Africa.

1813 David Livingstone born.

1819 Shaka's victory over Zwide, and Angoni begin northward flight.

1824 Bowdich's book published on interior of Africa.

1835 Angoni hordes cross Zambesi.

1840	Dr. Livingstone ordained as a missionary. Sultan of Muscat moved his court to Zanzibar.
c. 1840	Yao driven from Rovuma.
1845	Zwangendaba died.
1846	Candido visited Lake.
1851	Dr. Livingstone discovered Upper Zambesi.
1853	Dr. Livingstone set off from Linyanti.
1854	Dr. Livingstone arrived Loanda.
1856	Dr. Livingstone met Candido at Tete on journey to East Coast. Dr. Livingstone returned to England.
1857	*Missionary Travels* published.
1858	Zambesi Expedition sailed.
1859	Exploration of River Shiré begins. June 25th. Thornton dismissed. July 29th. Baines dismissed. September 17th. Rediscovery of Lake Nyasa. November 19th. Roscher arrived on Lake.
1860	Roscher murdered (March 19th). May–November. Livingstone's journey to return Makololo to Linyanti.
1861	January. Bishop Mackenzie arrived at Zambesi in *Pioneer*. July. Dr. Livingstone's skirmishes with Yao. Missionaries 'settled' at Magomero. September. Exploration of Lake began.
1862	January 7th. Livingstone passed Ruo on way to Zambesi mouth. January 11th. Mackenzie reached rendezvous. January 31st. Mackenzie died. February 1st. Dr. Livingstone met his wife. February 17th. Wilson went up river ahead of *Pioneer*. February 22nd. Burrup died. April 27th. Mrs. Livingstone died. June 23rd. *Lady Nyassa* launched at Shupanga.

1863   Thornton died.
May 19th. Charles & Kirk left coast for England.
June 26th. Bishop Tozer arrived Chibisa's.
July 2nd. Dr. Livingstone received notice of recall.
July 4th. Dr. Livingstone met Bishop Tozer.
September 10th. Dr. Livingstone arrived Kota Kota during his exploration of Lake shore.

1864   Dr. Livingstone steamed *Lady Nyassa* to Bombay.

1865   *Narrative* published.

1866   Dr. Livingstone reached Lake during his last journey.

1871   John Chilembwe born.

1873   Dr. Livingstone died.

1875   Young and Laws reached Lake and circumnavigated it.

1878   A.L.C. formed.
Rev. Duff Macdonald took charge of recently established Mission at Blantyre.

1882   W. P. Johnson and Charles Janson reached Lake.

1883   A British Consul appointed to Lake Country.

1884   A.L.C. established a store at Karonga.

1885   Berlin Act.

1886   Johnston spends a week-end at Hatfield.

1887   November 23rd. Fighting began with Mlozi.
December 23rd. Mlozi's stockade stormed by John Moir's party.

1888   March 3rd. Frederick Moir assumed command at Karonga.
April 10th. Incendiary attack on stockades.
May 28th. Lugard's party reinforced Karonga.
June 15th. Lugard's failure against stockades.
November. Johnston appointed Consul.

1889   February 21st. Lugard attacked stockade with 7 lb. cannon.
March 17th. Lugard left Karonga.

August 19th. Protectorate proclaimed over Shiré Highlands.
October 22nd. Johnston made truce with Mlozi.

1891 Nyasaland proclaimed a British Protectorate with Johnston Commissioner.

1892 Joseph Booth arrived Shiré Highlands.

1893 Chilembwe baptized.
A. L. Bruce Estates formed.

1895 July. Johnston paid a remonstratory visit to Mlozi
September 2nd. Chauncy Maples drowned.
December. Johnston defeated and hanged Mlozi.

1897 John Chilembwe went to U.S.A.

1900 John Chilembwe returned to Nyasaland.

1902 Dr. Hastings Banda born.

1905 Maji Maji Rising.

1908 Elliott Kamwana began preaching on Lake shore.

1909 Kanwana deported.

1914 August 13th. Rhoades' 'victory' at Sphinxhaven.
September 8th. Battle of Karonga.

1915 Dr. Hastings Banda left Lake shore.

1915 January 23rd.–February 4th. Chilembwe Rising.

1937 Hastings Banda qualified as a doctor in U.S.A.

1944 Nyasaland African Congress formed.

1946 July 30th. Sinking of M.V. *Vipya*.

1953 August 1st. Federation of Nyasaland with the Rhodesias.

1958 July 6th. Dr. Banda returned to Nyasaland.

1959 March 3rd. 'Operation Sunrise'.

1960 April 1st. Dr. Banda released from gaol.

1964 Nyasaland granted Independence under the name Malawi.

BIBLIOGRAPHY

Introduction and Chapter 1

Several detailed accounts of the formation of Lake Nyasa have been given by F. Dixey: a useful one is in *The Geographical Journal* LXVII, 2. A more recent study of this subject by J. G. Pike and G. T. Rimmington appears in *Malawi, a Geographical Study.* (O.U.P., 1965); these authors have also considered the variations in the Lake's level. Both these reports are written for the expert, and the general reader will probably prefer those in F. Debenham's *Nyasaland* (H.M.S.O., 1955) and S. S. Murray's *Handbook to Nyasaland* (Crown Agents for the Colonies, 1932). Archaeological evidence suggests that the pygmies settled on the lake shore several hundred years before the Christian era. But the earliest report I can find of the transitional culture of the Akafula is that given by the Arab Massoudi in his famous *Rivers of Gold* which he wrote about A.D. 915. Although not dealing directly with Nyasa country J. D. Clark's *The Prehistory of Southern Africa* (Penguin Books, 1959) and Sonia Cole's *The Prehistory of East Africa* (Harmondsworth, 1954) are standard works for this period. Much of our knowledge of the Akafula is due to the painstaking researches of my friend W. H. J. Rangeley, whose early death was an irreparable loss for all students of the Lake's history. Many of his papers have appeared in *The Nyasaland Journal*. There are few aspects of the Lake which have not been considered in this most admirable publication. The Akafula are considered in Vol. XVI, 2, by Rangeley, in Vol. IX, 1, by Clark, and in Vol. XIII, 1, by Pike.

Chapter 2

I have followed the most generally accepted version of the causes and sequence of the Bantu migration, but the dates given are necessarily approximate. The most useful sources on the subject that I have been able to consult are A. J. Wills' *An Introduction to the History of Central Africa* (O.U.P., 1964), D. L.

Wiedener's *A History of Africa South of the Sahara* (Random House, New York, 1962) and *History of East Africa* by Roland Oliver and Gervase Mathew (Clarendon Press, Oxford, 1963). An account by J. G. Pike in *The Nyasaland Journal*, Vol. XVIII, 1, is an excellent summary, and I found Basil Davidson's *Old Africa Rediscovered* (Gollancz, 1959) extremely readable on this subject.

The Portuguese on the Zambesi have told us a certain amount about the Amaravi, but it is not until after the arrival of Dr. Livingstone and his followers on the Lake that we obtain reliable first-hand descriptions of them. Some of the most vivid accounts of the Lake Africans as they were a hundred years ago are given by Henry Rowley in *The Story of the Universities' Mission to Central Africa* (Saunders, Otley & Co., 2nd edition, 1867), and in Dr. James Stewart's *Journals* published in the Oppenheimer series. Sir Harry Johnston's magnum opus *British Central Africa* (Methuen, 1897) is however recognised as the authoritative work on the subject.

Accounts of their traditional migration routes are still given today by the Lake people. They have been recorded by T. Price and also by J. Bruwer in *African Studies*, Vols. 9 and 11, while another equally good sketch appears under J. G. Pike's name in *The Nyasaland Journal*, VIII, 1. H. Gann's *A History of Northern Rhodesia* (Chatto & Windus, 1964) contains an informative section on the Bantu way of life, and is especially useful in helping to clarify their patrilineal and matrilineal affinities. A great deal of light has been thrown on recent local tribal history by Mary Tew in her *The Peoples of the Lake Nyasa Region* (O.U.P., 1950).

In considering the anatomical and physiological distinguishing characteristics of the Bantu, I have drawn heavily on Dr. J. C. Carruther's *The African Mind in Health and Disease* (W. H. O., Geneva, 1953) and on the several studies made by my friend Professor M. Gelfand, whose findings are lucidly summarised in *The Central African Journal of Medicine*, Vol. 5. No. 3. The note about the appearance of the name Lake Maravi on a Portuguese map of 1546 is taken from a paper by T. Cullen Young in *African Studies*, 1950, IX, p. 30.

CHAPTER 3

In considering the alien invasions of Maravi, I have depended again upon the sources mentioned in connection with Chapter 2. I found the history of the Yao ably dealt with in *Seven Tribes of British Central Africa* by Elizabeth Colson and Max Gluckman (Manchester University Press, 1951), by Rangeley in *The Nyasaland Journal*, XVI, 1, and by J. Clyde Mitchel in *African Studies*, 1949. Of course Livingstone touches repeatedly on the tribal history of the Yao in his books.

A vast bibliography of the Portuguese penetration of Central Africa is in existence, and much of it is now available in English. Many of these reports are more concerned with a patriotic claim to priority of discovery than with veracity and they make very confusing reading. Fortunately Eric Axelson has analysed these sources in scholarly surveys entitled *South-East Africa 1488-1530* (Longmans, Green & Co., 1940) and *The Portuguese in South-East Africa, 1600-1700* (Johannesburg, 1960). Rangeley collected a great deal of information about the Portuguese influence on the Lake, and some of it was published posthumously in *The Nyasaland Journal*, XVII, 1, while R. F. Burton's remarkable *Lacerda's Journey to Cazembe in 1798* (John Murray, 1873) is full of interesting sidelights on their history.

Mention has been made in the text of T. E. Bowdich's *An Account of the Discoveries of the Portuguese* (John Booth, 1824) and of W. D. Cooley's writings. *The Journal of the Royal Geographical Society*, Vol. 15, 1845, and *Inner Africa laid open* (Longman, Brown, Green and Longmans, 1852.) They make dull reading now, but all are adorned by delightfully inaccurate maps.

Nearly all the first-hand accounts written last century about the Portuguese emphasise their corruption and cruelty. Rowley for instance speaks of one planter whose 'whip was the most ferocious looking thing I ever saw. A few lashes were sufficient to reduce a child to insensibility.' He tells us too that his informant assured him 'if you keep slaves . . . you must degrade them by the whip' for they must be 'broken in and flogged to your will'.

Perhaps because the Angoni pride fascinated them, many writers have studied the traditions of this tribe. I found Margaret

Reed's *The Ngoni of Nyasaland* (O.U.P., 1956) to be one of the most relevant books. A small controversy exists about the date of Zwangendaba's crossing of the Zambesi. Some authorities maintain it took place on the 20th and not November 19th, 1835. The matter is discussed by E. H. Lane Poole in *Journal of the African Society*, XXIX, by J. H. Barnes in *Politics in a Changing Society* (O.U.P., 1954), and by Cullen Young in *The Nyasaland Journal*, V, 1. Elmslie's *Among the Wild Angoni* (Oliphant Anderson & Ferrier, 1899) is our most vivid description of the confrontation of the missionaries and Mombera. The dispute between the Angoni clans after the death of Zwangendaba is fully considered by Rangeley in *The Nyasaland Journal*, V, 1.

CHAPTERS 4, 5 and 6

The enormous bibliography of the Zambesi expedition may be divided into four groups: 1. The journals, dispatches and letters of Livingstone and his associates. 2. The books written by them. 3. Biographical material. 4. Commentaries on the expedition.

The first group is by far the most instructive. David Livingstone's own Journal gives a remarkably clear insight into the intentions, achievements and personal relationships of the venture. The Journal of James Stewart is scarcely less valuable in this respect. Both these Journals have been published in the Oppenheimer Series, while some important letters from Livingstone relating to the expedition appear in Volume 2 of this same series, to whose patrons a tremendous debt is owed.

Only second in importance to Livingstone's Journal is that of Dr. Kirk (ed. Reginald Foskett, Oliver & Boyd, 1965), which throws some fresh light on the characters of the expedition's personnel. Kirk's writing has a freshness and vitality not usually found in records of this sort. Among other things it reveals the cruel and wasteful slaughter of big game by the author and his companions, as well as the way Kirk relished (and then soberly analysed) the gossip bandied about during the expedition. These journals were used by Sir Reginald Coupland when he wrote his pioneering *Kirk on the Zambesi* (O.U.P., 1928). Owen Chadwick similarly has quoted many of the Waller papers in *Mackenzie's*

Grave (Hodder & Stoughton, 1959). The Journals of Charles Livingstone and Baines still await publication. The papers of Richard Thornton have recently been published as number 4 of the Robins Series by Chatto and Windus.

Fine collections of the papers of the Livingstone brothers are to be found in the National Archives of Rhodesia and in the Rhodes-Livingstone Museum, Zambia. Dr. Livingstone's journals are mostly written in stout leather-bound volumes with marbled edges and clasp-locks. It is a stirring experience to handle them and read the firm, familiar writing which gives an almost day-to-day record of the expedition. The pungency of the Doctor's comments is a constant stimulant, but every now and then one is pulled up sharply by his lack of charity for his associates. Almost as striking is the way his bursts of anger are recorded in his diary, and then repeated, often with increasing virulence, in later entries and in letters. The variety of words he uses unwittingly on these occasions pays tribute to the writer's wide vocabulary. His references to Thornton's transgressions are an example of this trait which intrigued me. In the February of 1859 he notes the youth 'has been inefficient of late', and 'terribly lazy'. A month later he 'has done next to nothing the last three months'. By June Thornton is 'inveterately lazy', has 'continued idle', and is 'incorrigibly lazy'. Later that year the Doctor informs various correspondents he had dismissed the miscreant because he was 'so extremely lazy', suffered from 'sheer laziness', 'had lost all appearance of energy', and was 'insufferably lazy'.

But it is Livingstone's occasional harshness which most startles the readers of his journals and letters. Knowing how attached he became to the Bishop, it seems difficult to believe Waller that soon after Mackenzie's death the Doctor remarked in the presence of his bereaved sister Ann, 'that the missionaries, dead, would be replaced by better men' (quoted Chadwick, p. 144). But it seems he did, for Livingstone uses similar words in a letter to Stewart (*Stewart's Journal*, p. 208) in April 1862: 'This sad loss will have one good effect: better men will be sent and no one hereafter come for a lark or to make a good thing of playing the missionary for a few years and then reaping laurels,' while two days later he informs his brother-in-law, J. S. Moffat, 'Bishop took fever . . .

and perished. .... The effect will be better men will come to the work' (*The Matabele Mission*, p. 170).

In some strange way, however, the radiance of David Livingstone's spirit is not dimmed but rather accentuated by those darker frailties of his soma which are exposed in papers he always intended to be kept private. In fact he emerges from his journals irritable and sometimes unjust, yet grown in stature, prodigious in energy, untouched by fear and urgent for the Right.

The *Narrative of an Expedition to the Zambesi and its Tributaries* (John Murray, 1865) is the account of the venture Livingstone wrote on his return to England. He made some use of his brother's diaries, and accordingly Charles Livingstone's name appears as its co-author in order that he might collect the American royalties. The book is far less absorbing than the earlier *Missionary Travels*. For one thing it is written in the third person which detracts from its intimacy. The unhappy personal relationships of the expedition are ignored or glossed over, while a listless, detached style makes it difficult sometimes to follow the sequence of events.

Narrative is nevertheless our best basic survey of the expedition. The only comparable account is Henry Rowley's studiedly discreet *The Story of the Universities' Mission to Central Africa* (Saunders, Otley & Co., 2nd edn., 1867). Its author was one of the clergymen who accompanied Mackenzie to Magomero. He was a prickly character. In his usual forthright style Livingstone describes him as 'a sad blethering fellow' who was 'red hot high church' (Chadwick, p. 144 and *Matabele Mission*, p. 165). Rowley considered Livingstone responsible for the Bishop's death but (although not hesitating to comment on the unfair treatment of Thornton and Baines) he avoids saying so in his book. He was less reticent, however, in his correspondence, some of which was later published, much to Livingstone's vexation. Rowley's book contains the best account I have seen of the Bishop's controversial decision to make war on the Yao slavers.

Biographies: Many studies of Livingstone have been written. W. G. Blaikie was the first in the field with his *The Personal Life of David Livingstone* (John Murray, 1880) and it is still valuable because it taps material (like the Doctor's Journal for 1862) which has disappeared. R. J. Campbell's *Livingstone* (Ernest Benn,

1929) is only useful for the L.M.S. correspondence it quotes. A more perceptive work is J. I. Macnair's *Livingstone the Liberator* (Collins, 1940), but it is Frank Debenham who gives us the first real insight into the character of his subject in *The Way to Ilala* (Longmans, Green & Co., 1955). Professor Gelfand has made a contribution to an aspect which is rarely noted in *Livingstone, the Doctor* (Oxford, Basil Blackwell, 1957).

The list of biographies might be almost indefinitely extended, but particular reference must be made to George Seaver's scholarly *David Livingstone* (Lutterworth Press, 1957) which I found the best and most informative of them all.

Notice has already been taken of Coupland's study of Dr. Kirk. The same author's *Livingstone's Last Journey* (Collins, 1945) is an enthralling account of the Doctor's final years. As are all students of the Zambesi Expedition, I am deeply indebted to Professor J. P. R. Wallis, not only for his biographical defence, *Thomas Baines of King's Lynn* (Jonathan Cape, 1941), but even more for his Introductions to the relevant volumes in the Oppenheimer series which are masterpieces of their kind. I have consulted *Stewart of Lovedale* by J. Wells (Hodder & Stoughton, 1908) for details of his life. Roscher's visit to the Lake is mentioned several times in *Narrative*, as well as in Coupland's *The Exploitation of East Africa* (Faber, 1939).

Commentaries: Owen Chadwick, in *Mackenzie's Grave*, already quoted, follows the missionary effort at Magomero in detail, and provides a scrupulously fair version of its tribulations. Some interesting light is thrown on the events which followed the arrival of the *Hetty Ellen* off the Zambesi by W. C. Devereux in his *Cruise in the Gorgon* (Bell & Daldy, 1869). It may not be out of place to make brief mention of what became of Livingstone's original companions. Of them only Thornton perished during the expedition. Bedingfeld's career was not affected by his dismissal: he went on to resume distinguished service in the Navy and retired a Vice-Admiral. Kirk sulked for some time after returning to England, and we find him informing Stewart that he considered Livingstone had behaved to him in 'an underhand way' (*Stewart's Journal*, p. 228). But Livingstone's gesture of naming the long line of mountains extending northwards from the Murchison cataracts to the Lake 'The Kirk Range' went far to heal the rift. Kirk became British Consul at Zanzibar, played a large part in suppressing the east coast slave trade and was knighted for his services.

At the end of the expedition Livingstone decided to steam the *Lady Nyassa* across to Bombay and sell her there. Rae refused to risk himself on so rash a venture. Livingstone rather ungratefully regarded this as cowardly desertion: 'he left us', he announced vindictively, 'out of sheer terror' (*Livingstone's Journal*, p. 387). In fact Rae would have been wiser to remain with his leader; instead he took up a post in the Comoro Islands and promptly died from a 'chronic ulcer of the stomach'. He does not appear to have been deeply mourned by his old colleagues. As with Kirk, Livingstone's influence secured a consulship for his brother. Charles' conduct had improved towards the end of the expedition, and his service at Fernando Po turned out to be exemplary; he died on the west coast of fever in 1873. His bad behaviour during the expedition is an enigma which still awaits solution.

Thomas Baines' rebuttal of Livingstone's charges were rejected by the Admiralty. Yet despite the clouds hanging over him, Baines' subsequent explorations and the quality of his art have made him second in fame among the expedition's personnel, only to Livingstone himself.

CHAPTER 7

I have relied largely for my account of the establishment of the Free Church of Scotland at the Lake on W. P. Livingstone's *Laws of Livingstonia* (Hodder & Stoughton, 1921). This itself takes a good deal of its material from E. D. Young's *Nyassa* (John Murray, 1877) which still makes exciting reading and contains an excellent contemporary map. Laws wrote his own *Reminiscences of Livingstonia* (Oliver & Boyd, 1934) but the book is disappointing, as is Stewart's *Livingstonia, its origins* (privately printed, 1894). The unpleasant events at Blantyre Mission are fully considered by A. J. Hanna in *The Beginnings of Nyasaland and North-Eastern Rhodesia* (Clarendon Press, 1956). Elmslie's book, already mentioned, is the best source for mission work at Bandawe.

The return of the U.M.C.A. to the Lake is well documented. Johnson's own account is given in the disarmingly written *My African Reminiscences, 1875–1895* (U.M.C.A., 1924), but his *Nyasa, the Great Water* (O.U.P., 1922) does not come up to expectations. A. E. M. Anderson-Morshead has provided a general survey of the Mission in *The History of the Universities' Mission to Central Africa* (U.M.C.A., 6th edn., 1955), but I found it unbearably sanctimonious. Much the same ground is covered in *History of the Universities' Mission to Central Africa* by G. H. Wilson (U.M.C.A., 1936). *Johnson of Nyasaland* by B. H. Barnes (U.M.C.A., 1933) is a useful record of the careers of Chauncy Maples as well as of Johnson.

CHAPTERS 8, 9 and 10

The descriptions given of the Wankonde are based largely upon A. J. Swann's *Fighting the Slave-Hunters* (Seeley, 1910), J. Thomson's *To the Central African Lakes and back* (Sampson Low, 1881), and J. F. Elton's *The Lakes and Mountains of Eastern and Central Africa* (Consul Elton's Journal, London, 1879). The horrors of the East African slave trade are recounted in many books. Sir R. Coupland's *East Africa and its Invaders* (O.U.P., 1938), and C. Lloyd's *The Navy and the Slave Trade* (Longmans, 1949) were among the most useful I was able to consult.

Both Hanna and Murray, in books already quoted, have given accounts of the Slave Wars at the north end of the Lake, while P. T. Terry has provided a summary of them in *The Nyasaland Journal*, XVIII, 1. Personal narratives of the fighting are, however, far more interesting. I have thus drawn heavily on Monteith Fotheringham's little known *Adventures in Nyasaland* (Sampson Low, 1891) and on Lord Lugard's largely autobiographical *The Rise of our East African Empire* (Blackwood, 1893). F. L. Moir's *After Livingstone* (Hodder & Stoughton, 1920) deals with his own contribution to the hostilities, while Sir Harry Johnston's somewhat smug *The Story of my Life* (Chatto & Windus, 1923) carries on the record. His *British Central Africa* is the standard authority for the war. I found Margery Perham's *Lugard. The Years of Adventure* (Collins, 1956) most helpful in attempting to unravel the motives that took this unusual man to Karonga. A rather fulsome biography of Johnston by Rowland Oliver (*Sir Harry Johnston and the Scramble for Africa*, Chatto & Windus, 1959) is a useful guide to his hero's career, and some interesting sidelights on Sir Harry appear in R. C. F. Maugham's *Africa as I have known it* (John Murray, 1929).

CHAPTER 11

Many studies of the partition of Africa are available. One of the most relevant is Griff Jones' *Britain and Nyasaland* (Allen & Unwin, 1964). The passages describing the life on the Lake prior to 1939 are based largely on the author's personal experience.

CHAPTER 12

It is unlikely that we shall ever obtain a more authoritative report on the Chilembwe Rising than *Independent African* by George Shepperson and Thomas Price (The University Press, Edinburgh, 1958) and I have been guided by it throughout this chapter.

CHAPTER 13

Much of my information for this chapter was given to me by Dr. Sanderson before he died. Sanderson was a most interesting man; he turned to Islam for his faith and completed a pilgrimage to Mecca. His account of Rhoades' victory was recorded in *The Nyasaland Journal*, X, 2, while G. D. Hayes has written on the same subject in that periodical XVII, 2. The German gunboat was 'demobilised' in 1918 and subsequently reappeared on the Lake as the Mission steamer *Mlonda*.

CHAPTER 14

In describing Barton's victory at Karonga I have used information given to me by survivors of the action. Cullen Young has written about it in *The Nyasaland Journal*, VIII, 2, and it is briefly reported in H. Moyse-Bartlett's *The King's African Rifles* (Gale

& Polden, Aldershot, 1956), Stier's letters are taken from *The Nyasaland Journal,* XVII, 1.

CHAPTER 15

The *Vipya* disaster was reported at length in *The Nyasaland Times* of August 29th, 1946, but a far more useful source is *The Record of the Proceedings of the Court of Enquiry on the loss of the M.V. Vipya* (Govt. Printer, Zomba, 1946) and the account of the two Appeal Courts. Some details were supplied by the author's friends, notably Dr. Whitfield.

CHAPTER 16

The account of the shooting at Nkata Bay is based on the *Devlin Report* (C. Cmd. 814/1959). This is written in a sparkling style unusual in papers of this kind. I found Griff Jones' dispassionate recording of the political unrest that followed Federation in Nyasaland most helpful. Dr. Banda still awaits his biographer. The story of his dismissal from the Examination Hall is taken from *Our African Way of Life* (Lutterworth Press, 1946) which he himself wrote in collaboration with Cullen Young. I have relied for some details in this chapter on reports in *East Africa and Rhodesia,* and for others on my personal knowledge.

INDEX

Achipeta, the, 34
Africa: individual personality of its people, 23; impact of Islam on, 37, 38; her conquerors, 37–8; denominational Christianity and, 139; Colonial competition in, 209–13; growth of nationalism, 219, 220, 252, 267
Africa, Central: negro invasion, 20; Bilharzia its major scourge, 27; impact of Islam on, 37, 38–9, 42; Portuguese intrusions into, 42–51, 52; search for gold, 43–4; outside interest in, 51; Livingstone's explorations and, 68, 70, 73; Mackenzie and, 104; Anglo-Arab conflicts, 153, 155–6; slave trade depredations, 163; naming of 'British Central Africa', 196 and n, 214
Africa, East: World War I and, 243, 251
Africa, Southern, 220; negro migrations into, 19–22; impact of Shaka, 58–9
Africa, West: introduction of Asian food-plants, 19; negro invasion into, 19–20; slave trade, 163
African Lakes Company, 154, 169, 172, 175, 181, 184, 194; becomes a Corporation, 197
African Rift Valley, 1, 3, 13, 151, 253, 282; geological origin, 12
Ajawa, the, see Yao
Ajawa Providence Industrial Mission, 226
Akafula: and Nyasa, 12–14, 22, 286; characteristics and origins, 14–15; daily life, 15–16; extermination, 17–18, 282
Amaravi, the: and Nyasa, 18, 23–6, 42, 209; characteristics, 22–3; their social habits and beliefs, 24–5, 28–34; prey to aggression, 34; known as Manganja, 34; white explorers and, 34–6; historical origins of their destruction, 37–8; and slavery, 40; Portuguese explorers and, 43, 48; terrorised by the Angoni, 62–3; Mackenzie and, 108; villages, 137
Angoni, the, 34, 51, 100, 152, 232, 234; ravages by, 57, 59–63, 110, 113, 137, 143, 223, 287; other names, 61n, 137; and Nyasa, 61–3, 110; mission influence on, 143; partition and, 210
Arabs, 1, 6, 7, 34, 93; reinvigorated by Mohammed, 37; invasions into

Africa, 37, 38–9; and slave trade, 39–41, 63, 98–9, 112, 125, 137, 150, 153–4, 156–63, 286; and Livingstone, 130; defence against Lugard, 183; Johnston and, 194–6; defence of Mpata, 199–203
Askaris, the, 234, 245
Atlay, George, 149
Atonga, the, 181–3, 185–6, 194
Aumann, Lieutenant, 245–6, 249

Bain, Rev. J., 164, 166
Baines, Thomas: and Livingstone's Zambesi Expedition, 83–4, 85, 87, 92, 96–7, 300; later career, 302
Banda, Dr. Hastings, 142, 224, 236; early life and career, 268–70; returns to Africa, 270–1; and Federation, 271–3; imprisonment, 273, 277; leader of Malawi Congress Party, 278–9; Prime Minister, 279–80
Bandawe, 62, 220; Laws and, 142–3, 181, 287
Bangweulu: Livingstone's death, 129
Bantu, 14, 15, 16, 286; and Nyasa, 17–18; origin, 19; migrations, 20–2, 39; racial pecularities, 22–4, 35; culture, 28, 29, 214; slave-trade agents, 40, 42; and Islam, 40, 154; Shaka and, 57–8; impact of denominational Christianity on, 139
Barreto, Fr. Manuel: and the Maravis, 25
Barros, Joao de (1496–1570): and Nyasa, 42–3
Barton, Captain, and Battle of Karonga, 245–51
Batoka Highlands: failure of expedition, to, 54
Bawe, 46
Beaumont, Lieutenant, 239, 242
Bechuanaland, 101, 115; Livingstone's mission station, 68, 79
Bedingfeld, Commander Norman: and Livingstone's Zambesi Expedition, 80–1, 88; later career, 301
Berlin Act (1885), 210
Berndt, Captain, 238, 241
Bilharzia: characteristics, 6, 26–8; and the Amaravi, 23–4, 26, 27–8; a world-wide scourge, 27
Bishop, Lieutenant, 246, 250
Blantyre, 233, 272; Mission, 140–1, 172, 174, 224

307